EXPLORING GR

GREEN CRIMINOLOGY

Series Editors:

Michael J. Lynch, *University of South Florida, USA*
Paul B. Stretesky, *Northumbria University, UK*

Now two decades old, green criminology – the study of environmental harm, crime, law, regulation, victimization, and justice – has increasing relevance to contemporary problems at local, national, and international levels. This series comes at a time when societies and governments worldwide seek new ways to alleviate and deal with the consequences of various environmental harms as they relate to humans, non-human animals, plant species, and the ecosystem and its components. Green criminology offers a unique theoretical perspective on how human behavior causes and exacerbates environmental conditions that threaten the planet's viability. Volumes in the series will consider such topics and controversies as corporate environmental crime, the complicity of international financial institutions, state-sponsored environmental destruction, and the role of non-governmental organizations in addressing environmental harms. Titles will also examine the intersections between green criminology and other branches of criminology and other areas of law, such as human rights and national security. The series will be international in scope, investigating environmental crime in specific countries as well as comparatively and globally. In sum, by bringing together a diverse body of research on all aspects of this subject, the series will make a significant contribution to our understanding of the dynamics between the natural world and the quite imperfect human world, and will set the stage for the future study in this growing area of concern.

Other titles in this series:

Animal Harm
Perspectives on Why People Harm and Kill Animals
Angus Nurse

Eco-global Crimes
Contemporary Problems and Future Challenges
Edited by Rune Ellefsen, Ragnhild Sollund and Guri Larsen

Exploring Green Criminology
Toward a Green Criminological Revolution

MICHAEL J. LYNCH
University of South Florida, USA

PAUL B. STRETESKY
Northumbria University, UK

ASHGATE

Published by
Ashgate Publishing Limited
Wey Court East
Union Road
Farnham
Surrey, GU9 7PT
England

Ashgate Publishing Company
110 Cherry Street
Suite 3-1
Burlington, VT 05401-3818
USA

www.ashgate.com

British Library Cataloguing in Publication Data
A catalogue record for this book is available from the British Library

The Library of Congress has cataloged the printed edition as follows:
Lynch, Michael J.
  Exploring green criminology : toward a green criminological revolution / by Michael J. Lynch and Paul B. Stretesky.
      pages cm. -- (Green criminology)
  Includes bibliographical references and index.
  ISBN 978-1-4724-1806-7 (hardback) -- ISBN 978-1-4724-1807-4 (pbk) -- ISBN 978-1-4724-1808-1 (ebook) -- ISBN 978-1-4724-1809-8 (epub) 1. Offenses against the environment. 2. Criminology. I. Stretesky, Paul. II. Title.
  HV6401.L96 2014
  364.028'6--dc23

                                                                    2013038853

ISBN 9781472418067 (hbk)
ISBN 9781472418074 (pbk)
ISBN 9781472418098 (ebk – PDF)
ISBN 9781472418098 (ebk – ePUB)

Printed in the United Kingdom by Henry Ling Limited, at the Dorset Press, Dorchester, DT1 1HD

Contents

List of Figures and Tables

Figures

Tables

About the Authors

Michael J. Lynch is Professor in the department of criminology, and an associated faculty member in the Patel School of Global Sustainability, at the University of South Florida, USA. He has been engaged in research on green criminology since 1990. His other interests include radical criminology, racial bias in criminal justice processes, and corporate crime and its control. He is the recipient of a Lifetime Achievement Award from the American Society of Criminology's Division on Critical Criminology.

Paul B. Stretesky is a Professor of Criminology in the Department of Languages and Social Science at Northumbria University, UK. In addition to his research on green criminology, he is engaged in research on families of homicide victims and missing persons, and the study of environmental justice. He is the co-author of *Guns, Violence and Criminal Behavior: Accounts from the Inside* as well as *Environmental Crime, Law and Justice*.

Chapter 1
Toward a Green Criminological Revolution

The earth is being destroyed as we watch, often as we do too little to stop the destruction. Today, for example, the Global Footprint Network estimates that it takes the earth one and one-half years to regenerate the resources that we have extracted from the earth in a year. This means that we are using the earth's resources at a greater rate than is sustainable. Unfortunately unsustainable business practices have been occurring since the early 1980s and are accelerating at such a rapid rate that we will consume nearly three times what the earth can regenerate annually by the year 2050 (Global Footprint Network, 2013). To be sure, there are those who take note of these alarming trends and are doing something to work toward sustainability. But, the efforts of a few individuals when compared to the majority of the human race are too little to overcome the devastating and unsustainable forces humans unleash on the planet. Thus we hide our head in the sand. We hope that divine intervention[1] or the next generation can prevent the impending ecological calamity. However, there may not be too many more next generations and time is running out to take care of the problem.

It is not our intention to write about the general neglect of environmental problems within society at large. Rather, our topic is much more limited, and is in many ways simply a microcosm of these broader social tendencies to turn a blind eye and a deaf ear toward environmental problems. In the scheme of things, the small area we address in this work appears to have little relevance to the vast problems of ecological destruction that lay before us as humans. Yet, that is, perhaps, precisely the point. All these small situations and contexts sum together to create our unsustainable and devastating behavior that result in massive ecological destruction. Since many people believe that the big ecological problems of the world are too big to tackle, the alternative is to approach these problems at smaller levels of aggregation. The hope is that changing each small situation will lead to large-scale change. Whether or not that is true is hard to determine and it is entirely possible that small change is an inefficient and ineffective strategy to prevent large-scale global harm.

Despite these observations, we, as criminologists, are concerned with the general neglect of ecological issues in criminology. We are concerned with teaching people lessons about crime, law and justice within the context of our biosphere. Indeed, a small number of criminologists continually call attention to the fact that criminology neglects widespread and important forms of harm such

---

1   Senator Whitehouse, a Democrat from Rhode Island, noted that one of his colleagues said, "God won't allow us to ruin our planet" (U.S. Senate Speech May 8, 2013).

as green or environmental crimes. And still other criminologists suggest that these green crimes present the most important challenge to criminology as a discipline. As criminologists, we are not simply concerned that our discipline continues to neglect green issues, we are disturbed by the fact that as a discipline, criminology is unable to perceive the wisdom of taking green harms more seriously, and the need to reorient itself in ways that make it part of the solution to the large global environmental problems we now face as the species that produces those problems.

We expect that most criminologists will reject the idea that they ought to be paying greater attention to the problems of green crimes and justice. After all, the history of criminology as a discipline is the history of an academic field devoted to the study of ordinary forms of street offending and efforts to control those offenses. In our view, these offenses and their consequences are quite small in comparison to the forms of environmental destruction taking place in the world around us. Yes, people are hurt by crime—but those are small hurts when one considers them in comparison to the end of humanity.

As criminologists we are dissatisfied to be part of a discipline that has become rather meaningless within the context of the modern world. The meaninglessness of criminology in that context will not change overnight, and this book may have little impact on that situation. Yet, at the same time, we feel that it is our obligation to propose that this situation needs to change, and to outline the ways in which criminologists can actively engage in research of importance in the contemporary world. While the research of criminologists is unlikely to change the world, any small step forward that addresses green crime and justice is a step in the right direction, and contributes to changing the social attitudes and practices needed to help reform the behaviors that have produced the ecologically damaging situation in which we now find ourselves. While our book is no solution to the ecological problems of our times, it exposes a way of thinking that pushes the discipline of criminology closer to being relevant in the modern context of ecological destruction.

To take this step forward, this book explores the parameters of green criminology, its theory and practice, and why environmental issues ought to become more central to the study of crime, law, and justice, or, more specifically, an integral part of criminological research and the criminological imagination. We argue that if harm is the primary concern addressed by criminology—that is, if criminology exists as a science designed to understand, address, reduce, or eliminate crime in the hope of reducing or eliminating harms *and* to promote justice for humans, nonhumans, and the environment—then criminologists need to recreate criminology, redesign its focus, open it to new understandings of harms and crimes, criminals, laws, corrective responses to crime and harms, victims, and justice. But how do we redesign criminology to consider environmental harm as an important area of study in an era when the destruction of the earth and the world's ecosystem is the predominant concern of our times? And, if we are correct in stating that this has yet to happen, we must ask why this has not been accomplished given that this situation has been known for quite some time.

The how question comprises a large section of this work, and is illustrated in various chapters that apply an environmental frame of reference that underlies a green approach to issues that can be addressed within criminology. Taking this environmental frame of reference as the starting point and applying it to criminological issues is the substance of green criminology. Such a perspective helps us to see criminology in a new way that is only apparent once this green-environmental frame of reference is adopted.

Toward a Green Criminology

In 1990, Lynch published the first work to suggest the need for a green criminology. It is now two decades later, and in the terms of generational language, an entirely new generation of criminologists has entered the world and has done little to transform the nature of criminology. To be sure, over the past generation, some advances have certainly been made in the area of green criminological research by a handful of pioneers in the field (Agnew, 2012; Beirne, 1999; Beirne and South, 2007; Benton, 2007; Bisschop, 2012; Croall, 2009; Eman, Meško and Fields, 2009; Gibbs et al., 2010; Groombridge, 1998; Hall, 2013; Hauck, 2008; Jarrell and Ozymy, 2012; Katz, 2010; Kramer and Michalowski, 2012; Lane, 1998; Lynch and Stretesky, 2003; Nurse, 2013; Ruggiero and South, 2010; Sollund, 2008; South and Brisman, 2013; Takemura, 2007; van Solinge 2010; Walters, 2006; White, 2008a; Wyatt, 2012).

Yet, despite these advances, one could hardly claim that green criminology has acquired a prominent place within criminology. Indeed, relative to many other varieties of criminology or criminological specialties, there is by comparison little in the way of green criminological research. That is, in reviewing the last generation of criminology, we can hardly say that the emergence of green criminology has had a dramatic impact on the field of criminology. As evidence of these claims, we observe that in the database Google Scholar the term "green criminology" makes up approximately 0.33 percent of the published material in the discipline of "criminology" between the years 1990 and 2013. This is equivalent to about three environmentally-related research publications for every 1,000 publications in the field. This low level of focus on environmental issues in criminology is hardly the type of attention that signals a shift in the discipline.

Why isn't criminology greener? To be sure, over the past two decades a number of criminologists have initiated efforts to build a green criminology, and we will discuss some of these efforts in detail later in this work. For now, it is sufficient to note that despite efforts to create a green criminology, the majority of criminologists have ignored the messages being delivered by green criminology. Again, the question of why emerges. Perhaps green criminologists have been ineffective in communicating the importance of their work. That might be a relevant argument if green criminologists were the only ones suggesting that the world is faced with intense and widespread ecological problems that demand the attention of the peoples of the world, including academics. One can imagine that criminologists read the news and understand that their academic colleagues in other disciplines are taking green crimes and harms seriously—more seriously than criminologists.

In that context, we must return to the question: Why have criminologists ignored taking an environmental frame of reference, especially in an era when environmental problems and concerns are so widespread? There are several potentially relevant explanations.

First, because criminology, as traditionally defined, is about human harms that are defined in criminal law, all other forms of harm tend to be excluded from criminology unless unorthodox approaches such as those found within critical/radical criminology serve as the foundation for criminological analysis. Given its focus on the legal definition of crime, it matters little to criminology that most of the harms that occur in the world are not criminal harms or socially constructed as criminal harms; or that the most serious harms of our times are not defined under criminal law statutes but by related legal codes such as environmental laws, corporate crime regulations, or administrative codes of agencies that police corporate, white-collar, and environmental crime. By definition, criminology was born from a specific and limited set of questions—who is a criminal? How widespread is criminal behavior? What are the causes of crime? How can crime be controlled?—and supported by a series of related assumptions criminology generated about crime and criminals (Beirne, 1993). For the most part, those assumptions about law, crime, and criminals limit the study of crime to behaviors most likely to be exhibited by the powerless (Reiman, 2006). By continually repeating these assumptions about the nature of criminology and crime within the criminological literature and criminological curricula, a boundary has been established and maintained—a boundary that has often tended to exclude a diverse range of topics relevant to studying harms and their consequences that ought otherwise to fit within the discipline of criminology if criminology were not so narrowly conceived of in the first place.

Second, because of the biases contained within criminal law, criminology focuses on the behaviors that others—lawmakers in particular—select as harms (White, 2008a). This focus on criminal law definitions of crime has meant that criminologists have failed to create an objective definition of harm that is independent of the social construction of crime in the criminal law, and instead have substituted the legal definition of crime for a scientific definition of crime as if the legal definition of crime were based upon objective criteria. That is, criminal harms are defined by law, and law is created by lawmakers, and lawmakers may not, and usually do not rely on objective criteria to make the distinction between say, criminal, regulatory, or administrative law, or even between behaviors that are defined as crimes and those that are not. Because there is no objective definition of crime, criminologists cannot objectively differentiate the legal forms of law—that is, criminal, regulatory, administrative, and so on—from one another nor the crimes those legal forms identify on the basis of the harmful outcomes produced by violating those laws. In criminology, a crime is a crime because criminal law defines it as a crime. That clearly tautological identification of crime has no objective, independent point of reference or definition of the type found in other disciplines identified as sciences. Physicists, for example, do not say gravity is gravity because of the law of gravity. Rather, the law of gravity is derived from the explanation of gravity to explain how gravity behaves.

To illustrate this point, consider the following. When an environmental crime results in a death, the vagaries of law allow this behavior to be treated as a regulatory violation even though there may be intent and knowledge that such an outcome is likely and, that as a result, the same behavior *could* be classified as violation of criminal law. Criminologists, however, have tended not to address this issue in any direct way, and instead tend to accept these legal definitions and their outcomes and distinction as if they are neutral, objective definitions of harms, and base the proper study of criminology on only the forms of harm pertinent to the definition of crime in the criminal law (Reiman, 2006). This tendency to privilege the criminal law as the starting point for analysis has directed the criminological gaze to very specific forms of behavior and to studying the kinds of system responses—criminal justice system responses—that are designed to control offenses and offenders who violate criminal law. This produces a very narrow range of issues that are, in turn, defined as legitimate criminological subject matter (see also Hillyard and Tombs, 2007).

Third, criminal law, by its design and in its applications—as a real process undertaken by police and courts—draws attention to those who are less economically advantaged, including those who are poor, uneducated, marginalized from the work force, or who comprise the blue-collar classes. These are the offenders to whom criminal law objects, not those who own and operate powerful corporations which are "regulated" through an entirely different set of legal mechanisms that exist outside of criminal law proper. As a result, corporate and environmental offenders are not typically treated as engaging in the same kinds of behaviors as street offenders, nor are they viewed as being equally liable or reprehensible for their crimes as street offenders. They are excluded by criminology as if these behaviors are irrelevant; as if these offenders produce no harms; as if these behaviors have little relevance to studying and understanding crime.

And fourth, because criminologists base their work in a frame of reference that reflects all of these assumptions about criminal law and criminal behavior, and because this frame of reference more generally includes assumptions common to all social sciences—that the starting point for all manner of social science is the human perspective—victimization of nonhumans is not considered important. In other words, social sciences, because they are socially centered on human societies, are human centered, and only perceive harms when humans are the victims. This frame of reference excludes other views of harm—any nonhuman entity or victim harmed by a legal violation, whether criminal, regulatory, administrative, or civil. And, in the event that the social science frame of reference acknowledges alternative views of victimization, it often treats those views as peripheral since they are outside the human frame of reference already narrowly defined by social sciences. This, perhaps more than the other issues raised here, orients criminology toward considering a limited range of harms. In that view, crimes are harms caused by humans primarily against humans that are defined in law as criminal harms.

In contrast to this human centered view, green criminology begins by imposing an alternative frame of reference, one based in nature, the environment, or natural ecology. We will discuss this frame of reference and the problems associated with human-centered frames of reference in more detail in a later chapter. For now, it is important to note that by selecting a natural ecology frame of reference, green criminology is a revolution in the making; a revolution that seeks to displace humans and human issues as the sole objects of study. In doing so, green criminology supplants the traditional criminological interest in personal crimes that, in comparison to environmental harms, are rather minor in their overall impact measured in terms of the scope and amount of harm caused. By moving away from this human-centered approach, green criminology points out that there are an extraordinarily wide range of environmentally-related harms that exist in the world, especially compared to the criminal harms to which criminology has been limited. This broader set of crimes that becomes the focus of green criminology is not the set of crimes committed by the poor that attracts so much criminological attention. In drawing attention away from these ordinary, powerless criminal offenses and offenders it is not only possible to view the crimes of the powerful as the most serious offenses that occur in society and as having the broadest scope of effect on human and nonhuman victims, it is also possible to understand the biased view that a criminology anchored to criminal law produces. In short, when criminology excludes an environmental frame of reference, it hides from our vision the vast array of harms perpetuated against and through the victimization of the environment. In the green view, the environmental frame of reference dominates, and the criminological frame of reference becomes secondary and subsumed within the broader environmental frame of reference. We explore this idea more fully later in this work.

Green Versus Traditional Criminology

Having laid out the purpose in this book in a rather small space, most criminologists may find themselves disagreeing with our basic premise that environmental harms matter more than criminal harms; that green harms are more widespread than criminal harms; that criminology maintains a bias against examining green harms because of criminology's basic assumptions about the criminal offender and the nature of crime. Thus, what we propose is a revolution in the way criminologists think about harm and crime. To be sure, most criminologists would not be in favor of such a green criminological revolution. They might argue that criminology is, after all, concerned with crime, especially crimes between people, the criminal law, and responses to those defined as offenders by criminal law. They are right that criminology has been practiced in that way. What we are objecting to is this practice and the consequences of the way in which criminology has been applied. Traditional criminology has been growing more irrelevant in a world that is increasingly being destroyed by green crimes.

In response to the traditional criminological position, we reply that the identification of a harm as criminal or otherwise in the traditional criminological approach involves a process of accepting the social construction of crime as an act identified as a crime because it is included within the criminal law. Again, as noted, that method of identifying crime and the scope of criminology is not objective because it fails to address the nature of acts that ought to be treated criminally because of their characteristics. The legal process of socially constructing crime contains subjective dimensions which criminologists, if they adhere to the principles of scientific investigation, ought to reject. Those subjective dimensions are reinforced by criminology when it employs the same subjective standards that lawmakers employ when they identify harm as criminal, administrative, regulatory, or civil. There is, in short, no criminological definition of harm that is independent of law or rulemaking that is employed by criminologists, and this very fact threatens the validity and objectivity of the criminological enterprise—of the entire disciplinary practice of criminology (Hall, 2011). Law is not an objective science, and as a result, neither can criminology be objective if it simply accepts legal definitions of crime as the origins of its research (Hillyard and Tombs, 2007).

In responding to the majority of criminologists, we should also point out that green criminology is based on a premise, justified by scientific studies in a wide variety of disciplines, that green harms are the most important concerns in modern society because they cause the most harm, violence, damage, and loss. Consider a brief example that illustrates this point. Under law, corporations can legally emit certain types and volumes of pollution. The fact that this behavior is defined as legal—that it is not a violation of law—does not mean that there are not harmful consequences associated with this kind of behavior. For instance, dumping pollution into a local waterway, even though allowed under law, may cause extensive environmental damage. Those pollutants may damage the local water supply and expose thousands or hundreds of thousands or millions across the landscape of a nation to toxins that affect their health. It should also be noted that the same detrimental consequences befall other, nonhuman species as well. Moreover, the pollution may impede the natural ability of the waterway to function, making nature a direct victim of the harm caused by pollution. This reinforces our point: just because a behavior isn't defined as criminal behavior doesn't mean there is no harm, that the harm is minor, or that the harm is adequately defined in law. And, it's the harmful outcome, not the behavior as defined by the rule of law that should be examined and should become the subject matter of criminology.

Further, as a response, we would point to the fact that the form of criminal justice criminologists ordinarily examine to discuss the control of crime is a rather narrow form of justice. There are other ways of conceiving justice that provide legitimate alternative frames of reference for thinking about crime and justice. Criminologists accept the criminological frame of reference as valid, and most work within that frame of reference. Consequently, it is difficult for them to perceive of an alternative to the traditions forged within criminology, to acknowledge that an alternative view of justice could, in fact, be useful or appropriate. For example, there is a significant literature on harm written from the perspective of environmental frames of reference in a variety of disciplines outside of criminology (for a review see Lynch and Stretesky, 2001). This literature has rarely made its ways into criminological literature, and is rarely acknowledged by criminologists as an alternative way of assessing justice (for an alternative view on this issue, see, for example, the various chapters in Merchant, 2005).

We recognize that most criminologists would not agree with our basic premises, which after all, suggest that criminology has a "wrong-headed" orientation, and that the criminological point of reference needs to be replaced with an environmental or green point of reference. Many of the arguments supporting our position will unfold throughout this book.

The Extraordinary Level of Environmental Harm

At this point, however, we would like to make it quite clear that environmental harms *are* much more important than personal harms associated with most ordinary crimes or street crimes—most of which are property crimes—and that environmental crimes *are* more extensive and damaging than the street crimes that occupy the attention of the majority of criminologists. This point about harm is really quite easy to illustrate and support, as we demonstrate in Chapter 5. In the first place, all one needs to do is review just a small portion of the scientific literature on environmental harms to come to the conclusion that these harms are well known, easily documented, scientifically verifiable, plentiful, and extraordinarily harmful.

There is little doubt that humans produce an extraordinary amount of pollution and harm the world in numerous ways by damaging the environment. Humans, however, tend to overlook the relevance of this form of harmful outcomes they produce. They also ignore that in harming the world they produce a wide variety of injustices through these practices and outcomes, and that the harms associated with green crimes *far exceed* those associated with ordinary street crimes. From a statistical or mathematical viewpoint, street crimes are such a small fraction of the harms humans commit that they are rather irrelevant to efforts to control harm and make the world a safer, more hospitable place. To be sure, the harms caused by street crime are real and painful, but these harms are not the most prevalent nor the most painful forms of harm that exist in contemporary societies. By reinforcing the common perception that street crimes are dangerous and require extraordinary resources and energy to control, the discipline of criminology aids in directing attention to those issues and, as a result, neglecting the other serious forms of harm that damage the world around us and promote a wide array of victimizations that make the world an unsafe place for human and nonhuman species.

Even if one were unfamiliar with the scientific literature on environmental harms, it has become increasingly clear in recent years that the environment around us is under expanded assault, that it is routinely harmed and damaged by humans, and that these environmental harms return to reap their vengeance on humans and other species. For example, as we outlined the content of this book, the U.S. Gulf Coast states and waters were under attack from the largest oil spill disaster in the history of the world. The more general and broader assault against the environment has threatened the very future of the natural world, at least the world as it has existed for quite some time in a state capable of supporting an extensive mass of life forms, including humans. Moreover, this environmental assault has, at a minimum, compromised the quality of life for the variety of species that inhabit the world.

If one were to doubt the scientific literature or was ignorant of the level of harm humans add to the environment, then one could turn to actual measures or data on the amount, extent, and type of environmental harm that exists in the world. There are a number of databases that catalog not only the number of such crimes, but their extent and volume (Burns and Lynch, 2004; Burns, Lynch, and Stretesky, 2008). For example, it is possible to estimate the number of acres of land impacted by various kinds of environmental harm such as deforestation or pollution; the number of species harmed by pollution or the number driven into extinction by pollution and the human invasion of nature; the number of miles of waterways polluted or buried by mountaintop mining; the miles of waterways and swamps buried by "land reclamation"; the quantity and concentrations of pollutants and toxins humans add to the environment in each environmental medium—air, land, water; the extent to which climate change has accelerated the melting of the polar ice caps, glaciers, and mountain snow caps, and changed the salinity and acidity of the oceans, and so on.

Criminologists may defend their focus on crime as defined by criminal law and the powerless criminal offenders, and reject the analysis of environmental crimes on other grounds as well. For example, criminologists might argue that one reason to ignore green harms is that it is not easy to identify green offenders—an argument that criminologists have made with respect to the study of corporate crime. The issue of ease of identification of crimes or criminals, however, is not a legitimate reason for ignoring the study of green harm and it is certainly not a scientifically grounded or valid argument that can be employed to reject the study of green harms and crimes. In contrast to what criminologists might ordinarily say, green harms can be measured and shown to outweigh the harms associated with street crimes. Moreover, in contrast to the assertion that is difficult to find green offenders, it is clear "who" the offender is when it comes to green harms. On the general level, we can say that the green offender is always human, either individually or collectively. At the more specific level, environmental databases do not always tell us the name of the human entity that does the damage. That is to say, green offenders are not unknown assailants; these are offenders who might not be a single individual, but they are humanly constructed entities that act only because humans act. That is to say, the important, cyclical, and persistent green harms that change nature aren't those produced by random acts of nature or by natural species. Rather, they are acts and outcomes created by humans. And, moreover, it is often possible, using data and scientific techniques, to locate these green offenders even when we may think that this seems impossible. Let us take oil spills as a brief example. It may seem impossible to link an oil spill floating on a body of water to a particular source. But doing so simply requires the same kind of investigative techniques used to solve street crimes. Oil spills, for instance, contain evidence of their origin. The U.S. Coast Guard maintains data on the "chemical finger prints" of oil from oil vessels, and this data can be used to link spills to their points of origins. Weather patterns, water currents, and geological data can all be used to trace oil spills to their origins (Burns, Lynch, and Stretesky, 2008; on the specifics of fingerprinting oil see: Daling et al., 2002; Wang and Fingas, 2003; Wang, Stout, and Fingas, 2006).

Humans have placed excessive demands on the environment both as a source of raw materials and foodstuffs, and as a depository for human waste. As we discuss in Chapter 8 and as political economic theories of the environment suggest, the pressures humans exert on the environment multiply each year as world populations grow, as efforts to accumulate wealth through increased production increase, as human cultures of consumption and a general disregard for the environment and its finite limits have evolved, continually crushing natural balance and altering the limits of human development the natural world imposes (Ehrlich, 1970; Schnaiberg, 1980). We often fail to understand the nature of these problems because, as humans, we see the world from our human perspective which is often quite upside down. For example, hunters or associations that represent hunting interests argue that we need to shoot deer each year in order to maintain the deer population and prevent them from starving and damaging the natural environment. This is true *only to the extent that humans have encroached* on deer populations' territories, and have altered the natural world for deer, and limited the scope of the natural world upon which deer may draw. Moreover, before there were humans, nature provided its own forms of balance for controlling the deer population, and humans were quite unnecessary to the equation. Deer populations rose and fell before there were humans, and nature provided the mechanism for balancing the natural demands of deer and other species. To some extent, the way this problem—controlling the deer population—is understood by humans and its human remedies are a matter of perspective or point of view. In the human-centered or anthropogenic orientation that elevates the importance of humans—an issue we discuss more in depth in Chapter 2—humans are needed to create balance. In the view of the world from an environmental perspective, however, humans are the problem, not the solution, to continuation of the world.

Our times—the circumstances in the world toward the end of the first decade of the twenty-first century—are defined by a number of green or environmental issues. It would not be unfair to say that this has been the case for the past 150 years. Industrial pollution of the air, water, and land, toxic waste sites, deforestation, species extinction, excessive pesticides use and pollution, climate change, the excessive use of fossil fuels, acid rain, a growing reliance on coal and oil, the environmental effects of drilling for oil or mining coal, the collapse of coral reefs and fisheries, and so on, these have been and are the problems of the modern world—problems that have not been adequately addressed or remedied; and, for the purposes of our work, problems that have not sufficiently been examined as criminological issues—as harms against nature, as green crimes in both their direct and indirect forms.

The problems listed above are also important because they are measures of the level of harm humans have done to the environment. Some reflect scope of harm, others the quality of harm. The most important of these measures directly assesses the impact of humans on the eco-system's imbalance—an imbalance that sometimes creeps and sometimes leaps closer and closer to a new point of environmental equilibrium incapable of supporting life on planet earth as currently constructed by humans (Lovelock, 2007; for further discussion of Gaia theory see also, Lovelock, 1979, 1991, 2009). It is these serious, large and expanding harms that we address in this book by exploring our perspective on green criminology.

The fact that the world has reached various ecological or environmental tipping points and that many such tipping points lie ahead in the not too distant future (see for example, Goodstein, 2004; Pearce, 2008) has been the subject of much scientific research for the past half century (Carlson, 1962; Colburn, Dumanoski, and Myers, 1997; Davis, 2002; McKibben, 1997), and for some issues expands to include nearly another half century of research (Markowitz and Rosner, 2003). Moreover, we know from historical research that the demise of societies has sometimes been due to ecological malfeasance of the human inhabitants of those societies (Diamond, 2005). There is now, however, an important historical difference—the environmental problems and conditions in question are no longer localized, or those that are limited to one society. Rather, like the world economy, these problems have become global in scope. And, it is the global nature of these problems that increasingly ties the peoples of the world together, requiring from them a united and unified effort that spans nations and cultures, and even academic disciplines to address.

We offer this book as an example of how these circumstances can be recognized within criminology. We cannot control whether criminologists act on these issues—we can only carry the message and hope that our message is heard.

Chapter 2
Defining the Parameters of the Problem

A Changing World

The world around us is in a constant state of flux. Some of that change is organic, natural, and evolutionary. These are things that humans can't control. Humans can't, for example, stop earthquakes, volcanic eruptions, tsunamis, or alter the orbit of the globe if it changes. To be sure, these natural disasters have large impacts in small areas. For example, some estimate that nearly 320,000 people died in the 2010 earthquake in Haiti, or that the 2004 Sumatra—Andaman earthquake-tsunami that affected parts of Sumatra, India, Indonesia, Maldives, and Sri Lanka killed up to 310,000 (BBC, 2010; USGS, 2004). Those single events caused extensive death tolls, injured many, and caused billions of dollars in damages. But these are the kinds of natural events humans must live with; they do not control them and cannot change their paths. While the death and injury tolls from these events are large, they are also unusual events, and many more people are killed annually by things we as humans can control—changes we make to the human environment that cause pollution that lead to death and disease, or lead to wildfires or floods, or erosion and landslides.

Humans also can't stop the long-term evolutionary changes in the earth that have been in the process of developing over the ages. Many of these evolutionary changes are the result of processes that are millions, hundreds of thousands, and thousands of years old, and are effectively part of the "nature of nature"—that is, they are part of the internal dynamic of the natural order of the world. From a human-centered point of view, what is problematic about "naturally" induced changes is that they may be detrimental to humans and, further, appear to be beyond human control. Thus, when naturally induced changes harm humans, there is no way to control this occurrence. But these are not the changes that concern us here.

Many environmental changes we observe have been forced by the demands of human populations. For example, according to the *Global Footprint Network*, in 2010 the world's sustainable bio-capacity was 1.78 hectares (4.4 acres) per person, while the total ecological footprint was 2.70 hectares (6.7 acres) per person, causing an ecological deficit of 0.92 hectares (2.3 acres) per person. In other words, even in a clean world, one where humans are not destroying the environment and limiting its sustainability though pollution of the air, land, and water, humans are using resources at an unsustainable rate—that is, faster than nature can produce those resources. The short story—between using up the world's resources at an unsustainable rate, polluting the remaining resources, and fuelling global warming, humans are transforming the world, and not in a positive way.

In this work we are concerned with the harms that humans create and how they relate to criminology. Unfortunately, forms of harm created by humans are often obscured from our view for two reasons. First, the human-centered perspectives through which natural ecological changes are viewed produce a narrow and biased view of ecological change. This human-centered orientation effects how we view, interpret, and understand unnatural changes such as the ones we as humans create when we pollute the natural environment. Because of this perspective, humans tend to view harm as something that affects them, not as something they cause. This human-centered view may sometimes allow us to recognize that we might harm other people, but it is not open to the suggestion that we as humans harm nature, that we harm the world and other species; that we are the criminal offenders in a series of wide-ranging, serial, and persistent crimes against the environment and its inhabitants that constitute a life course of offending against the environment.

Second, submersed within this human-centered view of ecological and environmental change is an idea that ecological changes are evolutionary—that is, that ecological changes are small, occurring over long stretches of time, and that nothing that humans can do changes the ordinary course of ecological evolution. Indeed, many natural ecological changes are small, small enough not to be noticed in the short span of a human lifetime. For example, one kind of ecological change that fits these criteria involves the slight changes that periodically take place the earth's orbit (Laskar, 1995). It is unlikely that humans induce these changes, unless, of course, they have moved a significant quantity of matter from one place to another, and that in doing so they affect the rotation and movement of the planet. Nevertheless, it is this general assumption that human actions have no impact on environmental evolution that is important to keep in mind, because it has had a strong effect on contemporary human perspectives on the environment and the role of humans in changing the environment. Generally, when humans imagine the way they affect the environment, they tend to understand their impact as being rather small, and only see their impact in relation to their immediate environment and not in relation to the operation or function of the world's ecosystem or the living earth system, Gaia (Lovelock, 2007). This is because when people think about their impact on the world, they think as individuals rather than as a species. This may have something to do with our understanding of how an individual impacts local ecosystems; but humans do not tend to view their impact on the ecosystem collectively—as part of the human species—and therefore tend to ignore the large-scale change in the world ecosystem that they produce. Humans do not tend to reflect on the idea that their behavior as a species changes the very nature of the world around them. A variety of ecological changes will tend to be ignored by humans not only because their impacts are perceived as small, or because those ecological changes are imperceptible to humans under ordinary circumstances, but also because they are sporadic. For example, the average person does not notice sun spots as they have a small and largely discreet effect and occur at somewhat sporadic intervals (Berdyugina and Usoskin, 2003). Today, humans are more likely to notice sun spots because they affect things like cell phone reception or satellite television.

Unlike sunspots, some sporadic natural events may be large and dramatic, such as volcanic activity or shifts in tectonic plates (Silver and Behn, 2008). These large events are certainly noticeable. Two additional points are relevant here.

First, none of these natural ecological events—the changing of the earth's rotation, sunspots, volcanoes, and earthquakes—are caused by, nor may they be controlled by, humans. They are, so to speak, truly part of the natural ecological cycle—part of the natural world's evolutionary process. Each is a small event in the natural history of the world that creates harm for a localized segment of the entire human population; say only for those affected directly by an earthquake. These events are mostly sporadic, and these natural events will occur despite the facts that humans occupy the earth. However, for the most part, these events don't possess the power to destroy the world and end life as we know it.

There are "natural events" that may be less than natural and have more than a minimal human dimension. Global warming or climate change is now widely recognized by scientists as having human origins and can impact weather events such as hurricanes, heavy snowfalls, melting of polar ice caps, rising sea level, torrential rains, and flooding, among other events (IPCC, 2001). In the Intergovernmental Panel on Climate Change (IPCC) 2001 synthesis report to policy makers, IPCC researchers report that "[t]here is new and stronger evidence that most of the warming observed over the last 50 years is attributable to human activities" (p. 5). While these human behaviors that produce climate change occur all across the globe, the outcomes of these changes can manifest themselves in extreme weather events. Thus, anthropogenic climate changes may impact weather events all across the globe. A recent study of flooding in Benin, Nigeria, for example, suggests that global warming has been one precipitating factor in the increase in excessive rainfall that interacts with expanding urbanization to induce severe flooding events that cause extreme levels of human suffering for the residents of the city (Atedhor, Odjugo, and Uriri, 2011).

Differentiating between natural and human-induced environmental cycles requires extensive attention to data. Nevertheless, in the contemporary era we have come to recognize, led by scientists, that these kinds of events are happening more often, and that they are not happening more often because of evolutionary, natural changes in the nature of the world. These events are happening more often and are being driven forward by human behavior—by the ability of humans to change the environment so dramatically by the forms of environmental damage they produce that the natural ecology must turn on humans and erase them to make the planet safe for other species (Lovelock, 2007).

Second, while natural events like a volcanic eruption or an earthquake may release an immense amount of power in a short period of time, and though its human consequences may be great within a given localized area, these are minor if not unnoticed blips in the evolution of the natural world. Each of these naturally occurring processes unfolds, sometimes slowly in evolutionary time, and the final event impacts the world around us only in very small ways with respect to the flow of nature.

At the same time, as humans we sometimes notice these changes and witness them, but only when the changes are abrupt and large in their scale—for example, earthquakes. Nature tends to change slowly in unnoticed ways when it is not under external stress. What humans do not often realize is that *they* are environmental stressors—the causes of accelerating ecological changes, and a reason that the path of ecological evolution changes sometimes in abrupt and new ways (Lovelock, 2007).

Human Stressors

Today, more so than at any earlier point in human history, the natural environment is under stress from human populations. These stresses have become constant, persistent, and wide-ranging. Over the past hundred years, these stresses have expanded exponentially. And because of their constancy and growth, these stresses have produced visible ecological changes—changes that are so dramatic that humans have now been able to view ecological changes within the unfolding of one human lifetime as opposed to an eon. Some of these changes have become quite obvious or evident to the ordinary person. For example, the average person may have witnessed the death of a waterway or the destruction of a natural area for the purpose of building residences or workplaces, or the transformation of fields or woodlands and so on for the expanded use of humans. And while average people have noticed such changes, they have probably not interpreted that change within the context of ecologically centered values that would allow them to view themselves and other humans as environmental stressors.

There are many human-forced ecological changes that the average person may not notice at all. Some of these are small, incremental changes such as when the temperature rises by a fraction of a degree in a year, or even the larger changes in temperature that occur over an extended period. There are other changes we fail to notice because we have become accustomed to change and to ignoring our role in that change process.

We live in an era of world history when the world changes rapidly, both with respect to world relations or in terms of human adaptations to the world around us, and with respect to the "world of nature" or the natural environment or ecology. For example, in just a few decades, human social relations and interactions have been transformed by the widespread availability of personal computers, laptops, and cell phones. There is no longer anywhere on the planet humans cannot travel except to the deepest parts of the oceans. And, if you have sufficient resources, you can even escape the earth for a few moments or hours by purchasing a ticket for space travel.[1]

---

1   *Virgin Galactic* offers flights to "space" for $200,000 (www.virgingatlantic. com, accessed October 2012). *Space Adventurers* (www.spaceadventures.com) offers four primary space travel experiences: lunar missions ($100 million), orbital space flight (with the option of being the first private citizen to walk in space), suborbital space flights ($102,000), and zero-gravity flights ($4,950). Dennis Tito was the first "space tourist" and

Social, political, and economic changes have been and are pushed forward constantly by the inter-connectedness of nations in a world economy and through an extensive international communications network that forms a world-wide linkage across nations of people with diverse social practices (McChesney and Schillar, 2003). In today's world, nations live on the edge of becoming "Blackberry nations," where individuals are embedded within an instantaneous and constant communication network that allows them to "reach out and touch someone" at every moment, where they can continually seek to discover if the other "can hear me now." These modern forms of communication have deeply impacted and changed our daily lives in rapid fashion, making us seek the next new communicative form, and leaving us unfulfilled when we do not have the latest technology or feeling unconnected when we are unplugged from the communication network.

But modern lives have also changed rapidly in other ways, ways that are at times imperceptible or ignored. These ignored changes are occurring, routinely, to the natural world around us, the world in which we are enveloped. These constantly changing natural world conditions have become a concern for policy makers in various nations across the face of the globe because these changes are undermining the ability of planet earth to sustain life—especially human life (Pearce, 2008).

The nature or environment of the world is changing, and at times is changing more rapidly than nature itself can accommodate in a balanced way (Lovelock, 2007; Pearce, 2008). In reality, nature—or Gaia, the living system of the world— is accommodating itself to changes in the environment, and is doing so by evolving rapidly, producing new and shorter periods of equilibrium and stability in response to human stressors (Lovelock, 2007). In this modern world, periods of environmental stability are becoming shorter and shorter, diminishing from tens of thousands of years to decades and perhaps less in the future (Pearce, 2008). This process is particularly evident, for example, in outcomes such as climate change, and in the generation of ecological tipping points (Lenton, 2011; Lyndsay and Zhang, 2005; Nobre and Borma, 2009; Pearce, 2008).

What we must come to grips with is that environmental changes have become a common aspect of the nature of contemporary ecological development, as these jumps and shifts in environmental equilibrium accelerate, that there is no longer the same kind of long-term, historical equilibrium that once characterized the stability of the ecosystem. Pushed to its extreme, this pattern of abrupt environmental change may result in tremendous transformations to elements of the natural world such as climate, which then feed back on other aspects of the natural world and induce widespread ecological changes that have potentially disastrous consequences (Lovelock, 2007; Pearce, 2008). These natural changes, which aren't natural with respect to the long-term trends in ecological stability and also aren't natural since they are driven by humans, have the potential to establish climate conditions unsuitable for the continued existence of species—including the human species, the

---

paid nearly 20 million dollars to be carried by a Russian rocket to the International Space Station in 2001 (Crouch, 2001).

species that is largely responsible for introducing the forces that drive environmental changes and new environmental stages of equilibrium (Lovelock, 2007).

To be sure, some portion of the new environmental problems that face humans—new in the sense that they have only been widely recognized for 50 years or less—are tremendous, so big and ominous that their names reflect the extent of their powers—for example, global warming and the ubiquitous nature of many environmental pollutants (Asakawa et al., 2008; Jansson, Asplund, and Olsson, 1987; Umemura et al., 2003). And yet, climate change is just one of the big environmental problems facing the inhabitants of today's world (Brown, 2008). In addition to the heat pollution humans produce that pushes global warming and climate change—and reflects well known principles in physics related to entropy and thermodynamics (Ozawa et al., 2003)—there are a number of other problems: for example, toxins and pesticides in foods; genetically modified crops; environmental pollution of air, land, and water; the disappearance of water; heavy metals in computing and communications equipment; toxic materials such as BPA in food-related consumption vessels, and so on. Many of these other problems are interconnected and stem from modern and past attitudes toward the environment and the natural world, the consumption of the resources the world holds, and humanly situated desires for economic "advancement," "success," "development," and "fulfillment" through the consumption of goods made from extracting raw materials from the natural world and dumping the wastes from these processes back into the environment. Whether described as "advancement," "development," and so on, what these changes in human society actually depict is the effort of some to profit at extraordinary rates by turning nature's resources into commodities, transforming those life-giving resources into socially constructed economic values supported by political and legal systems that have been built to legitimate transforming nature's resources into economic resources, and returning to nature the used up, transformed waste humans have manufactured.

Population Stressors

Some of the environmental problems that face the world today seem inescapable. This is true in a human-centered perspective because we fail to appreciate the causes of environmental harms correctly, or because we treat these outcomes as natural and inevitable consequences of life. We may assume, for example, that humans pollute and use up environmental resources at a rapidly expanding rate because they have no other recourse. Moreover, humans have come to view the aspects of modern life with its expectations of high consumption, overuse of resources, and tendency to waste and pollute as not only acceptable, but as the only way in which humans can live comfortably. Society assumes—wrongly, we believe—that technology and better governance structures will provide a solution to these problems. Because we as a species hold this belief, we also tend to believe that the solutions to these large-scale problems lay just around the corner, and that little work will be required on our part to correct these big environmental problems once the solution is discovered.

Consequently, the vast majority of people fail to force their governmental representatives to act *now* and seem content to wait for a solution to appear.

Not only have we learned to ignore our effect on the environment and accept it as normal, we have come to accept human population growth as inevitable, and to overlook its consequences as well. Worldwide, populations continue to expand, and while population growth has declined in recent years especially in more "developed" economies, the world population continues to grow as births continue to outnumber deaths (United Nations, 2009). Coupled with trends from prior decades and with expansive consumption of resources, population growth has added to environmental stress (Daily and Ehrlich, 1992; National Academy of Sciences, 1993). In other words, one of the big problems facing the world today is not only limiting population growth, but producing a decline in population growth especially in regions where natural resources are limited and hence over-consumed, or where natural resources are over-consumed as a consequence of socially-induced habits favoring consumption and the production of waste, or where over-consumption has resulted from a belief in the endless supply of natural resources, and high or even excessive standards of living.[2]

From a human-centered perspective none of these issues may be viewed as especially troubling. As humans we tend to view changes such as population change as inevitable. Consequently, we do little to address problems of population growth, and indeed tend to view population growth as a healthy sign of the vitality of human development. We fail to appreciate how population growth impacts the environment, or fail to appreciate the potential for population growth to create such great stress on the environment that it becomes a source of harm, not only for humans, but for other species and the future existence of the world as we know it. In contrast, in our human view, we are quite willing to see these population problems in other species, and argue for limiting animal populations through hunting or other forms of animal control, for example, in order to constrain their adverse impacts on the environment. In this human-centered view it is, of course, animals and not humans that are the problem.

What we omit by considering processes such as human population growth as "natural and inevitable" is the environmental stress population growth

---

2   There are a number of ways to calculate the minimum resources needed by people in different parts of the world for survival, and various interpretations of what economically and culturally relative terms such as "survival" or "adequate" life style means. For this purpose, we prefer a carrying capacity argument which calculates how much land is needed to produce the products consumed by one person in a given cultural/economic context. Moreover, our preference is to employ that calculation relative to localized economies of scale or with respect to the idea of bioregionalism—that the products people consume should be produced and available locally to minimize environmental impacts. This form of assessing survival/living needs also emphasizes variability in needs, but only to the extent that those needs are capable of being met locally and do not rely on imports for the purposes of either meeting needs or establishing acceptable consumptive tendencies.

produces, and the general tendency for humans to serve as a significant source of environmental deprivation and degradation. The environmental stresses presented by population growth are evident in expanded resource depletion and in the contemporary era, in outcomes such as the declining availability of oil, deforestation, species extinction, habitat loss, and water shortages among many other negative outcomes. Human population growth effects are widespread, and are not simply seen in the exhaustion of environmental resources. Population growth effects are also evident in the continued build-up of environmental toxins in the air, water, and ground associated with the massive quantities of human waste deposited there, and in other waste process cycles such as climate change which is the result of heat pollution.

As population growth and increased human demands for resources change the world around us, it is necessary to reevaluate what is at stake, to reconsider the structure and design of human societies, human values and lifestyles, how humans and nature interact, and how humans must adjust their behaviors in order to produce less environmental damage. In this contemporary world circumstance marked by extensive human harm to the environment, the world is evolving—or devolving?—into a less hospitable place. Recognizing this outcome some have called for new solutions and new ways of viewing and interpreting the world around us. And in creating these new solutions, it is also necessary to address other aspects of human cultures that have helped promote our declining environmental situation, but which in prior times have been excused from addressing their environmentally destructive activities. As far as criminology is concerned with respect to both theory and practice, this would include examining the meaning of justice, the practice of criminal justice—and the economic forces that shape that practice—and the defining of behaviors we count as or treat as crimes as these relate to environmental harms (see White, 2012). How can/will we redefine core human values and ideas so that they are brought into harmony with the limits, not of human desire and imagination, but rather with those that are a basic part of the limitations of the natural world? How should criminal justice practices be reformed to do less environmental damage while accomplishing their criminal justice functions? How can criminal justice and environmental justice be aligned?

One way of addressing issues such as human desire is to borrow from the ideas of well-known sociologists such as Emile Durkheim, who described a problem he called "anomie" or normlessness. Durkheim, writing in the late 1800s and early 1900s, saw anomie or normlessness as a problem of specific societies, and even within specific societies as problems related to subcultures or parts of larger societies (Durkheim 1951 [1897]). In the Durkheimian view, normlessness/anomie can occur at opposite ends of social organizations. That is to say, unorganized societies can exhibit normlessness, but so too can societies that are well organized. In a society that is well organized, the problem of anomie may occur when institutions promote goals that are unachievable, resulting in the famous interpretation of Durkheim's position that the goals and means in a society are misaligned so that societies promote values that are largely unattainable.

Durkheim's position can be extended to the relationship between the values promoted by a society and the ability of the ecosystem to provide the resources needed to meet those values. In the modern era, for instance, there is a good deal of emphasis placed on values such as economic advancement and accumulating wealth. In many economic views, wealth is a "stored reserve" of labor found in material goods, or the translation of wealth into material goods by using labor to transform the raw materials provided by nature into commodities in the human economy. One of the limitations of this view is that economics do not often address the fact that raw materials are finite, and that extracting and transforming those raw materials into socially constructed human items of value represented by commodities therefore has natural limits. In this sense, then we can think of an environmental version of anomie where human values are misaligned with the availability or quantity of natural resources available to produce wealth without destroying the ability of the ecosystem to function in a way that can continue to support both accumulation and life. In other words, the value placed on economic advancement and the idea that everyone can get ahead and obtain "the good life," is at odds with the level of resources available in the natural world. As noted earlier, currently humans consume natural resources at a rate that is unsustainable from an environmental perspective. This generates environmental or ecological anomie—the disjunction between human desires and environmental availability. It also generates environmental disorganization—an issue of concern in treadmill of production analysis—which we define as excessive waste streams that change the nature of the environment through polluting behaviors. In other words, the idea that economic advancement is limitless while resources are limited creates environmental anomie.

In framing this argument, we must also consider that Durkheim was writing in an age where the world was not as interconnected as it is today—today's global world market has pushed the ideas of economic expansion across borders, and societies now share a larger world "culture of consumption" that was once seen as limited to specific nations (for example, Veblen, 1899). As a result of this cross-cultural and cross-national expansion of consumption goals, today's world system can be viewed as pushing forward the state of environmental normlessness/anomie Durkheim described but without its previous national limitations. Human desire for progress, for consumption, drives us closer to world destruction as we increasingly devour the world around us for our own pleasure, a pleasure we experience by consuming and "advancing" our standard of living. In other words, today's world "culture" has become one of consumption, and world culture has become so all-consuming that it eats away at the very substance of its existence—the natural world.

Thus, one of the key issues we face today is addressing environmental anomie, and not simply in some locations, but across nations. If as we suggest, environmental anomie is one of the factors driving humans everywhere to destroy the world, there is little hope for a resolution to this situation outside of some form of joint, international recognition and response to this problem of the fit between consumption, production, and the limits of nature, an issue we address more fully later in this book when addressing the treadmill of production and consumption (Schnaiberg, 1980).

Human Responses and Perceptions

In the contemporary world affected by these pressing environmental circumstances—climate change, deforestation, resource depletion, the expansion of environmental toxic waste concentrations, over-consumption—the human inhabitants of many areas of the world and in different spheres of life have responded to the variety of environmental crises that face us as humans—some sooner, more forcefully or more appropriately than others. In recent years the governors of U.S. states, for instance, stepped up to organized climate change coalitions in the face of the failure of the federal government to respond to this need (Burns, Lynch, and Stretesky, 2008). International action has been underway for a longer period of time. In 1988, the United Nations established the International Panel on Climate Change (IPCC) that reviews research on and writes reports from those materials reflecting what is known about climate change. Related to the IPCC and international efforts is the UN Framework Convention on Climate Change and the Kyoto Protocol. The Kyoto Protocol has been signed and ratified by 191 nations. The United States has not ratified the Protocol, while Canada has withdrawn from the treaty (effective, December, 2012).

Sometimes, rather than follow the lead of responsible environmental steward nations, countries like the United States tend to ignore efforts to prevent further harm to the natural world. And unfortunately, the societies that tend to be the least willing to respond to environmental problems are those that cause the most environmental damage because of the economic gains involved. These are the societies in which environmental anomie is the most extreme. For some individuals living within those societies, it is simply easier to do nothing than to do something—to enjoy all the "modern conveniences" of life without paying for the costs of doing so—or so they think because they fail to consider how polluting the world affects their health and quality of life outside of the culture of consumption. For others, doing something would mean thinking about the problems facing the world, and rather than think about and remain conscious of the environmental harms that surround them, it becomes more psychologically comfortable to do nothing. And for still others, a range of responses lead to doing nothing. Some, for example, assume that it is unnecessary to protect the world from pollution because it seems improbable or impossible for humans to use up all of nature's resources, or to pollute the vast space of the natural world so extensively that it is harmed or that it becomes a source of harm, or that it becomes so damaged that it is changed in very fundamental ways.

Each of these "reasons" for doing nothing can be described as an excuse for inaction; or, in the language of criminology, as a technique of neutralization (Sykes and Matza, 1957). Techniques of neutralization are invoked by offenders to deactivate values that would otherwise prohibit their ability to engage in illegal, immoral, or other harmful behaviors. Only here, instead of neutralizing values that lead to conformity, people are neutralizing their effect on the environment— they are engaged in what we might instead label *environmental techniques of neutralization*. Thus, the idea that the world is too vast to harm neutralizes any worry an individual has that their behavior can harm the world—"after all, I am just one person. How can my behavior harm an entire planet?" Environmental neutralization may also take the form of other common assumptions such as: "the world is finite and will die anyway. What's the difference if my behavior causes the end of the world to occur sooner rather than later?"

The idea that the planet is so vast as to be immune from human harms is linked to assumptions about the endless supply of natural resources available in the "new worlds" during the period of world conquest and exploration associated with early forms of capitalism and mercantilism. At that point in history—beginning in the fifteenth century—human populations were fairly concentrated, industry was limited, and indeed, the world's supply of resources seemed vast and infinite, especially to Europeans who were discovering "new worlds" where the native peoples had not depleted the wealth of nature (Grove, 1997). This ideology of never-ending natural resources has managed to live beyond that period, continuing to drive the development of a world capitalist order, and to survive well beyond the historical era to which that assumption applied.

By taking this limitless view of the natural world in the contemporary era, what we have failed to realize or appreciate is that normal human uses of the environment do not have a small effect on the natural world that is easily absorbed and innocuous. Rather, at some point, humans use enough of a natural resource or have dumped a sufficient level of toxins into the environment that any additional strains are multiplied, and at some moment in time may cause a tipping point to be reached—that is, a point where environmental changes are accelerated dramatically, perhaps past the point where they can be reversed (Pearce, 2008).

A good example of this kind of problem is climate change. First, climate change is a large and significant environmental problem that spans the globe, cuts across national boundaries, impacting a variety of ecological forms and forces, and the various species of the world—including the smallest microbes. The process of climate change, driven by human use of natural resources in ways that generate heat waste, is not necessarily a slow and linear process. To be sure, during its early phases, climate change may be imperceptible to humans because of its slow course and the seemingly insignificant changes involved which are unobservable to those other than scientists with special equipment—for example, equipment to measure changes in atmospheric carbon dioxide concentrations. Over time, however, climate change accelerates, and it is only during its acceleration that the effects of climate change become obvious to more casual human observation. As the transformations associated with climate change become more and more obvious because they are accelerating, they have already reached new heights, and have edged continuously closer to tipping point levels. At the point where those ecological effects become obvious, we have waited too long to find the cure, and events such as the recent devastation of the United States' northeastern coastal areas by the force of Hurricane Sandy suddenly cause people to wonder why we haven't done something about climate change.

Equally important is the observation that because climate change has, for some time, occurred slowly, it seems to be a natural, evolutionary process. The fact that climate change has historically appeared slow and evolutionary, or that climate change has occurred at other points in the world's history tends to lead to the assumption that the current appearance of climate change is natural and inevitability, and that its driving forces must also be natural and evolutionary. Due to the characteristics of the process being observed, such as climate change's slow course, humans have failed to appreciate their role in forcing climate change. There is a significant scientific literature—dating back more than 100 years—which has warned people about this kind of outcome. Those kinds of warning seem to be irrelevant to most people, and to criminology.

The assumption that the environmental changes we are witnessing today are evolutionary, natural, and largely independent of human action permeates the general manner in which humans think about the environment and environmental problems. This view tends to stall human action, and makes it appear that human action cannot affect the course of environmental change. Because this view of a slowly changing, unlimited natural world has been quite widespread and prominent historically, it is only recently that humans have realized their role in producing environmental changes such as global warming that once appeared as long, evolutionary processes. At this point in history we have begun to realize not only that humans are the culprits behind dramatic and large environmental changes, but that in many cases humans are *the only cause* and that it is only the human species which possesses the ability to provide a solution to these problems.

We must recognize that there are other, extensive modern environmental problems beyond global warming that face the contemporary world. Many are connected to or intersect with climate change, such as deforestation, strip mining and mountaintop removal coal mining, shale oil extraction, and the use of hydrofracturing technology to extract natural gas. These practices not only exacerbate climate change, but also produce an array of other environmental problems such as the production of toxic waste. Other environmental problems exist independently from global warming, including widespread levels of industrial toxic waste that are also altering the conditions of nature. But, even these apparently independent environmental problems—climate change and toxic waste—are inter-related. For instance, climate change impacts the chemical structure and toxicology of the natural world, affecting how species respond to toxic chemicals in the environment, and in many cases may operate by increasing toxicity or diminishing toxicity thresholds (Lannig, Flores, and Sokolova, 2006; Mayer et al., 1991; Noyes et al., 2009; Patra et al., 2007; Richards and Beitinger, 1995; Ziska, Epstein, and Schlesinger, 2009). Other research indicates that global warming can affect the distribution of naturally occurring heavy metals in the atmosphere (Bargagli, 2000), and by extension, as precipitation in rain and snowfall, and consequently in bodies of water and surrounding land masses. In this way climate change can exacerbate the extensive problems already posed by toxic waste and environmental pollution.

Climate change can cause a broad scope of problems in natural ecological settings (Walther et al., 2002). The effect of climate change has also been documented with respect to the uptake and impact of toxins and the general effects of increased temperature on various species, and biodiversity more generally (Denton and Burdon-Jones, 1981; Kearney, Shine, and Porter, 2009; McGinnity et al., 2009; Parmesan, 2006; Porter et al., 2000; Portner, 2002; Rijnsdorp et al., 2009; Sokolova, 2004; Wohlersa et al., 2009). Studies also suggest that global warming will impact the spread of disease. One pathway through which this will happen is the spread of disease-carrying insects in terms of geographic scope, seasonality, and severity of appearance (Brownstein, Holford, and Fish, 2005). Likewise, global warming will affect another important contemporary environmental problem, the impact of endocrine-disrupting chemicals already present in the environment through various forms of pollution (Jennsen, 2006).

In other words, global warming isn't just a climate issue. By affecting climate, global warming's reach exceeds beyond hotter temperatures, rising sea levels, and changes in ocean currents and acidity. A number of serious concerns have been raised about global warming effects in Noyes et al.'s (2009) review of scientific literature on the interactions of temperature, toxicants—for example, persistent organic pollutants (POPS), organochlorine pesticides—precipitation, and salinity. Elevated temperature tends to amplify pollutant toxicity and concentrates tropospheric ozone, conditions likely to impact adversely not only human health especially in urban areas affected by accelerating toxin uptake and altering biological responses to toxins—for example, metabolism and excretion—but also the health of all species in affected regions. Beyond these human-centered observations, Noyes et al. note that climate change impacts the food chain, and may expand POP concentrations in water, soil, and biota, adversely affecting wildlife especially among species already affected by climate change. Areas experiencing increased precipitation due to climate change may also experience expanded exposure to POPs and other environmental toxicants through storm run-offs, while those with reduced precipitation will see concentrations of toxic air pollutants increase. Changes in ocean and fresh water salinity produced by climate change add stressors to the aquatic environment that may increase the toxicity of environmental pollution. These conditions may also be impacted and accelerated by climate change tipping points (Pearce, 2008). These expanded effects are one reason that climate change has global implications, and implications that expand well beyond human population effects.

But, the human effects of climate change should not be glossed over. If, as scientists observe, climate change intensifies the effects of some pollutants on humans, then the consequences of that process requires further examination. In green criminology, one of the ways that this issue can be examined is to explore the effect of environmental toxins on human behavior. Later in this book we examine this issue as part of a green criminological specialization we call green behaviorism.

Green Criminology and New Criminological Questions

To be sure, these environmental problems are large in scope and broad action is required to address them. There is also a need for these environmental concerns to be taken up more broadly in academic circles. And, this is one point of this book: to illustrate how these problems and issues can become and, moreover, must become part of the ordinary discourse of academic disciplines that focus on law, crime and justice, harm and victims—such as criminology. To do so, criminology must open up a dialogue that examines a host of questions:

- What kinds of environmental damage and harms ought to be considered crimes?
- What forms of law ought to be used to address these crimes?
- Should these harms be called crimes?
- What types of legal responses—formal or informal; regulatory, administrative or criminal—constitute the best legal response to environmental harms?
- What other kinds of response—non-legal—can be employed? Are licensing and permitting procedures adequate? Can these be used to reform corporate values, goals, and methods of production? Or even social values in consumer-oriented nations that facilitate corporate pollution of the environment?
- Does exposure to toxins impact criminal behavior? Can controlling toxic exposure help reduce street crime?
- Does society need to be reorganized to meet the goal of reducing pollution?
- Will global warming affect society in ways that might produce more crime? Will new forms of crime emerge? How can we prepare for these possibilities?
- Will international crimes related to resources and resource depletion become more problematic? What kinds of crimes might emerge in relation to scarce resources? Will these involve crimes of aggression between nations? What kinds of international responses will be needed to address these problems?
- Can the criminal justice system be restructured to produce more equitable outcomes, a greater sense of justice, and less environmental crime?

These, we suggest, are the types of questions—but not all of the questions— criminologists must learn to address, and the kinds of issues toward which criminology must become reoriented to remain relevant to the changing world around us in order to better understand and respond to the vast scope of environmental harms that characterize modern circumstances. By addressing these kinds of questions and issues criminologists can become involved in the intellectual work required to produce the knowledge needed to respond to environmental harms. And, important to the current work, it is or has been only green criminology that promotes attention to these kinds of issues, and which in doing so has created what has been up to this point in history a quite criminological revolution.

It is not our goal to explore each of the questions raised above within the confines of this book. Many of these questions are beyond the scope of our mission—establishing the parameters of green criminology, and addressing its usefulness as a new frame of reference for thinking about harms, crimes, laws, and justice, and providing some examples of how this can be accomplished. What we hope to accomplish in the pages that follow is an outline for practicing green criminology and for reforming criminology more generally. Before we can embark on this discussion, we need to lay the groundwork for our arguments.

Chapter 3
Science and a Green Frame of Reference

This chapter explores several issues relevant to establishing the parameters of a green criminology capable of addressing the issues laid out in Chapters 1 and 2. We begin this exploration with the science of the environment, discuss how science can and should influence green criminology, and address the kind of green frame of reference or thinking required to accomplish building a more expansive green criminology.

Science and the Environment

Scientists—physicists, chemists, toxicologists, epidemiologists, biologists, geologists, to name a few—have done much to discover, explore, chart, and reveal the many environmental problems and challenges that we confront in the modern age. These scientists have also documented the extensive harm to the ecosystem in which we are enmeshed as well as harm to the other species that depend on those ecosystems for their survival. But scientists on their own, even with their weighty evidence in hand, are not enough to protect us from harm. This is because scientists often approach their subject matter in an objective manner and they tend to reject taking an advocacy stance (Allen et al., 2001). In their view—in a completely rational and objective world—scientific findings are used by others to generate rational and sound policies that address the problems scientists have discovered. However, we do not live in a world where science and its methods, procedures, and evidence drive environmental policy. If the world worked in the way many scientists envision, we would long ago have addressed the environmental consequences that appear before us now and would be well on our way to solving the major environmental problems of our times. The problem of global warming and the science that supports the development of this process, for example, were discovered in the late 1800s (Fleming, 2005). And while it took decades for scientists to confirm what was observed in the late 1800s, it has taken governmental policy-makers even longer to recognize the problem. Moreover, the pollution problems that became evident to scientists in the 1940s, 1950s, and 1960s have been only partially addressed by policy-makers, while the reaction to emergent issues remains quite slow—for example, the BP-Gulf coast oil leak (see generally, Burns, Lynch, and Stretesky, 2008).

To be sure, modern scientists, though idealists with respect to the values and practice of science, are not naïve. They recognize that scientific evidence is not always accepted on its merits, and that science can be perverted to serve other interests. In short, science can be manipulated by political processes outside the realm of scientific objectivity (Davis, 2002; Markowitz and Rosner, 2002). Furthermore, because scientists are interested in the nature of the phenomena they study and may be more interested in those types of issues and in the pure application of science, they may not always promote the social application or policy implications of their work. Most certainly, some scientists also attend to policy matters and find themselves in the role of advocates (Davis, 2002). The problem this poses for the scientist is that they may be required to sacrifice their research efforts in favor of advocacy.

The point is that scientists may produce the kinds of knowledge needed to promote change, but they themselves are not also always agents of change. Of course, the same is true for the majority of social scientists as well. Nevertheless, social scientists should not overlook the knowledge produced by those in the hard sciences, and need to employ that knowledge in both policy matters and academic work.

Criminologists often tend to speak of criminology being a science, and more than that, of being an interdisciplinary science (Walsh and Ellis, 2006). They note that criminology is a science to the extent that it relies on—or attempts to rely on—scientific methods of inquiry such as the scientific method of analysis and discovery. Despite these efforts to reflect the methods of science, criminology is not a science in the same sense as physics, chemistry, or toxicology. In discussing the relationship between criminology and science, it is not our intention here to provide a critique of criminology as a science, nor to defend criminology as science. More simply, what we wish to point out here is that criminology, which also makes strong claims to being interdisciplinary, should draw upon the environmental research in the hard and natural sciences (see also Gibbs, et al., 2010; Jeffery, 1978). This evidence helps criminologists explore the implications of that body of research for the field of criminology. And, in our view, there are indeed many ways in which criminologists can learn from and apply the knowledge bases found in the hard, natural, and environmental sciences (for example, Lynch and Stretesky, 2001; Stretesky and Lynch, 2001, 2004).

Scientific findings regarding the effects, persistence, and fate of toxic chemicals in and on the environment have an extraordinarily wide range of criminological implications and applications. It is not our purpose to investigate all of these here, since these applications are far reaching—including criminal forensics applications (for example, Mieczkowski, 1999, 2004; Mieczkowski and Sullivan, 2007) and environmental crime investigations (Burns, Lynch, and Stretesky, 2008). Rather, at issues is the question of how criminologists can draw upon scientific knowledge in order to expand their understanding and discussion of environmental harms and their solutions, and to make environmental harms more central to criminological work. For example, by understanding scientific studies of toxins, criminologists can become involved in efforts to address policy, legal remedies, and regulations related to environmental hazards. How should science be incorporated into regulations designed to control environmental pollution and exposure to toxic hazards? What is the best way to implement scientific findings? Through administrative regulations? Criminal laws? Or through other, non-legal venues? If legal remedies are best, which types of regulations should have preference? And, is there a way to select from among the host of toxic pollutants those that ought to be targeted more fully or omitted from consideration? These are the kinds of questions an environmentally conscious criminology, like green criminology, can address.

When it comes to criminal behavior, criminologists also need to consider whether the knowledge produced by scientists has relevance to discussing the causes or influence behind criminal behavior (see Chapter 6). Can the science of toxins be applied to the study of criminal behavior? Should it be? What might be gained or lost by doing so? Should criminologists pay greater attention to heavy metal pollution as sources of aggression, learning deficiencies, and for their biological system impairment properties as these impact human development, the central nervous system, and brain development as these outcomes may relate to crime? How prevalent are the chemicals of concern in the environment? Are these chemicals located within geographic proximity to populations that have high or low rates of criminal offending? To begin to answer any of these questions, criminologists must be more willing to integrate the knowledge produced by scientists into their discipline (for example, see, Lynch, 2004; Lynch, Schwendinger, and Schwendinger, 2006; Stretesky and Lynch, 2001, 2004).

The applications of science to criminology briefly reviewed above are, in many ways, quite apparent. There are other issues that seem less relevant but which we contend have extremely important criminological implications. For instance, scientists have discovered the processes that produce global warming, one of the most important ecological problems of modern times. In what ways is the science of global warming relevant to criminology? Should criminologists address the policy implications of global warming with respect to policing? For instance, the New York City Police Department's patrol vehicles release nearly 100,000 metric tons of carbon dioxide annually (Dickinson, 2007). Can criminologists apply what they know about crime control to propose ways to produce green policing initiatives that reduce the impact of policing on climate change? In the American correctional system—the world's largest such system—how can the lessons of science be applied to control the harmful consequences of locking up so many individuals on the climate and natural ecology? And, in what other ways might global warming research be incorporated into criminal justice research? Should criminologists consider how the effects of global warming might impact crime in the future (Agnew, 2012)? If a warming trend is occurring, and this trend has its predicted impacts on agriculture, and if rapid inflation emerges as a result, how will crime change? And, how can criminologists plan for a future where these circumstances occur? Does this mean a greater need for the expansion of criminal justice processes? Does it mean that new, non-criminal justice remedies need to be pursued (Kramer, 2012)? These are just a few of the interesting questions that criminologists can raise when they take the science of the environment seriously, and when they adopt an environmental frame of reference over the more traditional criminological frame of reference (for example, see, Burns, Lynch, and Stretesky, 2008; Lynch, 2007; Lynch, Burns, and Stretesky, 2010; Lynch, Schwendinger, and Schwendinger, 2006).

In considering the knowledge science has to offer, we must come to grips with the idea that much of what natural scientists know has had little impact on criminology. This, in our view, is unfortunate, and limits the scope and shape of criminology, an issue we take up below.

Rethinking Criminology

It is in the context of modern circumstances filled with various environmental threats that criminologists must reconsider and rethink the scope and practice of criminology. In the context of the modern world, modern peoples must face the forces of destruction that they have created and unleashed on the environment; societies must reconsider their values and goals, the very structure of their societies and their economic, social, and political institutions. It is also in this context that humans must reconsider their understanding of nature and the environment, and in doing so, reevaluate assumptions about the relationships between humans and nature. Moreover, it is in the context of this great project of reevaluations that various disciplines, including criminology, must reconsider how they will incorporate environmental problems, their understanding of the environment, and environmental theories and perspectives. Doing so is, again, part of the green criminological revolution.

As noted, it is clear from an examination of current polices being enacted around the world that some societies have already begun to take steps to address the wide range of environmental problems facing human societies and the natural world. To be sure, some nations have long appreciated the need to think environmentally, and to accept a much different understanding of the interrelationship that exists between the natural world and humans than is common in, for instance, the United States. Moreover, some disciplines have already begun this type of reorientation, and questions about the intersection and interdependence of the natural world and humans have certainly been addressed beyond the realm occupied by traditional forms of criminological thought. These kinds of questions, for instance, have engaged philosophers for centuries. Indeed, over the past four decades, a number of academic disciplines have responded to the troubling findings scientists have produced concerning the state of the natural world, and new disciplines such as green chemistry, environmental toxicology, or global climate science have been the result. These reorientations take on a new environmental frame of reference, one which appreciates the central role of the environment in human affairs, and which expands our knowledge of how to identify and respond to environmental harm and disorder.

For its part, criminology has been slow to adopt green or environmentally oriented approaches. One only need consider that green criminology, now 20 years in the making, is only beginning to have a greater influence within the criminological literature and on bringing criminologists together to address green harms (for example, see the website of the International Green Criminology Working Group, www.greencriminology.org). As a consequence of the slow adaptation of criminology to environmental concerns, criminology has largely failed to appreciate how a green-environmentally oriented or centered view of the world influences an understanding or definition of central aspects of criminology such as justice, how this view might force a redefinition of crime, and how it might support the need to study environmental law, or the examination of agencies charged with enforcing environmental regulations, and so on.

Green criminology was created to provide the academic space in which environmental frames of reference and environmental problems and solutions can be better explored by criminologists. It is in the new space provided by green criminology that concepts such as justice can be expanded and explored and linked to an environmental frame of reference, where the definition of crime can be redefined and reexamined, where nature begins to take precedence over criminology's singular focus on the human-only aspect of crime and justice and the powerless offenders who comprise the sample of offenders criminologists tend to study.

In this sense, green criminology allows for a truly unique view of crime, law, harm, and environmentally linked problems to emerge. There is in this new view of criminology a revolution in thinking waiting to impose itself on criminology. This is, to be sure, at the present time a quiet revolution, one more appreciated outside the United States, and one which presently has been examined by a small group of researchers (Beirne, 1997, 1999, 2002; Beirne and South, 2006, 2007; Lynch, 1990; Lynch and Stretesky, 2003; South, 1998; White, 2008a, 2010). It is not our intention to review the contents of the green criminological literature here. Our concern spans beyond what green criminologists have done, and involves what green criminologists and criminologists more generally ought to be doing.

In order to appreciate the revolutionary nature of green criminology it is necessary to become situated within an environmental frame of reference or more appropriately a green frame of reference. Green criminology uses a variety of frames of reference (for example, for an overview see, Beirne and South, 2007; White, 2008a, 2010; on bio-piracy see, South, 2007; on defining green see, Lynch and Stretesky, 2003; on eco-global criminology as a variety of green criminology see, White, 2011; on environmental justice approaches see, Stretesky and Lynch, 1999, 2003; White, 2007; Zilney, McGurrin, and Zahran, 2006; on conservation criminology as a form of green criminology see, Gibbs et al., 2010; on agro-centered explanations see, Walters, 2006, 2007, 2011; on ecofeminism and green criminology see, Lane, 1998; on masculinities and green criminology see, Groombridge, 1998; on nonspeciest theory see, Beirne, 1999; on connecting state and green crimes see, White, 2008b), but has not sufficiently examined its frame of reference or what that frame of reference entails. Thus, in the sections that follow, we explore the contents of a green or environmental frame of reference, and what it means to take up or situate oneself and one's views of the world in this approach.

A Green-Environmental Frame of Reference

We suggest that green criminology opens up a new space within criminology specifically for the discussion and analysis of environmental concerns as these relate to environmental crime, law, justice, and harm. It is also in this analytic frame of reference that the criminological implications of adopting a green-environmental frame of reference can be explored and developed, and the scope of criminology expanded and enlivened. Thus, it is important that we define the scope of this space and the green frame of reference that supports that view. Moreover, it is important that we explore the scope of a green frame of reference, its content, and implications before tackling the more specific problem of defining green criminology both broadly and in its specific dimensions since doing so relies upon establishing its basis in a green frame of reference.

An environmental view of any topic or issue begins with *adopting an environmental frame of reference*. There are many possible environmental frames of reference, and each may contribute to developing the content of a green frame of reference in different ways (for example, see Merchant, 2005 on various environmental frames of reference including: deep ecology, spiritual ecology, social ecology, green politics, eco-feminism, and sustainable development).

To adopt a green frame of reference means to situate theory, interpretation, and understanding squarely within an environmentally grounded point of view or in relation to a theoretical understanding of nature. More importantly, it means *taking up that point of view or frame of reference above all other frames of reference*. While the green frame of reference may coexist with other frames of reference in any given discipline or analysis, it is, in the view we propose, the dominant frame of reference.

Stated in this way, our discussion may appear quite abstract and vague—what do we mean by taking up a green frame of reference? By the idea of situating oneself in a green view? Thus, to begin our exploration of taking up a green frame of reference, let us begin by contrasting a green orientation to other frames of reference or approaches more commonly employed within social science research. To start, let us take as our point of departure a sociological orientation or frame of reference.

A sociological orientation to research and explanation begins with a frame of reference in which the largest frames of reference are society, social organization and social relationships or the scope of human social organization. In this sociological frame of reference, the emphasis is on humanly created and constructed systems of relations, organization, and institutions, and, consequently, on humans as the key element that connects this frame of reference together and from whose perspective the key problems of society are defined and addressed.

When a researcher is squarely situated within a sociological frame of reference, all problems and issues are social problems related to human relations. Once this point of view is taken up, the analysis begins from an assumption that social problems can be interpreted, understood, and analyzed within the sociological frame of reference or in reference to humans and human relations. Further, in this view, social problems are conceptualized, contextualized, managed, imagined, and assessed in relation to humans or from a human or anthropocentric perspective on the world. In this view, then, the world is incorporated and interpreted within the human frame of reference. Thus, ecological problems are interpreted in ways that bring them into the sociological frame of reference.

Sociology is not alone in adopting this type of humanly situated or oriented perspective, and most social sciences exhibit a strong tendency to take up a human frame of reference. This may, for example, involve a psychological frame of reference, one based in economics, or one based on small group interaction such as in social work. In taking up one of these frames of reference social sciences are typically concerned with their subject matter in relation to humans, human relationship, human organization, human cultural values, or as the problems under study impact humans. In these various social sciences there may be sub-frames of reference, or frames of reference that are subsumed within the human frame of reference. But, even these sub-frames of reference typically fail to expand beyond the structural limits imposed by the human frame of reference that guides thinking within social science disciplines.

Often, when the environment is examined or included in human-centered social science frames of reference, it is treated as part of the sub-frame of a theory. It is important to note that the overarching frame of reference may be sociological or psychological, and so on. The point, however, is that regardless of the orientation of the frame of reference, it is capable of making room for an environmental view only as a sub-component or element or as a sub-frame or secondary frame of reference embedded within the larger frame of reference. Typically in the social sciences the primary or main frame of reference is anthropogenic or human-centered, and other frames of reference are viewed either in relation to the human frame or as sub-frames within this view.

As noted, in most social science views the environment is often accorded a place as a sub-frame of reference, meaning that environmental problems will be interpreted, understood, conceptualized, contextualized, imagined, and addressed relative to human-centered experiences, needs, and existence, and in relationship to its human impacts. This means that the environment is not fully appreciated in itself, in its independent status, or outside of its relationship to humans. Moreover, when the environment is treated as a sub-frame of reference it is viewed as being of secondary importance, and any effort to contextualize human social relationships is undertaken by framing humans within their social, economic, psychological, and political contexts first. This leaves environmental considerations as an afterthought, as appendages to the primary frame of reference.

As an example of this way of thinking, consider a sociological frame of reference in which the largest frame of reference is society. The sociological sub-frames of reference may consist of other large frames of reference. These large sub-frames of reference, however, are seen as being embedded within or subsumed within the larger sociological frame of reference. Thus, one might imagine a sociological frame of reference that begins with society in the abstract. From there, the frame of reference may identify empirically grounded reference points such as a specific society. Within that specific society one identifies and places sub-frames of reference such as the economic system, governance, education, family, and so forth, into the larger sociological frame of reference. Each sub-frame of reference may also be further divided into smaller units or sub-frame elements such as single-parent families, two-parent families, and so on. Thus, the sub-frame elements that a sociologist might focus on could include individuals, their bonds to society, institutions, family, peers, and so forth—the kinds of sub-frame elements commonly found within criminology analysis. To be sure, this approach appears to offer a logical and rational way to express and explore the human-centered aspects of society and the relations they entail.

It should be noted, however, that this logical and rational approach carries with it a set of problems based in the specific frame of reference approach that has been adopted as the anchoring point for the analysis. One problem is that this human-centered frame of reference has historically created a reductionist approach to sociological analysis that focuses on the lowest sub-frame elements—for example, social bonds—one that neglects their contextual connections and embeddedness (Mills, 1959). This style of thinking is often evident within criminology where a focus on sub-frame elements overrides the original orientation expressed in the social frame of reference from which such work often begins. For example, criminologists routinely examine the strengths and weaknesses of individual's social bonds to others as a source of crime and conformity. In doing so, they tend to isolate these bonds, and abstract them from their social frame of reference. As a result, the effort to conceptualize, contextualize, imagine, and address social bonds as an integral aspect of the social frame of reference is lost. This is a problem because it is reductionist. It is also a problem, as we shall argue, because it not only neglects, it loses other important frames of reference or points of orientation such as the green frame of reference, which quite often totally disappears from consideration in the vast majority of research produced by criminologists.

The reductionist tendencies we have briefly described, some might argue, are a minor problem, one which may become useful from an analytic perspective, or in terms of establishing whether or not bonds are, in the first place, even important elements in the study of the causes of crime. But this tendency toward reductionism that anthropogenically situated frames of reference encourage provides an example of our broader concern with this type of approach in general—that it focuses on the human or social frame of reference as the single, most important, and largest frame of reference, and in many cases, especially as far as criminology is concerned, as the *only* frame of reference recognized as legitimate. This occurs because human-centered frames of reference illogically take human societies as the largest frame of reference and in effect through a grand form of abstraction, leave out the largest frame of reference without which humans could not even exist—the environmental frame of reference.

In short, our contention is that in order to effectively examine and understand societies, it is necessary to begin with an environmental frame of reference, which may be green or otherwise. Absent the kind of environment found on earth, human societies of the type that have been developed would be impossible. Thus, it is therefore always necessary to acknowledge this point by including some kind of environmental frame of reference.

To illustrate our contention, consider how an environmentally situated approach forces researchers to begin with a broader contextual approach, one that eschews reductionist thinking in favor of a holistic appreciation of an entire network of relationships, many of which are displaced or ignored in the social science frame of reference. In an environmental frame of reference, for instance, a key point is that sub-frame elements of study are integral parts of the entire system or frame of reference.

From an environmental perspective, changes in the sub-frame elements can initiate feedback effects that alter the entire context of the frame of reference, including sub-frame elements. In other words, in an environmental perspective, the behavior of or changes in sub-frame elements impact the balance and health of the entire system taken as a whole. The reductionist tendencies of human-centered frames of reference, which we are socialized to accept within many academic disciplines and which we tend to appreciate given that we are humans, are hidden and encouraged by anthropogenic frames of reference.

Our point is that an environmental frame of reference is to a large degree entirely different than the anthropogenic-centered social frame of reference found, for example, in economics, sociology, criminology, or any one of a number of other social sciences. It is a common practice for sociologists or economists to treat society or an element of society as the frame of reference. What happens, however, when we ask the sociologist or economist to think about environmental issues and problems? They are likely to think of this dimension of the problem in the same way as they think about other problems they examine—as a sub-frame within the larger human frame, or as a sub-element within that frame of reference. As an example, let us imagine that we ask a social scientist to think about the social, economic, and environmental frames of reference. They are, perhaps, likely to think of them as outlined in Figures 3.1-3.3.

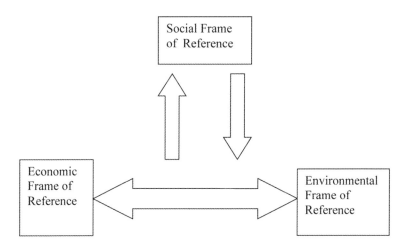

Figure 3.1   Social frame of reference interactions with other frames of reference in a hidden hierarchical format

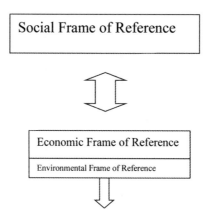

Figure 3.2   Social frame of reference interactions with other frames of reference in an obvious hierarchical fashion

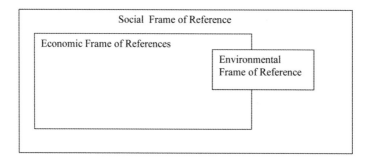

Figure 3.3   Overlapping frames of reference showing hierarchy

In the social science view, the environment is likely to be included as a separate frame or sub-frame of reference, and may be thought of more precisely in the manner depicted in either Figures 3.1, 3.2 or 3.3 as typical models. In general, this means that in a social science view, the environment will be treated as a distinct, unique, independent area for investigation with different levels of overlap or feedback. In Figure 3.1, feedbacks between the various frames of reference are depicted, with the social frame elevated in the diagram to indicate its—often hidden—hierarchical domination over other frames of reference. In Figure 3.2, the economic and environmental are depicted as sub-frames of reference. Both the economic and environmental sub-frames of reference here are depicted as having diminishing importance and effect on the social frame of reference. In Figure 3.3, both the environmental and economic frames are viewed as encapsulated sub-frames in the social frame of reference. Here, the economic and environmental sub-frames are not viewed as independent, but having much less importance than the social frame of reference, which is hierarchically the most important frame of reference. All these diagrams carry with them a message about the subservience of the environment and the environmental frame of reference to the human-centered orientation of this way of thinking. Here, it is clear that the environment is considered as secondary, and perhaps often not at all, or as potentially unnecessary to the examination of any specific issue.

There are, in our view, several deficiencies to these approaches to the environment. First, it is likely that these frames and sub-frames of reference are not so clearly distinguishable from one another—that they tend to overlap in ways that an anthropogenic-centered orientation promotes, but which in reality obscure from view the real relationships between these different entities. Second, this anthropogenic-centered orientation is not the only or perhaps the best way to perceive the relationships between these frames of reference, and, we would argue, that this view misidentifies the frames and sub-frames of reference, their connections, interconnections, and relative importance. This interpretation becomes clear once we situate ourselves in an environmental orientation.

Toward a Green Frame of Reference

An environmentally situated orientation or frame of reference forces us to recognize the limitations of a humanly situated orientation to environmental problems and issues, and, more broadly, to understanding the environment, its importance, and the context in which environmental, social, economic, and other matters are framed and understood. When we take up an environmental orientation, the very nature of how we interpret and understand the environment and its interactions, its importance, and the ways in which humans are enmeshed in the environment changes (Daly, 1998).

In the anthropogenic-centered orientation, the frames of reference are most important and the relationships between the frames of reference distort the actual relations between these entities. Anthropocentric views are distorted because they depict the frames of reference in isolation from one another or as conceptually separate frames of reference. This occurs because they privilege the human frame of reference and because of the way they determine the order of importance of these frames of reference and their degree of interaction. To be sure, the frames of reference depicted in Figures 3.1, 3.2, and 3.3 do occur—and it is not our intention to deny that these interactions do not occur. Rather, our point is that the way these interactions are depicted by a humanly centered orientation is inaccurate. And, while the three diagrams presented above may have heuristic value at times, we cannot rely on these depictions since they are distortions of reality.

In what ways are these diagrams distorted? In his discussion of a similar issue, economist Herman Daly (1998) described a suitable realignment of this diagram that reflects an environmental orientation as depicted in Figure 3.4

In other words, Daly suggests that the predominant frame of reference ought to be the environment, and that the human frames of reference—society and economy—

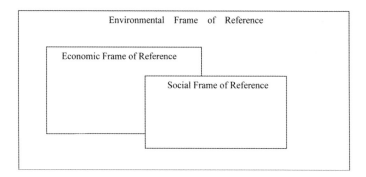

**Figure 3.4   Adaptation of Herman Daly's (1998) model
of environmental thinking**

are sub-frames within the environmental frame. This view suggests that there is
no true independence of any of the reference frames. Further all human frames of
reference are constructed within the limits imposed by the environmental frame
of reference. As a result, the environmental frame of reference dominates thinking
and is larger than the human frames of reference. Moreover, nothing in human
frames of reference eclipses the boundaries of the environment.

To some, the distinction between the diagrams in Figures 3.4 verses those
found in Figures 3.1, 3.2, and 3.3 may appear subtle, a mere simple reordering of
relationships. We suggest that the diagram in Figure 3.4 actually contains the starting
point of reference for thinking about the environment and its relationship to humans
that is really quite revolutionary with respect to much social science theory and
certainly with respect to criminological theory. In the view represented by Figure
3.4, human frames of reference can never be independent of the environmental
frame of reference, and consequently, all aspects of human societies must be re-
imagined in relationship to the boundaries imposed by the environment. In effect, all
human relations, developments, structures, and so forth, are limited or constrained
by the environment and can never exist independently of their intimate connection
to the environmental and, in thinking about these relationships, to the environmental
frame of reference. The environment is, in this view, the largest structural frame of
reference and constrains all other frames of reference.

Why should the environmental frame of reference be granted this kind of
theoretical privilege as the anchoring point for analysis? First and foremost, the
environmental frame of reference ought to be privileged in this way because the
environment defines the maximum scope of human possibilities. As humans we may
not like to imagine this option, but this is true especially with respect to the physics
of the natural world. Humans cannot create things from nothing, and must start the
human creative processes from the materials provided by the natural world. These
materials may be combined, reshaped, and reorganized, but they are never, in the
truest sense of the word, created by humans, for humans cannot create something
from nothing. Nor can the products human create expand the physical world—they

cannot add "volume" to the physical stuff in the universe. Human products may change the environment, may reorder it, but they cannot escape its boundaries.

In addition, we must recognize that the organizational forms of human societies are constrained by the limits of the environment. We cannot endlessly populate the world beyond its natural capabilities; we cannot use more materials than the natural world provides. By depicting the relationship between humans and the environment in this way we are admitting that our possibilities as humans are not limitless—they are less than the scope of possibilities presented within nature. How much less? The answer to that question is open for debate and depends on how much of nature humans use or leave untouched for other species, and how much of nature we can use before we destroy the sustainable capacity of nature upon which human life depends (Lovelock, 2007).

In our view, much social science, both in theory and in practice, originates from an anthropogenic-centered orientation and thus fails to consider the environmental frame of reference in the way we have described above. As Daly (1998) has argued with respect to economic ways of thinking, the consequences of human-centered styles of thinking are essentially two fold. On the one hand, social and economic theory and consequentially policies have been imagined and understood only from the human frame of reference. This means that the consequences of these modes of thinking and their derivative policies will tend to omit their environmental ramifications from consideration where those ramifications are not viewed as having human impacts. On the other hand, a human-centered orientation carries with it the additional problem of preferencing human frames of reference. This kind of orientation continues to isolate human and environmental issues from one another unless, of course, linking the two cannot be avoided given the nature of the problem under examination. The real issue here is that the environment becomes an after-thought—that is, it is only considered when it forces itself into consideration by "misbehaving," by making its natural boundaries evident and forcing itself into human consciousness because the feedback effects it produces in response to the forms of ecological damage humans produce can no longer be ignored. Indeed, it is just this type of situation that is evident in the modern world—in the discovery of global warming, or the build-up of toxins in the environment, and so on.

The environmental feedbacks we are currently experiencing have produced a lesson we need to acknowledge. That lesson is that humans have discovered that they cannot treat nature as endless and robust and beyond the impact of modifications created by human disregard, neglect, or noxious behavior; that humans cannot continually add toxic pollutants to the environment without suffering from that form of behavior or without that behavior impairing the environment and affecting non-human species and environmental subsystems or local ecological units; that human use of energy creates heat, and that the heat pollution produced by humans is changing the very nature of the environment and consequentially producing further constrains on human development and societies. In understanding that these things are happening to humans, it does not necessarily follow that humans perceive or understand that the ecological damage they cause not only affects humans and constrains human life, but also constrains the life course of other species, ecological units, and the total ecological system. These are big issues, and how humans respond to them is a major contemporary concern. Here, we have a more modest goal, and must shortly turn to the issue posed by the following question: How do these concerns affect criminology? Before doing so, however, we wish to extend our discussion of the environmental frame of reference by drawing an analogy to the argument C.W. Mills (1959) made about the sociological imagination more than half a century ago.

From a Sociological Toward an Environmental Imagination

In his well-known work, *The Sociological Imagination*, C. Wright Mills presented a critique of sociology that applies not only to the sociology of his era, but which remains relevant today. The relevance of that argument expands well beyond the scope of sociology.

Mills stated that ordinary people "do not possess the quality of mind essential to grasp the interplay of man and society, of biography and history, of self and world. They cannot cope with their personal troubles in such a way as to control the structural transformations that usually lie behind them" (1959: 4). Mills' point here was that the average or ordinary person doesn't think about social problems contextually. Rather than viewing themselves as interconnected to one another and as part of a larger social and economic system, individuals tend to view their own circumstances as personal troubles or individual troubles. Interpreted in this way, the average person sees in social problems a personal trouble, and can only manage to understand that social problem as an individual concern that is unconnected from the personal troubles others are also experiencing. Mills suggested that this view of social problems leads people to understand their own place in the world from a subjective standpoint, and to see themselves in isolation from others. The consequence of this form of interpretation and perception is that it hides from view how individuals and the troubles they experience are connected, and that those connections are needed to produce an accurate and useful understanding of the nature of modern social problems.

In making this point, Mills was also drawing attention to the critique of sociology he presented; a critique which basically noted that contemporary sociologists had, like the ordinary individual in society, overlooked the importance of thinking contextually, of linking together individuals in ways that reflect the nature of society and the webs of interdependence that characterize societies and social relationships. Before ordinary people could see these connections, Mills argued that it was necessary for those who analyzed social problems not only to see but to make these connections in their work; that it was the job of the social scientist to make these connections obvious. And it was only by setting "an example" that the work of sociologists would become relevant to ordinary people. Thus, for Mills, it was the task of those who analyzed contemporary social problems—artists, journalist, scientists, editors, and scholars—to enlighten the public about making these connections by using what Mills called the sociological imagination.

In describing the sociological imagination, Mills (1959: 5) wrote

> The sociological imagination enables its possessor to understand the larger historical scene in terms of its meaning for the inner life and external career of a variety of individuals. ... [T]he individual can understand his own experience and gauge his own fate only by locating himself within his period, that he can know his own chances in life only by becoming aware of those of all individuals in his circumstances.

Mills proposed that this kind of analytic frame of reference was employed by classical sociologists, and that taking this view "enables us to grasp history and biography and the relationship between the two in society." In this way, the sociological imagination provided self-consciousness concerning the place humans occupy within society, and thereby enabled new interpretations of social relationships and social problems that expressed how individual troubles were linked to each other and were influenced by prevailing structural conditions. This would allow individuals to see that they were not alone, and that their personal troubles were social problems.

Mills' (1959: 55-68) discussion also explored the reason that this kind of thinking was not widespread within the social sciences. For example, Mills argued that sociologists failed to grasp the importance of the sociological imagination because they were preoccupied with employing reductionist thinking both theoretically and empirically—that is, sociologists, like the average individual, had fallen into the trap of thinking about people as isolated, abstract individuals, and it was the characteristics of those individuals more so than social structure which has occupied sociologists in the twentieth century. In taking up this view of the individual in society, the contemporary sociologist and other social scientists such as psychologists and, we would assert, criminologists, created a human subject for study that was an empirical and theoretical abstraction. For Mills, the individual was treated abstractly when they were discussed and analyzed as individuals—as an individual unit separate from their social-structural connections. This tendency to treat individuals as abstractions was best illustrated for Mills in psychologism, by which Mills meant the "attempt to explain social phenomena in terms of facts and theories about the make-up of individuals" (1959: 67). Using psychologism, researchers endeavor to collect facts about individuals and to reach conclusions about social structure, an idea more generally referred to as the ecological fallacy. Mills' point was that much sociology and perhaps all of psychology had misinterpreted the individual and the importance of social structure.

The critique and perspective Mills proposed in his work have had an important influence on sociology and are widely cited especially for their call to situate human actors and actions within their social context (Fuller, 2006; Phillips, 2001; Phillips, Kincaid, and Scheff, 2002). To be sure, Mills' view is important, and by calling for contextualized analysis he highlights a point important to our own work—the need to place humans in an environmental context and frame of reference.

In our view, however, Mills' critique, perhaps because it was written in the 1950s and was therefore explored during a period in history when environmental issues had not reached the heightened levels of concern they have today, needs to be expanded to address environmental problems. Mills' concern with context situated individuals within relevant historical social, cultural, and economic structures, but did not explicitly recognize environmental/ecological frames of reference as important dimensions of human context and social structure. In hindsight, we believe that Mills would agree that his approach could be extended to considering the environmental frame of reference as part of the structural context in which individuals must be situated.

Following Mills' lead, we argue that any approach that fails to appreciate the connection between humans and the environment is likely to treat humans abstractly. Outside of the natural environment or removed from the ecological context, or thought of in ways that disconnect them from an environmental imagination, human beings, as such, do not exist. Once extracted from the natural ecology, from the substance of life, humans become analytical abstractions, divorced from the larger context in which they are enmeshed and on which they depend for life. To be sure, humans create social, political, and economic structures—cities, towns, neighborhoods, and so forth—to enhance their existence. But these are only the most immediate social environments which humans construct, and these immediate social contexts could not exist without, in the first place, the resources of nature. Our view suggests, then, that humans cannot be understood fully in relation to only the structural edifices that they erect. To take the human context as consisting only of social structure is to ignore that the ability of humans to create these structures, while dependent on human labor, is not possible in the first place without the material resources nature supplies. Moreover, the way human societies have evolved and continue to evolve has a direct relationship to nature. Human settlements, cities, and so forth do not spring up where resources are few or absent; where there is no water or food, or where material to build the structures upon which human settlement depend are absent. Certainly in the modern era, humans now have the ability to settle in many places, having developed the apparatus for moving raw materials and food stuffs across the face of the globe. But, even these forms of settlements are limited by costs and by the feasibility of such endeavors.

The environmental imagination or more appropriately in our view, the green imagination, forces us to recognize that when we treat humans in isolation from the environment or ecology in which humans are intimately enmeshed, we have before us an artificial construction—the abstract human, the individual cut off from the ties to nature that affect the very being of this subject's human qualities. It is in this abstract sense that humans as human, as real living, acting thinking beings, cease to be so and become nothing more than a theoretical construction that appears to have use for analysis. But for analytic strategies that seek to understand the full implications of the contextual network associated with being human, it becomes imperative to include a larger green imagination that connects humans to the environmental frame of reference.

We view our analysis of Mills' position on the sociological imagination as more of an extension than a critique of Mills. Certainly, we have great respect for Mills' point of view, and understand that the limitations that adhere in his view are a product of the era in which he lived. Having made that point, we need to move beyond Mills' version of contextual social analysis so that it incorporates nature as an important structural force. But, more than this, we need also to move beyond the human-centered orientation that is also dominant in Mills' perspective. It is only by doing so that the full importance of the green imagination and the green frame of reference becomes more apparent. And, it is only in doing so that we can escape the anthropocentric arguments of social science.

Toward a Green Imagination

Environmental problems—pollution, global warming, resource depletion, and many others—cannot be fully understood or analyzed when the theoretical frame of reference emphasizes the importance of those problems only for humans. To be sure, from an anthropogenic perspective, environmental problems are important precisely because they affect humans. Still, this emphasis is not consistent with a green frame of reference. In our view, a green imagination is employed to extend the analysis of environmental problems beyond humans and the myopic focus of the effect of environmental problems on humans. A green frame of reference should be employed to recognize that when environmental harms and problems are the focus of analysis, that there are a variety of nonhuman victims that need to be considered as well (see Beirne, 1999). Moreover, these non-human victims are not limited to non-human animals, but include other species and the environment itself as a living entity.

Borrowing from Mills, we can say that a green imagination places environmental problems within an historical context that pays attention to ecology as the primary frame of reference, and traces connections between sub-frames of reference—for example, human, non-human, local ecological units—to illustrate their interconnection. This idea has multiple dimensions, and is best illustrated by example rather than by specific theoretical explanations.

Consider, for example, the problem of environmental pollution generally, and for the purposes of our example, water pollution in particular. In our example, Big Company's production process generates 10,000 gallons of waste water a day. This waste is emptied into a lagoon, which holds the waste for evaporation. The waste sediments are collected, dried, and burned at high temperatures. For many years, local residents have complained that the lagoon leaks, contaminating local groundwater, which seeps into the drinking water supply. In addition, the burning process creates noxious pollutants which contain heavy metals and dioxins. On days when the company burns waste, residents complain of various problems, including shortness of breath, asthma, burning eyes, and itchy skin, which are probably the result of particulate pollution as well as noxious chemicals. A number of the residents have become ill, and children seem especially affected. Moreover, Big Company is one of several local companies that pollute the local area.

Thus far, our scenario describes the connection between manufacturing, pollution, and the health of local citizens through environmental contamination of the local ecology. This description, at this point, takes only a human-centered perspective. To expand on this human-centered perspective, we need to consider the following.

The problem of pollution in this case is described by its local effects. Yet, once expelled into the environment, these pollutants can exert an influence well beyond the local area. Air pollutant, for instance, can travel great distances. Nriagu (1990) described the widespread distribution of heavy metal pollutants across the surface of the world, and argued that the source of most trace metal pollution is industrial waste. Compared to natural background sources of environmental heavy metals, the emission of heavy metals by industry were found to be extensive. The level of lead in the environment was 28 times higher, cadmium six times higher, and vanadium and zinc six times higher than would be predicted from background sources alone. For copper, mercury, arsenic, antimony, and nickel, pollution levels were 100-200 percent higher than expected. Nriagu also noted that heavy metal concentrations in urban areas normally exceeded those in rural areas by five-to-ten-fold, and for some pollutants by 100 times or more. Evidence of the ubiquitous nature of environmental pollution stems from an extensive literature on the distribution of these pollutants which have been discovered in diverse locations and media ranging from Antarctic marine mammals (Aono et al., 1997) to Siberian ice core samples (Eyrikh, Schwikowski, and Papina, 2004).

It is evident from these studies that not only is pollution mobile, the first "victim" is nature itself; the land on which pollution is poured; the water into which it seeps or is emptied; the air into which it is emitted. In this way the very nature of ecosystems, both proximate and distant from polluting sources, are altered. These ecological victims are hidden from view when we adopt an anthropocentric view in which the victims must be humans.

Once the air, land, and water are polluted, they impact all forms of life which draw from and come into contact with those environmental media. These forms of exposure may occur through direct contact with a contaminated environmental medium, and indirectly through the food chain (Colborn, Dumanoski, and Myers, 1997). Once in the food chain, toxins accumulate upward and have their most dramatic effect on species higher up the food chain. It is through direct and indirect exposure that all species are affected by toxic pollutants. All of these non-human species, including insects, fish, flora, and fauna become part of the chain of victimization. It is here, in both primary ecological exposure and damage, and indirect damage to all living species that come into contact with the contaminated environment, that we see the limitations of even Mills' perspective on the sociological imagination with its anthropocentric view which can only seriously entertain the human social context and human victimization.

Criminology and a Green Frame of Reference

Above we have argued in favor of a need to reconceptualize how humans think about their relations to and place in the world by describing a green-environmental frame of reference and a green imagination that we believe needs to be employed in place of human-centered frames of reference. What does this mean in practice? And, more precisely, what does this mean in terms of the practice of the academic work of criminologists?

First, it means that criminologists must re-think the framework upon which their discipline is built, which, after all, tends to begin and end with a human frame of reference. Little criminological research extends beyond the human frame of reference, and even when criminologists entertain environmental research, their studies have been criticized for their limited effort to take a broader view of environmental harm (for discussion and exceptions see, Beirne, 1997, 1999, 2002). Undertaking this reorientation to a green frame of reference and a green imagination is no easy task, since much of the thought processes of humans are essentially self- or species-centered. Criminologists, like most other humans, are not trained to think environmentally, to step outside of their humanness and to reconsider the place of humans in the world around them and the broader implications of a green frame of reference. Green criminologists have, however, made use of this kind of approach. Van Solinge (2010) takes a broad, green view of environmental victimization in his analysis of deforestation crime in the Amazon. As he notes, crimes of deforestation have significant impacts on local human populations, especially those whose lifestyles are more traditional. His argument also draws attention to victimization of future human populations. In addition, however, van Solinge notes that deforestation has profound impacts on non-human species. Of particular concern is the effect of deforestation in the Amazon on non-human species in one of the richest ecological areas in the world (see also, van Solinge, 2008; for a discussion related to air pollution see, Walters, 2010).

Second, re-thinking the framework upon which criminology is built means transforming criminology so that it begins with a green frame of reference. To do so, as we have noted above, the environment must become the starting point for analysis, and the starting point for thinking about criminological matters. This reorientation is no small step, because it is not readily apparent how crime, justice, and law can be treated outside of a human frame of reference, and to be sure, the history of criminology is written as if this were not possible. Thinking about crime, law, and justice outside of an anthropocentric model may lead criminologists to discover new ways of thinking about crime, law, and justice that provide a better understanding of those processes. Again, this is not an easy task. Criminology has a long, intellectual history, and the manner in which criminologists think about crime, law, and justice is structured by that history. Contemporary researchers have established reputations based on research derived entirely from human-centered frames of reference, and those frames of reference are not likely to be given up for a new way of thinking. But, what criminologists must keep in mind is that the frame of reference they employ most often is not uniquely criminological—it is, rather, broadly shared within society so that it will also be difficult to convince the public or law makers that an environmentally situated frame of reference is useful for understanding crime or producing crime- and justice-related policies.

Third, in taking up this green frame of reference, criminologists must make an effort to view problems that were previously only imagined in the social frame of reference in their constant interconnection to the green frame of reference. There are a number of examples that could be offered here. For instance, the criminological definition of crime focuses rather exclusively on crimes between humans. While there is nothing in a green frame of reference to prevent the study of these events and behaviors, recognizing that there are other types of harms that can also be called crimes—crimes of toxic waste, crimes of depletion, crimes against nature, crimes of global warming, and so forth—opens up new ways of seeing crime, the vast array of human activities that produce environmental harm, new types of environmental victims, and perhaps new ways of conceiving the idea of justice from a broader green frame of reference (for example, see, Beirne, 1999; Green, Ward, and McConnachie, 2007; Lynch and Stretesky, 2003; Walters, 2006, 2007; White, 2008a).

What we have offered here are guidelines for thinking in new ways within criminology that promote green thinking. We do not, at this point, develop a specific position or prescription for replacing all the work criminologists do and have done with this green frame of reference. We cannot at this point in the development of this idea say here is how you would look at gun control, or domestic violence, or terrorism, or any other criminological topic from a green frame of reference. How specific criminological topics might be addressed depends on how the idea of a green frame of reference is employed, and whether criminologists begin to lay the groundwork for such a view, and how they lay that groundwork. In the chapters that follow, we provide some specific examples of the kinds of issues that emerge when one begins to think by employing a green frame of reference and a green imagination. We realize that in one book we cannot remake all of criminology or address all of its issues from the perspective of the approach we have outlined here. And, we recognize that our approach to a criminology based in a green reference point may have its limits. This view may not be able to explain gun crimes or domestic violence, or terrorism. But certainly, criminologists might learn something about the topics they study and ones they fail to study and the nature of their discipline by opening up to the possibilities of thinking green.

Moreover, we recognize in our own work the limits of our ability to think in a green frame of reference that eclipse an anthropocentric orientation. To be sure, at points our work can be subjected to the critique we have laid out above. For example, when we count human victims of environmental harms as we do in a later chapter, we openly admit to taking an anthropocentric view. To some extent, as criminologists our knowledge of how to count and study non-human victims of environmental harms is limited, and moreover is a product of available data that would allow us to address the problem of environmental victimization more broadly.

With these initial ideas in mind we turn to further applications of research that is consistent with green criminology. Green criminology is, as we have noted, a revolution in the way criminologists think. It is an idea that is so revolutionary it holds out the possibility of potentially remaking a discipline or perhaps spawning a new discipline. In the chapter that follows, we explore this revolutionary idea—green criminology—further.

Chapter 4
Toward a Typology of Green Criminology[1]

As noted in the previous chapter, green criminology is a means for studying problems related to environmental harm and crime, victimization, law, environmental justice, environmental regulation, and moral/philosophical issues as these issues relate to humans, non-human animals, plant species, and so on, and the ecosystem and its components (Benton, 1998; White, 2008a). Green criminology has largely emerged and been defined by the kinds of research that researchers identify as being green rather than as a theoretical concept (Lynch, 1990; Lynch and Stretesky, 2003; South, 1998). This approach to defining green criminology as "what green criminologists do" has both advantages and limitations. The advantages of this emergent properties approach to green criminology is that its subject matter is not confined by pre-existing ideas that may limit the kinds of academic advancements green researchers pursue. The limitation of this approach is that there is no clear theoretical or definitional consensus on green criminology which impedes describing that view and generating a concise explanation about the scope and mission of green criminology. This makes this view unlike other, more precisely defined criminological approaches.

One way to address the scope and definition of green criminology issues is by creating a typology that organizes green criminology into types of approaches. This chapter takes up this challenge and builds a green criminological typology by examining the kinds of research recognized as falling under the green sciences.

Natural scientists have long taken up environmental issues, and their attention to green studies predates the emergence of green criminology. Thus, the concepts natural sciences employ to organize their green research efforts may be useful for developing a similar approach within green criminology. One reason for taking this approach to developing a green criminological typology—that is, for relating it specifically to the kinds of green research that have been undertaken in the sciences—is that this orientation can be employed to illustrate the interconnections and intersections between green criminology and green science. The advantage of specifically focusing on and exposing this overlap between green criminology and green science has to do with encouraging green criminologists to draw on relevant scientific literature to support their views and contentions and makes the connections between green criminology and green science visible and obvious.

---

1   Note: This chapter represents and adaptation and significant revision of an article we previously published: Lynch, Michael J. and Paul B. Stretesky. (2011). "Similarities Between Green Criminology and Green Science: Toward a Typology of Green Criminology." *International Journal of Criminology and Criminal Justice* 35,4: 293-306.

Green criminology cannot, in our view, make a substantial contribution to the study of crime and justice without being able to admit to and making its connection to science obvious.

To illustrate these connections and make them more obvious, we review the overlap between green criminology and green science in three primary areas. First, we draw attention to what we call *eco-approaches* or research that addresses environmental issues in relation to non-human species and their intersections with the natural ecology. Second we examine what we term *enviro-approaches*, that is research that addresses pollution issues that impact human species in interaction with the environment. Third, we explore *green policy approaches* that address solutions to and the prevention of environmental harms.

These three approaches, however, do not exhaust all possible types of green criminological research, and there is a significant volume of research left that is omitted by these three primary areas of intersection. In other words, there are issues green criminologists address that are not included within green natural science approaches. We identify this unique green criminological contribution that stems from research which connects environmental issues to economic, social, political, and philosophical theories either by their initials (ESPP), or by the term *green contextual approaches*. Green contextual approaches explore the causes and development of environmental harms, environmental policy and law, and social control reactions—law enforcement—to environmental harms that exist independently of green scientific research. The issues examined by green criminologists under the heading of ESPP involve issues green scientists do not ordinarily address. Thus, ESPP issues also stand out as a form of research that green scientists can draw upon to deepen their discussion of environmental problems.

To explore these connections and the development of a typology of green criminology, we begin with a discussion of environmental issues found in the general toxicological literature. The more general literature in toxicology identifies ways to study environmental pollution and its toxic effects. Concern with specific environmental problems found in the world around us, however, eventually produced specializations within the toxicological literature and the practice of toxicological research. For the present discussion the most important of the specialties are the sub-disciplines known as eco-toxicology and environmental toxicology. While sharing the same basic methodological approaches to the study of toxins in the environment, these approaches differ with respect to their focus on specific species categories—humans, animals, plants, and so on— and the environment itself as "victim"—although in the scientific literature the environment is not described as a victim, but is rather examined as an affected entity. In taking specific views related to species and the ecology as different affected groups, eco- and environmental toxicology move beyond the general issues explored within toxicology more generally which focus more directly on the mechanisms of toxicity.

Environmental Issues and Toxicology

Toxicology, which can be defined as the study of the "adverse effect of chemicals on living organisms" (Klaassen and Eaton, 1991), has produced a significant literature related to examining the effect of environmental toxins. In general use, the term "environmental toxins" applies to any toxic substance found in any given environment. In that view, the environment need not be an ecosystem, but might also include home or workplace environments. This means that the term "toxicology" is not limited to the study of toxins in nature, but rather is concerned with the effects of toxins in any environment, whether it is a natural environmental or a humanly created environment. In contrast to Klaassen and Eaton's definition, toxicology sometimes is defined more generally as the study of the impacts and detection of poisons and the treatment of toxic conditions in or the study of antidotes for toxins in living organisms. In either case, the general concern is exploring the deleterious effects of toxins on living organisms.

In pursing the study of the impact of toxins on living organisms, toxicologists draw on knowledge contained in multiple sciences. As a result, toxicology, like criminology, is often described as an interdisciplinary science because it draws on research from related natural sciences including chemistry and biology (Sipes, 2002).

Toxicological studies are often concerned with identifying the specific biological and chemical mechanisms involved in generating toxic effects within organisms (Forbes and Forbes, 1994: 2). As a result, the level of analysis for general toxicological studies is typically the individual organism. That is, toxicologists might ask "what is the effect of chemical X on species A?" Because of ethical considerations, toxicologists can only examine the effects of certain chemicals on humans when those exposures occur "naturally"—that is, when toxicologists cannot create the exposure because of ethical considerations. As a result, they must sometimes generalize from studies of the effects of a chemical on other species to humans. But, in many cases toxicologists can employ epidemiological methods and derive knowledge from the study of humans exposed to toxins through, for example, pollution of the environment in which humans live.

By using general toxicological methods, toxicologists can identify toxicity thresholds and differential effects of toxins across species. As an example, toxicological research demonstrates that ionized (+2) copper is toxic to bacteria, fungi, microbes, and other simple life forms at low concentrations (Debelius et al., 2009; El-Gendy, Radwan, and Gad, 2009; Serra and Guasch, 2009). At the same time, it is also known that other species require low levels of ionized copper as an essential element of their diet to ensure normal biological functioning (Chen and Chan, 2009). And while available in nature, the concentration of ionized copper in the natural environment is typically not high enough to induce biological harm or toxic effects for most species exposed to ionized copper in nature. This leads to a common toxicological conclusion—it is not necessarily *the mere presence* of a chemical in the environment that makes it harmful, but rather its *concentration* and more specifically its *dose* in a specific individual that leads to toxic outcomes.

Toxicologically speaking, any foreign agent or substance—that is any chemical not found within an organism's basic biological structure—can act as a toxicant. Identifying which foreign agents act as toxicants requires assessing the dose-response relationship between a chemical and a harmful outcome for an organism that can be traced to biologic mechanisms within an organism (Forbes and Forbes, 1994). Thus, even ionized copper, which is an essential trace element for some species, can act as a toxin when its concentration or dose exceeds a given and identifiable limit that can be linked with a harmful outcome.

Toxicology is designed to examine the general relationship between chemical dose-response relationships in the biologic mechanisms of organisms. For example, humans sometimes purposefully ingest substances such as illicit drugs for their psychic effects. For the toxicologists, the interesting issue here is the dose at which ingesting such chemicals causes harm. That harm may include detrimental effects on biological processes or even result in death at a certain dose. With respect to the focus of this book, it should be pointed out that there is no inherent link between toxicology and the study of environmental chemical harms. Indeed, general toxicological research or what is also called classical toxicology is ordinarily considered a branch of pharmacology (Bazerman and De los Santos, 2005)—which is defined as the science of drugs and their preparation. Pharmacology draws attention to the effects of classes of chemicals identified as pharmaceuticals and includes the study of addictive drug agents and chemicals purposefully ingested for their effects (Lynch, 1966).

Toxicology, however, can be divided into sub-fields or specialties. Some of these sub-fields directly deal with the issue of environmental exposure to toxins including sources of exposure and exposure doses, length and concentrations. For example, some forms of toxicology limit their analysis to the study of xenobiotics or chemicals that are foreign to or not normally found within an organism (Sipes and Gandolfi, 1991). Because xenobiotics are not normally found in a given organism, they can be interpreted as not playing a role in the normal biochemistry of the organism being examined (Walker et al., 2006: 57). In this sense, xenobiotics can be thought of as a chemical found within an organisms that is unexpected with respect to the normal biological functioning of that organism. Above we provided an example of the effect of exposure to +2 copper. For species or organisms that normally do not require or contain +2 copper, the presence of +2 copper would be identified as a xenobiotic. However, for other species or organisms that employ +2 copper in their normal biochemical processes, +2 copper would not be a xenobiotic.

Xenobiotic toxins may include both human-produced and naturally occurring substances that act as toxins. Xenobiotic research may therefore include the study of the effects of naturally occurring and/or human-produced xenobiotics on humans and non-human organisms as well as on the environment or on the functioning of ecological units or natural ecological processes (Walker et al., 2006).

In toxicological research, xenobiotic studies are further subdivided in a way that fits fairly well with the distinct research emphases that have already been established within green criminology. In toxicology, studies that focus on the effects of toxins on non-human organisms and the environment are termed *ecotoxicology* while studies that examine the effect of environmental toxins on humans are called *environmental toxicology* (see Figure 4.1). These approaches are described further below.

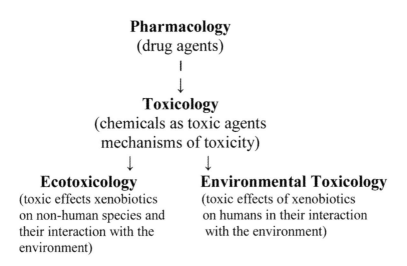

Pharmacology
(drug agents)
|
↓
Toxicology
(chemicals as toxic agents
mechanisms of toxicity)
↓   ↓
Ecotoxicology   **Environmental Toxicology**
(toxic effects xenobiotics   (toxic effects of xenobiotics
on non-human species and   on humans in their interaction
their interaction with the   with the environment)
environment)

**Figure 4.1   Relationship of pharmacology, toxicology,
and toxicological subfields**

Ecotoxicology

As a subfield of toxicology, ecotoxicology began in 1969 and is linked to the work of René Truhaut who defined it as "the branch of toxicology concerned with the study of toxic effects, caused by natural or synthetic pollutants, to the constituents of ecosystems, animal (including human), vegetable and microbial, in an integral context" (Truhaut, 1977).

Forbes and Forbes (1994: 2) argue that the academic origins of ecotoxicology emerged from the integration of toxicological with ecological science proposed by Truhaut's work for the International Council of Scientific Unions (ICSU) (Forbes and Forbes, 1994: 4). This was an important unification that for the first time identified ecosystems as organisms that could be examined from a toxicological perspective.

In the ICSU report, Truhaut proposed that ecosystems should be treated as what he called "supraspecific" organisms. As Forbes and Forbes note in their discussion of Truhaut's work, Truhaut did not provide a specific definition of what he meant when he referred to ecosystems as supraspecific organisms, so this term is open to interpretation. In our view, this is an important term, but in order to explain why, we must first define our understanding of this term.

The term supraspecific is a biological term which relates to the aggregation of organisms above the species level. This term is used to illustrate how species are connected. Truhaut's point seems to have been that a similar aggregation scheme can be applied to the environment. In this sense, a supraspecific ecosystem is an aggregation of the elements and constituent parts of the ecosystem into a whole that resembles, in its aggregation, a living organism. In our view, this concept implies that the species and ecosystem elements that are often treated or understood as separate entities—for example, birds, fish, land, waterways—are actually joined together by the environmental context they share and to which they contribute. That is to say an ecosystem is the sum of many parts, and while those parts may be, in a strict scientific or taxonomic sense, unrelated to one another at the individual species level, their combination creates a unique organism—a supraspecific ecosystem. Those separate elements of the supraspecific ecosystem, like individuals in the traditional approach to social science research, are likely to be treated as individuals or as independent units that are unconnected in scientific research. Keeping in mind our discussion of C. Wright Mills and the sociological imagination, we see Truhaut's use of the term supraspecific as an example of how individual units in an ecosystem can be linked together when researchers employ a green imagination or green frame of reference.

In our view, the importance of this concept of ecosystems as supraspecific allows an ecological unit to be described as an interrelated and interconnected unit that shares space or habitat, and which, as a result, forms a singular living unit that is greater than the sum of its separate parts—much like the Durkheimian sense of society. This would mean, for example, that in a given area, the supraspecific ecosystem could include a vast array of elements, such as wildlife, trees, waterways, and so on, and, if present, humans. This understanding of Truhaut's definition not only fits well with our definition of a green imagination, it is also important because of the position he took on pollution.

According to Truhaut (1977) the effects of chemical pollutants could be observed and studied in supraspecific ecosystems. Specifically, Truhaut stated that this approach included studying the fate and cycling of pollutants in ecosystems. In our view, this would mean examining the spread, concentration, and effects of chemical contaminants and pollutants across the span of the supraspecific ecosystem—or in each part and in the whole of the elements that make up the supraspecific ecosystem. In other words, the idea of the supraspecific ecosystem implies that the presence of toxicants in one element of the supraspecific ecosystem would lead to efforts to trace and locate those toxins in other parts of the supraspecific ecosystem.

Truhaut's focus on the supraspecific ecosystem was an effort to go beyond the more traditional definition of an ecosystem as previously defined by Tansley (1935). As Forbes and Forbes (1994: 5) note in their discussion of the origins of ecotoxicology, ecologists had studied the impact of chemicals and pollutants on ecosystems for nearly four decades before Truhaut (Forbes and Forbes, 1994: 5). These studies, however, were treated as part of either general ecology or general toxicology. Truhaut's contribution was to separate these studies into a specialized field of investigation that was distinct from classic or general toxicology and ecology, and in which the study of toxic chemical effects were linked through their appearance in an ecologically joined unit.

Despite the fact that the science of ecotoxicology was identified as a specific field of study by the 1970s, in the 1990s Forbes and Forbes (1994: 6-8) observed that there was—and is—still much confusion when it comes to separating ecological and toxicological studies and specifically in identifying ecotoxicological research even among those engaged in this type of research. In an effort to clarify its definition, Forbes and Forbes (1994: 6) argue that ecotoxicology proper focuses on "determining the effects of pollutants on the structure and function of intact ecosystems, communities and assemblages." In providing this clarification, Forbes and Forbes also note that the very definition or concept of ecotoxicology contributes to the difficulty in accomplishing its tasks. Specifically, Forbes and Forbes (1994: 6) note that "the complexity at this level of biological organization has generally precluded direct measurements of effects on natural ecosystems and has directed study toward separate components making up the system."

As an example of Forbes and Forbes' point, consider that following Truhaut's initial broad definition of this area of research, a number of additional definitions of ecotoxicology have been offered (Forbes and Forbes, 1994: 2-4). Some definitions of ecotoxicology maintain its broad focus on the effects of toxins on ecosystems (Maltby and Naylor, 1990; Moriarty, 1983); other views restrict the definition of ecotoxicology to examinations of the effect of environmental toxins on biota (Butler, 1984), or to the effect of environmental chemicals on non-human biological organisms (Klaassen and Eaton, 1991), or in general as the study of "ecology in the presence of toxicants" (Chapman, 2002). As an example of a very specific definition consider the definition of genetic ecotoxicology proposed by researchers who attended the 1994 Napa Conference on Genetic and Molecular Ecotoxicology, which states that genetic ecotoxicology is "The study of chemical- or radiation-induced changes in the genetic material of natural biota. Changes may be direct alterations in genes and gene expression or selective effects of pollutants on gene frequencies" (Anderson et al., 1994).

Over time, a number of specializations emerged within ecotoxicology, dividing this specialty into smaller subfields. Many of these subfields encourage a focus on very specific applications of toxicological studies to highly focused environmental-species interactions. For example, these subfields include the analysis of the fate of toxins in aquatic environments (Rand and Petrocelli, 1985) or on aquatic species (Gallo and Doull, 1991). Given the wide variety of definitions that have emerged to identify the scope of ecotoxicology, we employ Walker et al.'s (2006: i) more general definition of ecotoxicology as the "study of harmful effects of chemicals upon ecosystems and includes the effects on individuals and the consequent effect at the level of populations and above." By individuals, ecotoxicologists do not mean human individuals, but most often—though not exclusively—individuals in non-human species.

With these various definitions in mind, it is necessary to summarize the key point—that ecotoxicology is concerned with the effect of pollutants and environmental contaminants on ecosystems and the organisms that inhabit affected ecosystems. Because of the unrestricted scope of Truhaut's or Walker et al.'s definitions and similar definitions offered by other ecotoxicologists, the study of ecotoxicology may sometimes be identified as including humans as affected organisms. While some definitions of ecotoxicology include humans, as we shall see below, toxicologists have developed a specialty area devoted solely to examining the effects of environmental pollution in ecological systems that affect humans called environmental toxicology (Walker et al., 2006; Zakrzewski, 2002).

What's in a Name: Pollution, Pollutant, Chemical
and Environmental Contaminants

A problem in the definitions of ecotoxicology briefly examined above is the introduction of some new terms that have specific scientific meaning that may not be apparent to criminologists. Among these terms were pollution, pollutants, chemical contaminants, and environmental contaminants—keep in mind that this terminology also applies to the discussion of environmental toxicology that follows. Though often treated as interchangeable concepts, there are subtle but important distinctions between these terms, and the appropriate use of these terms has important implications for helping establish useful connections between green criminology and toxicological studies, and aiding green criminologists in using these terms in scientifically legitimate ways.

Walker et al. (2006: i) define *pollutants* and *chemical contaminants* as "chemicals that exist at levels judged to be above those that would normally occur in any particular component of the environment." More technically, a chemical becomes a pollutant or chemical contaminant when its level in the environment exceeds its normal background level. In other words, the existence of a chemical emission in an environment does not make it a pollutant. It only becomes a pollutant when the chemical being emitted exceeds its naturally occurring background level. What we should also take away from this discussion is that the terms pollution and pollutant are equivalents, while the terms chemical contaminants and environmental contaminants are also equivalents.

While pollutants/pollution and chemical/environmental contaminants are, in the first instance, defined by the same initial criteria, they can also be distinguished from one another. The characteristic that distinguishes a chemical/environmental contaminate from pollutants/pollution is an effect outcome. A pollutant or pollution consists of chemical contaminants that *cause actual environmental harm*. In contrast, the existence of chemical contaminants in the environment may not produce harm, or does not have to cause harm to be identified as a contaminant.

That is to say, a chemical contaminant is present in an environment when it exceeds normal background levels for that chemical in the environment. The chemical contaminant only becomes a pollutant *if* it also causes harm to the ecosystem and species within the ecosystem. In relation to the earlier discussion of Truhaut's work, we can say that the emission of chemicals into the environment are chemical contaminants in a supraspecific organism, and only become pollutants once they cause adverse consequences or harms for the supraspecific organism.

It should be noted that it is also possible for a chemical to appear in the environment as both an environmental contaminant and a pollutant in different contexts. In other words, the definition of an emission as an environmental contaminant or as pollution does not depend on the specific chemical being emitted, but rather is a definition related to the outcome that is also associated with the emission of that specific chemical into the environment. As an illustration, let us return to our +2 copper example. This copper ion can exist in the natural world. When copper ions exist at a level that is at or below their normal background concentration, they are not considered pollutants or environmental contaminants. This status may change over time or from location to location, however. For instance, if a local manufacturer adds chemical waste to the environment that contains +2 copper, the level of +2 copper in the local environment may exceed the background level of +2 copper. In that case, the +2 copper becomes an environmental or chemical contaminant. If the copper begins to poison local organisms, it is then considered a pollutant to those organisms. But, +2 copper may also exist in an environment, cause harm to micro-organisms but not be at high enough concentrations to harm other species in the environmental system such as humans. In this case the +2 copper is a pollutant to micro-organisms but a chemical contaminant with respect to humans. Moreover, even if the concentration of +2 copper in the environment is high enough to *potentially* cause harm to humans, it may not be considered a pollutant unless it *actually* causes harm to humans. The lack of actual harm to humans in this case may be related to the proximity of the +2 copper contamination to human settlements, or if nearby, to the fact that the +2 copper is contained and does not cause human exposure. Even if the +2 copper causes human exposure, it may not be a pollutant for humans because it doesn't cause harm if the dose of +2 copper remains below toxicity thresholds.

This may all seem very complicated and far afield from green criminology. This discussion is useful, however, because clarifying these terms allows criminologists interested in green issues to understand scientific terminology and to use that terminology appropriately in their research. Green criminologists may, for instance, refer to the disposal of a chemical as a pollutant. From a toxicological perspective, this definition would only be accurate *if* the disposed chemical caused actual harm. Toxicologically speaking, even if the disposed chemical was highly concentrated and above background levels, it would be considered a chemical contaminant until direct measures could be used to demonstrate that the contaminant caused harm.

Environmental Toxicology

Toxicological specialties share similar methods to detect, assess, and study the presence, concentration, and effects of toxins on living organisms and ecosystems. While the methods are shared across toxicological specialties, toxicological specialties focus on different units of analysis. For this reason, ecotoxicology and environmental toxicology are often treated as distinct variations of general toxicological research (Forbes and Forbes, 1994). This is not always the case, however, and the division between ecotoxicology and environmental toxicology is not always observed or defined in a wholly consistent manner (Forbes and Forbes, 1994; Zakrzewski, 2002). For purposes of the current discussion, the primary distinction between environmental toxicology and ecotoxicology is environmental toxicology's focus on the anthropogenic origins of chemical pollutants and the specific effects of those pollutants on human health and behavior (Walker et al., 2006; for extensive analysis and alternative interpretations see, Bazerman and De los Santos, 2005; for specific examples of research focusing on behavioral effects of pollutants see, Colborn, Dumanoski, and Meyers, 1997).

Prior to the 1960s there were numerous yet isolated efforts to examine the effects of environmental pollutants on human health and behavior in the scientific literature (for discussion see, Markowitz and Rosner, 2002; Rosner and Markowitz, 1989, 1994). These studies can be described as isolated to the extent that they were not unified under any specific disciplinary rubric that defined the boundaries or methods of research that should be employed to study the effects of environmental pollution on human health and behavior. Moreover, these studies were isolated because they appeared in a variety of different scientific literatures: medicine, epidemiology, biology, toxicology, and ecology, for example. Many early studies that focused on what is now defined as environmental toxicology, for example, were originally undertaken as studies of general toxicology, epidemiology or as applications of occupational health and medicine (Zakrzewski, 2002).

Research on the effects of environmental toxins on human health coalesced in the mid-1950s around several widespread environmental disasters (Burns, Lynch, and Stretesky, 2008; Davis, 2002) and was highlighted by the publication of Rachel Carson's book *Silent Spring* in 1962 (Bazerman and De los Santos, 2005). Carson's book brought widespread attention to the problem of pesticides' effects on birds, and argued that these effects were also a growing concern for humans. Though these scientific claims generated public concern they also brought public opposition from the chemical industry which questioned Carson's research, conclusions, and even her motivation for writing the book. In light of this controversy, President Kennedy asked his science advisory committee to review the claims made in Carson's work, and she was completely vindicated by their conclusions (Field, 1997).

The growth of environmental pollution and chemical contamination, and an expanding number of scientific studies on environmental problems coupled with growing public awareness of environmental harms led to the passage of several national environmental laws in the United States in the late 1960s and 1970s. These laws included the: National Environmental Policy Act (1969), The Clean Air Act (1970, 1977), The Clean Water Act (1972, 1977), The Endangered Species Act (1973), and the Safe Drinking Water Act (1974). These negative and deteriorating environmental conditions also led to the establishment of the U.S. Environmental Protection Agency (1970) (see, Burns, Lynch, and Stretesky, 2008). With the exception of the Endangered Species Act, each of these Acts focused on addressing harms to humans associated with anthropogenic sources of pollution.

One of the central concerns of environmental toxicology is addressing human or public health with respect to anthropogenic sources of environmental contamination and pollution. To do so effectively it was necessary to create methods for measuring the effects of pollutants on human populations and for determining the origins of human pollution exposure. General methods for determining the presence of toxins in various species and media—for example, water, air, and so on—were at the core of classic toxicology methods. Those methods, which were already in use in the study of occupational exposure to toxins, were extended to environmental toxicology (Forbes and Forbes, 1994).

As noted, the key issues in environmental toxicology include: (1) measuring the association between environmental toxins and negative human health outcomes; and (2) linking exposure to environmental toxins to their origins in human industrial production and the generation of chemical contaminants and pollution, including sources where industrial wastes were contained, such as hazardous waste sites. Given the central concern in environmental toxicology of linking human exposure to toxins to their anthropogenic sources, new measures that aided in this task were created. One example of this kind of tool is the anthropogenic enrichment factor (AEF), or the study of how human activities enhance the presence of pollutants in the environment (Walker et al., 2006; on distinguishing AEFs from background pollution see, Reiman and de Cariatt, 2005).

By measuring AEFs, environmental toxicologists were able to identify the level of environmental pollution that humans created. The AEF is a complex measurement produced by a scientific method that requires calculating chemical concentrations in the environment, and comparing the current levels of chemical contamination to known preindustrial levels of pollution in the environment. When the preindustrial level of contamination is unknown, it can be calculated with the use of the threshold of significant contamination (TSC). In determining the AEF, three criteria for classifying the pollution effect are employed:

1. The *no effect threshold* (NET), which corresponds to an average preindustrial level—in the case of metals—or defines the concentration below which no effect is detected in organisms—in the case of organic compounds. NET effects occur when the current contamination level and the preindustrial concentration of a chemical in the environment are the same, or even if current levels are below the preindustrial level.

2. The *minimal effect threshold* (MET), or the level of a chemical's concentration in the environment at which those organisms most sensitive to toxic effects of a given chemical contaminant are impacted. In terms of definitions provided above, the MET indicates the point at which chemical contaminants become pollutants for some but not all species.

3. The *toxic effect threshold* (TET). The TET is the empirical measure of the concentration of pollution, above which 90 percent of organisms in an environment are affected by a given pollutant (Pelletier, 2002).

Research employing the AEF has found numerous examples of widespread pollution caused by humans. For example, in their study of AEF for mercury for North America, Selin et al. (2008) were able to identify the amount and sources of mercury contamination and pollution in the environment. Their study indicates that 68 percent of mercury in North American originated from anthropogenic sources, meaning that the majority of mercury in the North American environment exists in the form of chemical contaminants produced and released by humans into the environment. Of those mercury deposits, Selin et al. estimated that 31 percent originated in emissions outside of North American, 20 percent were from North American emissions, and 16 percent were the result of prior anthropogenic contamination of soil and the oceans (see also, Pacyna et al., 2006; Roos-Barraclough et al., 2002).

At this point, awash in much science and the story of environmental toxicology, we need to return to criminology for the moment to illustrate, at least briefly, the importance of environmental toxicology for green criminology. One clear connection that can be made is to forensic criminology where these kinds of scientific procedures can be used to investigate crimes. Certainly, the methods used by environmental toxicologists have a role to play in the investigation of environmental crimes. These methods, for example, can be used to trace pollutants through environmental media or to their sources (for example, Cloquet et al., 2006; Fatta, Nikolaou, and Meric, 2007; Schaper and Jofre, 2000). But there is another important issue that we need to raise because we will expand upon this observation later in this chapter. That issue involves environmental toxicology's focus on human victims and on the human origins of harm human victims of environmental pollution suffer. Addressing these harms is a key component of green criminology, and in taking up this issue green criminologists have followed along, perhaps unwittingly, the path blazed by environmental toxicologists. This is an important connection for green criminology, because it can be employed by green criminologists to establish the scientific basis of their arguments about the destructive impacts of green crimes. Green crimes, in other words, are not harms that green criminologists imagine; rather they are real harms with scientifically derived indicators. Thus, in contrast to the definition of crime employed in most criminological research, there is a scientific basis underlying the identification and definition of green crimes. Conceptualized in this way, it should be quite clear that when green criminologists examine pollution as a green crime, they are—or should be—referring to a scientifically measureable phenomenon, one with an independent basis in objective measures of harm. The orthodox or traditional definition of crime cannot, by comparison, stand up to this kind of scrutiny. The traditional crimes examined by criminology are social constructions, and must always be so since the traditional definition of crime is derived from law, and law offers no objective mechanism for distinguishing crimes from one another or from behaviors that escape the purview of the criminal law.

Green or Sustainable Chemistry

By the late 1980s, studies of environmental pollution produced through ecotoxicology and environmental toxicology coupled with persistent environmental pollution and lax efforts to enforce environmental regulations created an interest in facilitating increasing efforts to control the industrial sources of environmental pollution. There are different mechanisms for addressing the control of industrial pollution, and to illustrate that point we draw attention to one such pollution control strategy that is widely used in industries. In the United States, the most common of these industrial pollution control strategies is referred to as "end of stream" technology. End of stream technology includes methods for dealing with the waste generated from industrial production after it has been produced. In this sense, end of stream technologies involve mechanisms for controlling pollution as an output (for example, Nemerow, 1963; Nemerow and Agardy, 1998), and only responds to the conditions found at the end of the stream of technology that generates pollution.

End of stream technology has a number of limitations. Perhaps its biggest limitation is that because it comes into play at the end of the production process, end of stream technology can do little other than try to control waste that is already being produced. This can be accomplished by, for example, containing polluting waste in secure locations—this is, secure from an environmental standpoint, meaning an effort is made to contain the waste in "small" or geographically "isolated" locations unlikely to contaminate the entire environment—or by minimally processing the waste and reducing its volume—for example, scrubbing of air releases to remove toxins; evaporation of water waste into solids; burning of reduced toxic wastes—or by treating the waste in different ways to minimize its environmental impacts. None of these techniques, however, significantly reduces the massive volume of waste that is produced by industry. Moreover, some of these end of stream techniques, such as the burning of hazardous waste, end up producing more dangerous toxins such as dioxin. The dangers of dioxin have long been known in toxicology (Schwetz et al., 1973), and end of stream approaches that transform pollutants into this more dangerous pollutant fail to solve the problems presented by industrial toxic waste.

End of stream technology can be seen as a control response that accepts the fact that industries produce waste, and that there is little that can be done to the production process to reduce the production of toxic and hazardous waste products. This attitude toward toxic waste production is attached to an assumption that the costs associated with changing the productive process to minimize or eliminate the production of toxic and hazardous waste are prohibitive, and as a result, will have negative economic impacts. In such a view, these assumptions mean that the only options to deal with toxic waste and pollution are remedial solutions that deal with the waste products from production after they have been generated. That is, the end of stream approach assumes that the best response to the problem of toxic waste production is to design a response to those toxins once produced. In other words, end of stream technology only responds to toxins after they are produced, where the role of technology is to minimizing the effects of pollution by treating, reducing, transforming, and storing the toxic wastes generated by production. There is no effort in this view to see the production process itself as problematic and to deal with production practices as a technique that can be altered to reduce pollution.

Because current production practices generate such large volumes of toxic pollution, end of stream technologies are an inefficient mechanism for dealing with the polluting materials left over from production. Consequently, in order to reduce the volume of waste produced and make it less harmful, new production techniques other than new end of stream techniques are needed.

McDonough and Braungart (2002a) argue in their book *Cradle to Cradle: Remaking the Way We Make Things* that it is essential to reconsider how we make things in order to reduce pollution and constrain the toxic harms caused by industrial production. At the same time, redesigning production also eliminates the need for end of stream waste management techniques. In a related work, McDonough and Braungart (2002b) addressed how traditional business assessment techniques contribute to industrial waste streams and pollution-related harms. McDonough and Braungart argue that traditional business assessments are dependent on addressing the cost and benefits of production techniques, but do so within a limited horizon that makes sense from a purely short-term perspective on corporate profit making. Moreover, not only are costs and benefits judged in the short term, they are judge in the traditional business sense of monetary profit. The result of this traditional business model is that the costs of investments in pollution reduction technology and inventive production techniques are under-valued relative to their benefits for society. Thus, given this short-term economic orientation, short-sighted profit-related decisions about inefficient and ineffective end-of-line technologies tend to win out over other environmentally beneficial solutions that would be of greater benefit to society.

McDonough and Braungart argue that it is necessary for business leaders to think in new ways in order for the problem of toxic waste production to be solved. The solution is to produce less waste that needs to be managed, or, as McDonough and Braungart show in *Cradle to Cradle*, to produce no waste at all by changing the way things are made. This involves rethinking and redesigning production and includes changing the chemicals involved in those processes, the way energy is generated and applied to production, and so forth. McDonough and Braungart are exemplary in their views, because not only do they make these arguments, they show that these kinds of production technologies can be implemented. To do so, they have engaged with a number of large corporations to change the ways things are produced. In fact, some of the real world projects McDonough and Braungart have implemented have been so successful that the "waste" stream leaving the plant they have redesigned—for example, water—is cleaner than the raw natural materials—for example, water—that entered the facility (McDonough and Braungart, 2002a).

Instead of relying on the traditional economic view related to end of stream technology, or which simply uses chemicals to design a cost-efficient production process without regard for its environmental consequences, McDonough and Braungart describe an alternative, environmentally conscious production process. The new system of business management they propose integrates traditional, profit-oriented economic goals with environmental perspectives in order to promote social goals and a healthy environment. Their new environmental business model promotes sustainable design strategies and a new business ethic of sustainability and social consciousness that can produce profit while promoting socially responsible business practices. They call this new strategy "triple top line growth."

The idea of triple top line growth is to design production practices that generate value while also restoring nature and enhancing human culture. Doing so is based on replacing the old business ideology produced by firm-level cost-benefit decision making with a form of socially oriented business philosophy which sees businesses not only in their isolated profit role, but as important, integrated societal mechanisms that drive society toward a profitable, healthy, and sustainable future. To do so, short-term profit planning must be replaced by a long-term growth model oriented toward ecological sustainability and environmental enhancement. In effect, what McDonough and Braungart have done is reinvent business philosophy so that it is oriented toward the social good and does not assume that social goods are produced simply through the pursuit of profit in an unregulated market where everyone pursues their own individual interests. The triple top line growth approach reverses the common idea that what is good for capital is good for society. Often times, what is good for capital promotes unhealthy environmental conditions that have expansive negative impacts on society, and social and ecological costs that cannot be sustained in the long run. In contrast, McDonough and Braungart suggest that what is good for society are healthy outcomes, and the goal of triple top line growth becomes joining healthy outcomes and the opportunity for profit making into a single task where profit making becomes subservient to ecological and social sustainability.

In short, McDonough and Braungart's position can be summarized as follows. Traditional business practices may produce positive outcomes for the business itself—for example, profit and growth—and for business owners, but does so at the expense of a healthy natural environment and at the expense of public health. There is no reason in their view, however, that these three outcomes—profit, healthy natural environments, and positive conditions for public health—cannot exist in harmony.

To be sure, not everyone would agree that McDonough and Braungart's approach can, as they suggest, be instituted within the confines of a capitalist system. John Bellamy Foster (2000), drawing on ecological Marxist theory, has criticized this view. He, along with Paul Burkett (2008), argue that capitalism and nature are in constant conflict with one another, and that it is part of the nature of capitalism—even a requirement of capitalism—that it destroys nature to furnish the raw materials required for the constant expansion of capitalist production. While we agree with that critique, we also believe it is worthwhile considering the possibility that ideas similar to those proposed by McDonough and Braungart can at least be useful in terms of minimizing the effect of capitalism on nature. In the long run, we agree with Foster and Burkett that capitalism and nature are in a constant struggle with one another, and that capitalism is dependent on the destruction of nature for its expansion. To be sure, the history of the relationship between capitalism and nature indicates that Foster and Burkett have a point.

In terms of the subject of this chapter, however, it is also useful to consider McDonough and Braungart's view to the extent that their suggestions have relevance for organizing the content and subject matter of green criminology. On that point, the comparison McDonough and Braungart make between triple top line growth assumptions and the clearly environmentally destructive tendencies of traditional end of stream pollution control also draws our attention to a related area or philosophy of production, green chemistry.

The term "green chemistry" was created by two researchers at the U.S. Environmental Protection Agency (EPA) in 1991, Paul Anastas and John Warner. Green chemistry is considered a philosophy of chemical research and engineering that directs attention to reconceptualizing how things are or can be made in order to reduce waste streams and environmental hazards. Green chemistry would, for example, direct attention to the reduction or elimination of end of pipe-line toxic wastes by altering production practice as well as the elimination of the use of toxic substances in the manufacture of goods (Anastas and Warner, 1998; Lancaster, 2002).

The 12 principles of green chemistry identified by Anastas and Warner have had broad influence on efforts to reconfigure productive practice, and became the basis for establishing Presidential Challenge grants in green chemistry during the early years of the Clinton administration to enhance the development of green technologies through green chemistry. These 12 principles are also referred to by the EPA Office of Chemical Safety and Pollution Prevention (www.epa.gov/aboutepa/ocspp.html, accessed August 2013) as part of the Pollution Prevention and Toxics program (www.epa.gov/oppt/, accessed August 2013; for the 12 principles see, www.epa.gov/gcc/pubs/principles.html, accessed August 2013).

The idea behind green chemistry grew out of and differentiates itself from the more general study of the fate of chemicals in the environment known as environmental chemistry. Environmental chemistry shares many common analytic techniques and procedures with environmental toxicology and ecotoxicology. More specifically, the use of environmental chemistry to examine the fate of chemicals in the environment focuses on the distribution, dispersion, transport, and effects of chemicals in the natural environment. As noted, in contrast to this quite specific "mechanical" view of chemistry and environmental pollution, green chemistry has been depicted more as a "philosophy" of chemistry than as a specific chemical technique. As a philosophy of chemical production, green chemistry seeks ways to reduce chemical pollution at its source or in the production process (Keys, 2008). Green chemistry, in short, encourages the rethinking of productive practices so that they produce less harmful outcomes. The philosophical orientation of green chemistry emphasizes consideration of waste streams and the effects of chemical pollutants on ecosystems and species that inhabit ecosystems, and sits in stark contrast to older industrial models of economic production where cost was the primary concern and the focus was on containing end of pipe waste streams as an afterthought (Anastas and Warner, 1998). The end result of green chemistry is stimulating a concern with minimizing the harms of industrial production or with controlling the negative consequences of industrial production at its source rather than at the end of the pipeline.

Green chemistry has developed into a substantial subfield of chemistry research. In order to demonstrate its usefulness, it has been necessary for green chemistry to generate criteria for measuring and assessing harmful chemical effects and the reduction of those effects in manufacturing processes. Again, a substantial literature exists addressing this particular issue (Constable, Curzons, and Cunningham, 2002; Henderson, Constable, and Jiminez-Gonzalez, 2010; Selvia and Perosa, 2008). As another example of the influence of this approach, the rapid growth and importance of research in this area has also given rise to the specialty journal *Green Chemistry*, founded in 1998.

Green Science and Green Criminology: Overlapping Concerns

Above we reviewed some of the essential characteristics of ecotoxicology, environmental toxicology, and green chemistry. That review also explored the development and history of these natural science approaches to the study of environmental issues and harms. The history of these views helps illustrate how green science developed and how different specializations emerged within the green sciences. These specializations promote the scientific analysis and definition of ecological harms. At the same time, the emergence of specialization or specialized areas within the green sciences restricted the scope of inquiry taken up in each view, and followed a typical scientific pattern of specialization of knowledge.

At points in the previous discussion, some technical information was included to illustrate the practices and differences between these various green scientific views, and to clarify the focus of each approach. Taken together, that discussion produces a general typology of green science research that can also be recognized within or extended to green criminology. This green science typology, therefore, can be used to help organize green criminological research into areas of specialization.

Before proceeding further with the discussion of the overlap between green sciences and green criminology, it is useful for us to answer the following question: Why use the trends and practices in the green sciences to organize green criminology? As we suggested above, there are a number of benefits to such an approach. Most important among these in our view is that basing green criminology's organization on the green sciences facilitates integrating these views and promotes drawing on the scientific knowledge base of green sciences to enhance the examination of green crime and justice issues explored by green criminology. Doing so is important because it illustrates the extent to which green criminology can be linked to scientific values and principles. By making that link green criminology can demonstrate that its objectives are not simply a reflection of moral principles or philosophies or of preferences, but that at its base green criminology involves a reliance on objective, scientific standards for its views about environmental harms, crimes, and justice.

With this background in mind, we now take up the issue of how these three green sciences overlap with issues addressed by green criminologists. In the material that follows we explore these overlaps and make them evident in order to produce a typology for green criminology. We begin this discussion with an examination of the basis for a green typology tied to the type of victim associated with environmental harms.

Green Victims

There are numerous ways to build typologies of knowledge. Typologies can be useful ways not only to organize knowledge, but also to build theory (Doty and Glick, 1994; McKinney, 1950, 1969). By slicing off, so to speak, smaller areas of knowledge from larger areas, the function of a typology is to make it easier to comprehend the content and scope of research related to a specific issue and perhaps to identify facts, connections, and concerns that can serve as the basis for developing theories. Because this process of dividing knowledge generates specialty areas, the theories which emerge may be limited to specific concerns.

One of the themes that can be derived from the green science types identified above is that green sciences have been, at least in part, organized around examining the effects of toxins on specific elements found in ecosystems including ecosystem elements themselves—for example, waterways, air, soil—and the various species that inhabit ecosystems. A similar approach is evident in green criminology. This focus, which draws attention to different kinds of green victims—an issue we pursue in greater depth in a subsequent chapter—began to emerge in green criminology, for example, not only from the kinds of issue-specific research green criminologists have engaged in, but also from green criminological discussions of various approaches such as biocentric or anthropocentric views and the ways those views influence the content and form of green criminology. These kinds of discussions make it clear that a central concern in green criminology has been research and analytic issues that focus on types of victims.

As a general description of this victim focus, Carrabine et al. (2008: 316) identify four primary types of green crimes that generate victimization: crimes of air pollution, crimes of deforestation, crimes of species decline and animal rights, and crimes of water pollution. This list is not exhaustive and excludes other issues that have been the focus of green criminology such as toxic and hazardous waste crimes that impact the land and water (Lynch and Stretesky, 2001), distributive justice or environmental justice issues and their differential impacts across populations with unique characteristics (Stretesky and Lynch, 1999; 2003; White, 2007), and inequities in the enforcement of environmental regulations (Lynch, Stretesky, and Burns, 2004a, 2004b), food crimes (Croall, 2007b), and bio-piracy (South, 2007). Regardless of the issue examined, as White (2008a: 14) notes, there is no specific theory of green criminology. As a result, green criminology contains no central set of assumptions guiding the development of these forms of research. In considering this situation, White (2008a: 9) observed that the general focus of green criminology has been on "who or what" is being victimized by "environmental degradation and destruction." Thus, following White's observation, it can be argued that it is useful to build a typology of green criminology around a discussion of victims and victim types. As noted, this idea is quite similar to the organizational format that has come to characterize green science research.

In green criminology victims come in a variety of forms. These victims include logically distinct groupings:

1. humans
2. non-human animals
3. flora or plant life
4. ecosystems of various sizes—for example, a local freshwater ecosystem; a regional air-shed—which may include the entire ecosystem or Gaia (relevant to discussions of global warming; see, Lovelock, 2006)
5. constituent elements of ecosystems treated as separate entities—for example, air, land, water
6. insects
7. microbes
8. the chemical processes in an ecosystem

While we can logically divide victims into these groups, and perhaps add others, one of the considerations in developing a typology is generating a useful framework for differentiating things from one another. Another consideration is parsimony. It may, for example, be possible to extend the above list quite far. But in terms of the issues green criminologists are likely to address and the distribution of green issues across a large number of categories, extensive divisions are illogical from the standpoint of practice and parsimony. Thus, based on the discussion above that examined ecotoxicology and environmental toxicology, we suggest that these various victim groups can be divided into two types that correspond with the view already established within green sciences: the distinction between human victims in interaction with the environment, and non-human victims or affected classes of species in affected ecosystems. Following the logic of the green sciences, we label green criminological studies that focus on human victims as *enviro-approaches* (or enviro-green criminology). All other studies, those that focus on non-human species and the environment and its components, can be combined into a separate category called *eco-approaches* (or eco-green criminology). Admittedly, this is not a complex theoretically driven distinction. We have not derived some set of guiding principles that explain why these divisions should be followed. Nevertheless, we believe this distinction is important for several reasons.

First, during the development and expansion of green criminology, disagreements emerged concerning green criminology's proper focus. These disagreements were not "serious," meaning that they did not challenge green criminological assumptions or its legitimacy. Rather, these disagreements involved efforts to draw attention to different types of concerns and related explanations so that they were not excluded but rather would be included as central green criminological issues. Thus, for example, green criminologists who focused research efforts on human victims were criticized for neglecting non-human victims and the environment and taking an anthropocentric view of environmental harm. At the same time, those who focused attention on non-human species and the environment were likewise criticized for ignoring humans and adopting a biocentric perspective (see White, 2008a). In our view, these criticisms were not substantive critiques of the subject matter of green criminology, but rather were intellectual discussions that contributed to defining what the scope of green criminology ought to entail.

Certainly, both forms of criticism described briefly above are valid. Green criminology ought to pay attention to the broadest set of victims possible. In recognizing this goal, however, it should also be noted that it may not be possible in all cases to draw out the kinds of explanatory or theoretical connections that allow all forms of victims and forms of environmental harm to be examined simultaneously. This is an issue that has been recognized and addressed in the green science literature and described in brief above. To be sure, as green scientists have argued, at times an integrated research approach is precluded by the question being addressed; by the breadth or narrowness of the specific issue under examination; or at other times, the scope of study may be reduced by the context of the discussion which may include specific cultural or legal examples. Nevertheless, each of these forms of study contributes to the mission of green criminology and contributes to its base of knowledge and should be recognized and appreciated for those reasons.

While academic discussions and critical appraisals of green criminology ought to be appreciated for their contributions, these discussions and critical appraisals shouldn't distract attention from the broader goal of green criminology. In our view, *that broader goal is to draw attention to the various ways in which human manipulation of the environment and pollution of natural environments produces harmful outcomes whether those harms affect humans, ecosystems, or nonhumans, and even non-human-non-animal species.* This is the chief contribution of green criminology, and that goal should not be lost in debate and discussion over the terminology, theory, or methods employed within green criminology.

Consequently, one of the primary reasons to follow the approach that has already been devised within green sciences is to avoid promoting internal conflict among green criminologists. In our view, it is useful to adopt a position on organizing green criminology that allows the work of different varieties of green criminology to flourish. In pursuing each type of research green criminologists can contribute to the overall goals of green criminology while appreciating the perspective others take as well. At the same time we recognize that there is a need to be able to classify these views simply because classification of this type is useful for the purposes of understanding and presenting the content of knowledge developed within green criminology.

A second issue, related to the first, has to do with the scope of a broadly conceived green criminology that addresses all victims within the confines of ecological systems or frames of reference. As green scientists have recognized, it is difficult to undertake studies of environmental harms that are comprehensive in scope and include the ramifications of environmental pollution, for example, on all aspects of ecosystems and their inhabitants—the goal of Truhaut's perspective on supraspecific organisms. If such work is complex empirically, it will also be complex from a theoretical standpoint and that complexity may undermine efforts to explore the development and content of green criminological theory. Until such a unified position can be undertaken sensibly, there is utility in dividing green criminological research into studies that focus on humans and those that focus on non-human and ecological harms.

Third, by following similar distinctions made in green sciences, not only is the compatibility between green criminology and green science made evident, but this distinction clarifies how evidence produced by green science can be applied to issues of interest to green criminologists. The harms discussed by green criminologists are not harms that, in general, green criminology discovers. Rather, these are harms exposed by scientific studies that, for example, have explored the negative impacts of toxins on specific species or aspects of the living environment or the environment as a living system. By aligning green science and green criminology, the scientific basis of green criminology is underscored. While some may not believe this to be an important point, without scientific evidence of harm the claims staked by green criminology become little more than moral judgment which consequently can be subjected to debate and challenged by, for instance, "philosophical musings" or uninformed discourse on the nature, scope, and degree of harm environmental crimes or pollution present. As an example, consider the "debate" over climate change. By ignoring the scientific evidence and the scientific basis of climate change, anti-global warming rhetoric has been able to promote and sustain a challenge to the science of global warming (Lynch, Burns, and Stretesky, 2010). In many, but not all instances then, green criminologists can employ the green science victim-based typology to refer to the scientific discoveries that provide support for their perspectives.

Green Policy Approaches

A third dimension of the overlap between green criminology and science centers on policy issues. As noted above, green chemistry directs attention to technological issues and promoting technologies of production that reduce and eliminate environmentally connected harms. For green scientists, the policy issues that have dominated those discussions are those related to applications of the principles of green chemistry.

The principles of green chemistry have had broad impact. For example, as noted above, this approach has been attached to incentive-based policies such as the U.S. EPA's Presidential Green Chemistry Challenge Awards program. In the policy approach to green chemistry, the effort to reduce environmental harm is attached to economic rewards for establishing compliant and innovative pollution reduction technology rather than on coercive forms of social control such as laws and regulations related to the control of end of pipeline pollution.

A similar theme is found within green criminological research. Within green criminology, however, the focus has not been entirely on technological issues (for examples see, Croall, 2007a; Lynch and Stretesky, 2001; South, 2007), nor on voluntary compliance with environmental regulation (Stretesky, 2006; Stretesky and Lynch, 2009b) but extends to legal, economic, and social policy as well (White, 2008a) and to examinations of the effectiveness of formal social control processes for controlling environmental harm (Lynch, Stretesky and Burns, 2004a, 2004b; Stretesky and Lynch, 2003). Thus, while green criminologists are more likely to focus on formal social control responses and the coercive effects of law and regulation, and green chemistry selects an incentive-laden, economically based voluntary compliance model, each view shares a focus on examining the kinds of policies that may be effective in controlling environmental harm. With these similarities and differences in mind, it is nevertheless evident that both green criminologists and green scientists share a concern with environmental harm reduction policy or an interest in what we identify as green policy issues, which therefore constitutes the third area of overlap between green science and green criminology.

Economic, Social, Political, and Philosophical Issues

One of the areas in which green criminology and green sciences demonstrate little overlap is in respect to discussions of the relationship between economic, social, political, and philosophical (ESPP) theory and environmental harm. More specifically, discussions of ESPP issues, concerns, and applications are much more common within green criminology as compared to the green sciences. This has much to do with the difference between the nature of green sciences and green criminology.

Green scientists, for example, are not concerned with explaining why environments, humans, non-humans, and so forth become exposed to pollutants—but with why these entities become victims. The goal of green sciences, in other words, is to document and study harms, not to explain the causes of those harms. Rather, the green sciences have a practical concern—these various living things are exposed to toxins and pollutants, and the question is whether this exposure causes observable harm. Thus for the green scientists the concern is measuring exposure to pollutants and being able to demonstrate whether there is an association between exposure and adverse outcomes for ecological systems, humans, and so forth. While the green scientists may be motivated to take up this kind of research out of personal or social concern, they will tend to express this concern in relation to objective criteria of harm or consequences that can be measured scientifically. Again, in that view there is no reason to insert morality as a basis for evaluating harms, since the evaluation methods include objective scientific standards for discovering harms.

In addition, unlike green criminologists, green scientists are not concerned with exploring *why* humans pollute environments. Green science begins with the simple observation that pollution happens, and green scientists are interested in observing its effects. They aren't necessarily interested in why it happens; in exploring the ESPP dimension of pollution—they are just concerned with the consequences of polluting behavior.

Likewise, not all green sciences are concerned with studying the effectiveness of social controls designed to minimize environmental pollution. Indeed, as noted, scientists who examine pollution control tend to take, as one might expect, a scientific view toward the control of pollution. The issue for a green scientist is how to control pollution from a technical, scientific standpoint, and as the history of pollution control illustrates, it matters very little that these controls were often viewed as involving end of pipe technology. For natural scientists more generally, there is a tendency to view applications of research as applied science and beyond the scope of basic scientific research. In many respects, applied science, especially in certain contexts, is viewed as a policy matter and simply put, many scientists see policy matters as existing beyond the realm of science. This is not to say that scientists don't think that their discoveries ought to serve as the basis for social policies designed to control environmental pollution (Burns, Lynch, and Stretesky, 2008; Lynch and Stretesky, 2003)—they simply don't often see themselves as having the training or knowledge to turn their discoveries into social policy or law. This outcome is left to others—but again not always and certainly there are organizations of scientists such as the Union of Concerned Scientists that take up policy matters almost exclusively. Nevertheless, the discoveries of science open up application possibilities that researchers in other fields such as green criminology are interested in applying.

Theory or Not and the Organization of Green Criminology

To this point we have described the organization of the green sciences and demonstrated a parallel though not a perfect reflection of that form of organization within green criminology. As noted, the typological view taken above focused on organizing green criminology in relation to the green sciences, and also with reference to victim types, policy matters, and attention to ESPP issues that have been prevalent in the green criminological and green sciences literatures. In taking this view we have avoided discussing green criminological theory or a single theory of green criminology, or dividing green criminology based on differing theoretical premises. To be sure, the latter typological view would be consistent with the approach taken in orthodox criminology, where criminology has been divided by differences in theoretical approaches that, for example, group and contrast different theoretical approaches employed to examine crime, such as learning theories, or biological theories, or psychological theories, and how those theoretical explanations for crime compare to one another. Currently, there has been a dearth of green criminological theory, if by theory one means a theoretical approach employed to orient the study of the causes of green crimes. Until the theoretical parameters of green criminology are developed in this way—assuming that they need to be developed in this way, and given that green criminology is, in our view, a revolutionary way to think about crime and justice, though that outcome may never occur—there is little reason to develop a typology of green criminology based on its possible theoretical orientations. Indeed, Lynch's (1990) political economic view, Barnett's (1999) land ethic, and Beirne's (1999) nonspeciesist approaches may be the only theoretical approaches to green criminology that have been entertained or which are needed. We leave open the discussion of whether these theoretical models ought to be the basis for a typology of green criminology to others to consider.

While green criminology may not presently be identified as aligned with any particular—or multiple—theoretical approaches, it is worth commenting on the potential impact of such a development on green criminology. The possible division of green criminology into different theoretical orientations raises the possibility of the potential for green criminology to become divided into specialty areas. Moreover, that division can lead to competition between those theoretical areas. In the process, that theoretical competition can potentially undermine the goal of green criminology which is to expose environmental harms and address the correction of those harms. That is to say, researchers may become more interested in promoting their particular theoretical orientation over some other view, and the outcome of that conflict could cause criminologists to neglect the real concern of green criminology—exposing and addressing green harms, crimes, and injustice.

In order to understand our view, it is necessary to first posit a few assumptions. One of the goals of criminology is to explain the causes of crime. In the process of explaining crime criminologists have invented a variety of "theories" of crime that attempt to explain the origins of the motivation or opportunities for crime. These theories offer different explanations, and therefore compete with one another for dominance or to be recognized as "the best" theory for explaining crime. The competition between these theories is also a competition between theorists aligned with different theories.

In examining a theory, researchers endeavor to investigate the explanatory validity of theories, and may offer their own variation of a theory as part of that process. As a result, we do not only have theories A, B, C, D, and so on, we have theorists 1, 2, 3, and 4's versions of each theory—for example, Professor 1's version of theory A, and so on. The differences between these approaches may be small and hinge on the inclusion or exclusion of a given variable, the combination of some set of variables versus their independent measurement, the location of a variable in a sequenced explanation, and so on.

In short, the explanation of crime becomes a highly competitive process in which it matters whether criminologists refer to Professor 1's version of theory A, or Professor 5's version of theory C. And rather than becoming or resembling the idea of a normal science where one theory is selected as the best explanation because of its scientific evidence, the process of academic competition in criminology— perhaps because the theories are weak in the first place with respect to explanatory power—tends to prevent cooperation in producing the best explanation of crime. In other words, in criminology theories do not necessarily prevail because they are the best theories, but rather have dominance because of their attachment to particular people or to some set of values that emerge in the process of academic competition within criminology. In short, academic competition appears to have a tendency to undermine rather than promote the development of knowledge to the extent that academic competition and academic stakes in recognition associated with promoting a particular argument prevents the development of knowledge. This act of academic competition may reflect, for example, the worth of having one's name associated with a given argument or a specific interpretation of crime to which others refer.

This tendency to value the identification of an idea/theory/explanation/finding and so forth with the work of a given individual(s) has consequences for the development of knowledge. One of those consequences relates to the training of the next generation of scholars who recognize that this form of academic competition not only occurs, but is encouraged. Thus, a new generation of scholars may learn that one way to become recognized and respected is to offer a modification of some argument because that modification will become linked to some particular person or group of people. These various theoretical approaches are in a continual competition with one another, and in the history of criminology, no particular approach tends to win or become dominant. And, as a result, what tends to get lost in this whole process of academic competition in criminology is the reason for undertaking research on the causes of crime in the first place.

We have summarized the issue related to the effect of academic competition here as a cautionary tale because we fear that a similar process has and will continue to unfold within green criminology, preventing progress of that view as researchers stake claims to different versions of green criminology or different segments of its application. To be sure, in some cases it is certainly justifiable, especially in a rather new area of research, to divide—as we have here—green criminology into areas of focus or specialization, such as identifying the distinction between research focused on human versus non-human animal harms, or studies that examine both, or approaches that instead examine ecological victimization or distinguish ecological from species-specific effects and victimization. That kind of argument is, in our view, very different than, for instance, debating whether green criminology ought to be called something else—which, again in our view, is simply an expression of the form of academic competition into which criminologists are normally socialized.

In reality, it doesn't matter if we call green criminology by another name unless, of course, that alternative name is used to indicate that the named approach is entirely distinct from green criminology. In the latter case, it would indeed seem appropriate to accept the new approach and named area as something different than green criminology. But, doing so should depend not simply on some naming preference—it should be a consequence of whether the new approach is indeed unique and promotes solving the particular problem of concern that led to the development of green criminology in the first place. That problem, we would argue is:

1. that humans damage the environment;
2. that the damage they cause has direct and indirect effects that produce violent outcomes;
3. that humans need to control this damage in order to maintain the health of the ecological system so that it can operate efficiently as intended without causing negative consequences; and
4. that these environmental consequences would not normally occur were it not for human's impacts on the environment or their interference with nature.

In light of these comments, we do not feel the need to justify the use of the term "green criminology," nor to defend our use of this term as opposed to other proposed terminology. Nor do we believe it necessary to offer an elaborate argument for linking green criminology and green sciences as we do here. As noted, we do so to facilitate the use of green scientific knowledge by green criminologists in the examination of green harms and their consequences and remedies. At the same time, we recognize that by linking green criminology and green sciences we are implicitly defending and justifying green terminology. But, again, this is not our goal. Rather, our goal is to illustrate how green sciences, broadly defined, intersect with green criminology, and how recognizing that intersection allows green criminology to draw on a scientific base of knowledge produced by green sciences that can contribute to the study and prevention of green harms.

To be sure, if all criminologists who studied the harms associated with environmental damage, victimization, and the control of those outcomes agreed with respect to terminology, the path of green criminology's development would be simpler and more efficient. Moreover, the unified perspective taken by green criminologists would be more difficult to ignore and easier to defend. We recognize, however, that academic culture and the competitive aspects of economic relationships that influence that culture will, until academic culture and economic relationships change, continue to influence terminological debates.

Having addressed the issue of competition and the use of specific terminology, we should note that despite the current coexistence of different views with respect to the identification of green criminology, alternative names have not proposed distinctive approaches to green criminology in any theoretical sense. Indeed, the green criminological literature is rather weak in comparison to orthodox criminology with respect to the identification of specific theoretical approaches to green criminology. Nevertheless, while green criminology may not, at this point in time, be able to be organized from a theoretical standpoint, there is nothing that would preclude such as organizational structure from emerging in the future. Our effort to illustrate the overlap between green sciences and green criminology offers one way of shaping that form of disciplinary organization.

The lack of one singular or several competing green theories in criminology has been noted in the literature. To be sure, while green criminologists have often staked claims related to specific theoretical issues and employed these to examine green harms, crimes, and policies, there is no singular green criminological theory. This circumstance has led others to note that "There is no green criminological *theory* ... Rather, as observed by South (1998), there is what can be loosely described as a 'green' perspective" (White, 2008a: 14).

As the term "perspective" indicates, green criminologists express shared interests in exploring environmental harms, crimes, and policies. At the same time, these analyses have offered quite divergent theoretical views toward this subject matter. South (1998), for instance, takes an issues-orientated approach in which the theoretical nature of green criminology is subservient to the nature and kind of problem under examination. Benton (1998, 2007) and Barnett (1999) have described the parameters of ecophilosophies in relation to green criminology, while Beirne (1999, 2007) has taken up the development of a nonspeciesist criminology that avoids making anthropocentric claims. Other approaches such as ecofeminisms (Lane, 1998) and masculinities theory (Groombridge, 1998) have also been employed in theoretical discussions of the parameters of green criminology. Likewise, political economic and activist theories (Lynch, 1990; Lynch and Stretesky, 2003), corporatist views (Lynch and Stretesky, 2003), and environmental and social justice theories (Stretesky and Lynch, 2003; White, 2007,

2008a) have all been subjects of theoretical discussions within green criminology. Again, this diversity of theoretical approaches has prevented the emergence of a unified green criminological theory.

There is, of course, no specific reason that green criminology ought to be unified in supporting a single theoretical approach anymore than, for example, one would expect a unified or a singular theory of crime to prevail even within orthodox approaches for understanding and explaining crime. It could be argued that, for instance, the scope of issues of concern to green criminologists is narrower and the behaviors under consideration more similar than the scope or range of behaviors examined by orthodox criminology. This assertion may or may not be true. For example, one of the reasons researchers offer support for green criminology is that it opens up a wide range of behaviors normally excluded from orthodox criminology to examination and discussion (South, 1998). Moreover, the behaviors green criminologists study are only similar to one another to the extent that they involve outcomes that are similar in effect—that is, they impact the environment or species living within the environment. In other respects, green crimes are extraordinarily diverse, and include the behaviors of corporate and state offenders—two groups of offenders who are not typically the subject of orthodox theoretical explanations of crime. In addition, green criminology focuses on a rather wide range of crimes from pollution to the dumping of toxic wastes, to global warming, food crimes, and crimes against non-human species—not just animals—which are ordinarily not the subject of orthodox criminology. And finally, one might also note that widely cited criminologists such as Gottfredson and Hirschi have asserted that ordinary crimes that are the subject of traditional criminological theory are really all the same in the end to the extent that each involves the use of force and fraud (Gottfredson and Hirschi, 1990; for a critique see, Lynch and Groves, 1995).

Despite the fact that green criminologists examine similar subject matter and often draw upon similar background literature and concepts, the specific problem under investigation, though joined to a broad environmental context and theory, may contain parameters that distinguish seemingly similar subjects from one another. For example, while there is much green criminological research on air or water or land pollution, air or water or land pollution is not a simple, objective outcome or indicator of harm. Rather, the exact nature of air or water or land pollution harm is dependent upon the context in which that specific form of pollution occurs, which means that green criminologists must pay attention to theories that respect the connection between environmental harms—as an example—and the social, political, and economic content in which those harms occur. Take as an example a criminological discussion of global warming, which might, as the name implies, seem to force the use of broad or global theories and explanations. While this is true to some extent and studies of global warming at *specific levels of analysis* will be required to draw on similar theories, there is a difference between explaining global patterns in climate change, the relationship between international trade and global warming (Stretesky and Lynch, 2009a), global warming's effects on local areas, or even its impact on populations of interest such as the poor or women, or even with respect to other power relationships that may be of interest, each of which would impact the theoretical stance taken by green criminologists.

In short, unlike other divisions in green criminology that we have described above—for example, the focus on who or what is the victim—while it is apparent to us that the typology of green criminology ought to include theoretical work, it may be necessary to produce, at some point, an independent typology of green theories of environmental harm, crime, law, and justice to further demarcate the scope of green criminology. Given the current diversity of theoretical approaches that have been used to explore these issues within green criminology, the lack of scholarship that has emerged to address the creation of a specific green criminological theory, the current stage of development of green criminology, and its issues-oriented approach generally, it is useful to postpone an effort to create a theoretical typology until some point in the future when the existence of competing theoretical issues requires the production of an organizing typology.

Conclusion

This chapter has employed the existence of parallel developments within green criminology and green sciences to suggest a four-fold typology of green criminology which consists of: (1) eco-approaches; (2) enviro-approaches; (3) green policy; and (4) theoretical explanations of environment harm, crime, and law that draw on economic, social, political, and philosophical (ESPP) orientations. We view this typology as a useful guide for organizing the types of research in which green criminologists have engaged and, therefore, as a general outline of green criminology's compartmentalized subject matter. To be sure, the typology that we have offered here can be developed further especially with respect to further divisions within each of the four areas of green criminology identified herein.

In exploring a typology of green criminology it was our intention to highlight areas of compatibility between green criminology and green sciences in an effort to illustrate that much of green criminology is connected to a scientific basis, and that without this basis in science it would be difficult to discuss environmental harms outside the limited scope of moral philosophies and subjective evaluations. Indeed, one of the important distinctions between green criminology and orthodox criminology is precisely the ability of green criminology to illustrate that the forms of harm it has explored and with which it is often concerned has a scientific foundation in which the harmful outcomes can be precisely measured. This observation is not, of course, true of all green criminological discussions (for example, Benton, Barnett, Beirne), and there is much green criminology which, like orthodox criminology, depends on exploring moral-philosophical positions that define harm and crime.

We should also point out that while green criminologists may never actually engage in the forms of basic scientific research that undergirds many of its arguments, this does not make the scientific basis of green criminology any less important. Indeed, without hard science data and information, much of green criminology would be impossible. Moreover, we would agree with Halsey's (2004) assessment that there is no need for a green criminology, but not for the reasons he suggests. In our view, the need for a green criminology would disappear *if* much of that view were not connected to the science of environmental harm. Perhaps ironically to some, it is indeed this connection to science as one of the primary concerns and mechanisms for discerning harm that actually distinguishes green and orthodox criminology. For, while orthodox criminology has made much of its scientific basis, it has been unable to create a basis for that claim with respect to the measurement of harm, and offers no objective, scientific measures of terms such as "crime," or "injustice." This, however, is precisely where green criminology has eclipsed orthodox criminology and where, more so than orthodox criminology, green criminology has been able to connect itself to science.

Chapter 5
Green Victimology

Criminologists have not always been concerned with the victims of crime. The origin of interest in the victims of crime—victimology—can be traced to the efforts of researchers in the late 1940s and early 1950s (Wallace and Roberson, 2011). More extensive development of victimology as a criminological specialty emerged during the victim's rights movement of the 1980s and 1990s. Interest in victimology also spread with the broader emergence of the restorative justice perspective within criminology. As with other criminological specialties, victimology incorporates a well-developed or identifiable literature that includes typological approaches, theories of victimization, and efforts to count victims of crime. And, like many other areas of criminological research, victimology has tended to exclude an examination of the relationship between power and victimization. That neglect has meant that the major studies of victimology and major textbooks on this topic (for example, Karmen, 2010) exclude the examination of victims of corporate, white collar, state, and environmental crimes. Given the history of criminology and its focus on street crime or the crimes of the powerless, it is completely possible to understand *why* victimology has excluded the crimes of the powerful and the victims of the powerful from its research program.

While we may understand *why* this has happened, this circumstance nevertheless remains unacceptable. One of the goals of victimology is to empower the voice of victims and to promote the protection and rights of victims of crime. By excluding the victims of powerful offenders, victimology has excluded those who most need to be empowered and to have their rights protected because of the extraordinary power differentials between powerless victims and powerful offenders. In addition, by excluding the victims of powerful criminal offenders, victimology excludes an extraordinarily large number of crime victims and a broad array of forms of victimization.

It is not our intent here to discuss all such crime victims, but to focus attention on the victims of green crimes. In doing so we are not only endeavoring to expose the tremendous extent of green victimization that occurs, the ways in which it occurs, and the extensive variation in the kinds of victims these crimes produce, but also laying the ground work for a *green victimology*.

Traditional Victimology

Pick up any victimology textbook and examine its content. You are likely to discover chapters defining victimology along with a number of chapters focusing on specific kinds of crime victims: children, the elderly, domestic partners, victims of hate crimes, and so forth. The chapters may examine victimization by focusing on particular types of crimes such as homicides, rapes, assaults, and sex crimes. There is likely to be a discussion of the rights of crime victims, how laws protect crime victims, and the ways in which the criminal justice system also contributes to reinforcing the rights of victims. In none of these typical discussions does the reader encounter the examination of some very widespread forms of crime committed by the most powerful people in society—corporate crime, state crime, or environmental crime. To be sure, some have addressed the effort to create a victimological approach to the crimes of the powerful. Kauzlarich, Matthews, and Miller (2002), for example, have proposed a victimology of state crime. Szockyj and Fox's book (1996) examines corporate victimization of women, while Stitt and Giacopassi (1995) and Croall (2007a, 2009) have examined corporate victimization in broader terms.

Modern criminologists who have an interest in victimology and victimization, have spent a good deal of effort both justifying the study of criminal victimization and criminal victims and collecting data on criminal victimizations and victims. Criminologists, however, tend to define victimizations rather narrowly, focusing largely on criminal victimizations associated with street crimes. Little effort has been made to build a broader victimology that includes the victims of other forms of legal harm. Indeed, research on corporate, white collar, and environmental crime has detailed the numerous forms of harm these crimes cause. It is not uncommon for these latter crimes to involve hundreds and even thousands of victims in one offense. Yet, criminologists do not often focus attention on the victims of corporate, white collar, or environmental crimes, and thus omit a large number of crime victims from their efforts to estimate the level of crime and victimization in society.

One argument against including victims of corporate, white collar, or environmental crimes—which taken together forms what we call crimes of the powerful—that may be encountered in the victimology literature, is that these offenses are not criminal offenses and therefore ought to be excluded from victimology research. Yet, the difference between criminal victims and victims of the crimes of the powerful is a matter of legal definition and legal decision making and not a difference based upon academic substance or an independent, objective definition of crime. For example, the authorities in charge of prosecuting powerful criminals often have to make a choice between proceeding criminally, administratively, or civilly. Many such cases are pursued civilly and administratively because the prosecution requirements are lower than in criminal cases. Thus, it is not the form of harm, its degree, or necessarily even the intent of the offender that comes into play in such cases as the factors that differentiate criminal and non-criminal forms of victimization; rather, it is a matter of administrative convenience. And administrative convenience is not a good standard to use to define the difference between street crime and the crimes of the powerful, or as a basis for deciding which behaviors deserve the attention of criminologists as crime or as serious forms of victimization.

Putting aside this debate, the problem that remains is the failure to treat victims of powerful offenders as if they deserve the attention of criminologists. In other words, it should not matter if you are victimized by a bank robber or a banker; what should be of interest is that there are entire classes of victims criminologists see fit to exclude from their studies, and that the exclusion of those victims isn't based on a theoretical premise or an objective definition of a crime victim, or a definition of victimization. Indeed, the exclusion of corporate, white collar, and environmental victims seems to be driven by non-objective criteria and concerns. Consequently, that method of excluding certain kinds of crime victims says much about the practice of criminology and its standing as an objective social science.

This exclusion of certain kinds of victims also tends to promote an assumption that because criminologists focus on victims of criminal offenses, that these victims must outnumber the victims of other forms of harm. This is a difficult position to prove using criminological research since so few criminologists devote their attention to studying the victimology of powerful crimes.

One of the goals of victimology is to demonstrate criminological concern for and interest in victims of crime. To be sure, this is an admirable goal and certainly any individual criticizing criminologists for evincing concern for crime victims would be taken to task. At the same time, however, the focus of victimology on crime victims has, perhaps, shielded it from criticism. Moreover, since a wide variety of criminological views including those on the left are sympathetic to the goals of victimology and have done much to promote victim-centered policy and programs, the usual sources of criminological criticism have been largely silent when it comes to criticizing how criminologists have constructed the study of victimology.

Like other areas of criminological research, however, victimology can and should be critiqued. For example, victimology is open to or susceptible to the same kinds of class-bias criticisms that apply to many fields of traditional criminological research and theory. Traditional forms of criminology have, for example, tended to place little emphasis on the crimes of the powerful, and instead devote the majority of their attention to explaining and exploring the crimes of the powerless. Since traditional victimology has largely followed the path of orthodox criminology, it should come as no surprise that it suffers from the same kinds of biases and that it can therefore be subjected to the same kinds of critique. There is, for instance, no victimology of corporate, white collar, state, or environmental crime—although as we illustrated earlier, some have certainly called attention to these issues. Indeed, if one were to read the victimology literature closely, there is little mention of the victims of powerful offenders. After reading that literature one would be hard pressed to suggest that there was indeed a significant social problem related to the crimes of the powerful or that these crimes cause any appreciable level of victimization in society, or that criminologists believe the issue to be important and deserving of study.

Here, we addresses this deficiency in the criminological literature by comparing counts of criminal victimizations in the National Crime Victimization Survey (NCVS) to our own count of victims of environmental crimes or what we call green victims. We estimate the number of victims of green crimes from government and other accounts of the number of people victimized by air, water, and hazardous waste exposures in the United States. The latter victimizations, though not as sensational or evident as criminal victimizations, are numerous and can produce serious consequences for exposed populations including illness, disease, and death. The green victimizations we count may be unseen or less obvious than those that result from street crime, but they are nevertheless serious.

Background

Criminologists estimate criminal victimizations in the United States employing the National Crime Victimization Survey (NCVS; http://www.bjs.gov/index.cfm?ty=dcdetail&iid=245, accessed September 2013). The NCVS is based on a random survey of residents in 50,000 households, and asks them questions about their victimization experiences that resulted from street crimes. Based on this survey, the 2007 NCVS estimated that there were 17.508 million property crime victims and 5.177 million personal crime victims, or 22.685 million criminal victimization incidents in these categories (Rand, 2008).

Since the NCVS applies only to the population 12 and older, estimates of victimization rates need to take only this population into account. Of the 301,621,157 U.S. citizens the Census Bureau estimates as U.S. inhabitants on July 1, 2007, approximately 48.7 million (16.1 percent) were under the age of 12. Thus, for those over 12 (approximately 252.9 million people), there was 1 criminal victimization for every 11.1 persons. On a daily basis, this figure comes to 62,151 victimizations due to street offenses—excluding homicides which are not addressed by the NCVS since the victims cannot report the offense. In 2007, there were approximately 14,136 homicide victims over the age of 12 (Crime in the U.S., http://www2.fbi.gov/ucr/cius2007/, accessed September 2013), a number so small that it does not affect the prior calculations—for example, this figure adds 38.7 victims to the daily victimization estimate, or changes that estimate by 0.06 percent. This small percentage change does not alter the estimation of the per capita rate of victimization.

On the face of it, these street crime victimization figures seem quite large. To be sure, 22.7 million street crime victimization incidents is a large number. Yet, proportionately this figure indicates that only about 9 percent of the U.S. public—excluding corrections for multiple victimizations to any individual—is the victim of a street crime in a year. These victimization incidents can be further subdivided into other time units that will be used below to describe some comparisons between street crime victimizations and green victimizations:

> 2,591 criminal victimizations per hour
> 43.2 criminal victimizations per minute
> 0.72 criminal victimizations per second

Below, we illustrate that the number of criminal victimizations produced by the NCVS, which appear quite large in an absolute sense, are quite small in a relative sense when compared to the number of victimizations associated with environmental crimes or what we call green victimizations. Green victimizations occur in a number of forms, and here we limit our discussion to those associated with exposure to air pollution in violation of air pollution standards, water pollution exposures in violation of water pollution standards, and to proximity measures related to distance from a known hazardous waste site.

Before describing those measures, it also bears note that there are a wide variety of environmental or green victims that will be excluded from the present discussion. Green crimes harm eco-systems and their constituent part—for example, water, air, land; non-human animals; plant species and their aggregations—for example, forests; insects; microbes; and even the living system of earth, Gaia. Each of these affected entities should also be considered green victims. These victims are not easy to count, and we will provide a few examples of these forms of victimization later in this chapter to illustrate this concern.

In order to restrict our discussion of green victimization and make a comparison to the NCVS, we limit our analysis to human victims of green crimes. In restricting the present discussion to human victims, we are in no way implying that we believe that other groups—for example, non-human species, and so on—are not also victims of green crimes or that they are less worthy victims than human victims. It is, at this point in time, not possible to create a measure of victimization that can be compared to the NCVS except by limiting our focus to human victims. Moreover, it is beyond our knowledge to be able to construct a useful victimization measure for these other categories of victims at this time. With some additional work on these problems, it may be possible at some point in the future to create an adequate measure of green victimization that can include animals or ecosystems as victims, and we do not dismiss that possibility. But, these measures require population counts for species, or other measures of victimization—for example, miles of streams or rivers, acres of lakes, and so on—for which adequate data are, to our knowledge, currently missing.

Green Harms to Humans

To begin our discussion of green harms to humans and the effort to construct a measure of green victimization, we review a study by Environmental Health Watch that employed U.S. Environmental Protection Agency data from the Cumulative Exposure Project on outdoor air pollution across all U.S. census tracts—approximately 60,000—and which also included exposure measures for 148 chemicals (http://www. ehw.org/community-environmental-health/air-pollution/sources-of-air-pollution/ air-toxics-hazardous-air-pollutants-sources/, accessed September 2013). That study indicated that seven airs toxins exceeded cancer benchmark concentrations across *every* U.S. census tract. The study also reported that the average U.S. census tract contained 14 air pollutants that exceeded cancer benchmark standards. In some census tracts, cancer benchmarks were exceeded for as many as 32 air pollutants. The fact that there are seven carcinogenic pollutants found in every U.S. census tract provides a very rough estimate of the extensive scope of green victimization that exists in the United States. Given that the aggregation of all census tracts includes the entire U.S. population, these seven pollutants are very likely causing the entire U.S. population to be exposed to some form of carcinogenic pollution.

For purposes of the present discussion, we refer to these violent air-based victimizations caused by air pollution as EVAPEs (environmental victimization due to air pollution exposure). This data roughly indicates the very widespread nature of EVAPEs in the United States. Though Environmental Health Watch's study provides no direct measure of population exposure, the fact that there are seven air pollutants that exceed cancer benchmark standards on average across all U.S. census tracts would indicate that the majority of the U.S. population is the victim of environmental air pollution exposure—in every census tract, there are seven chemicals that exceed regulatory limits for clean air. That means that every person in the U.S. is exposed to seven chemicals that violate the law, every day, and with every breath they take.

That's a lot of victimization. To put that rate of victimization in a rough comparative context, recall that above, we estimated from the NCVS that about 9 percent of the U.S. population was the victim of a street crime in a given year. Environmental Health Watch's victimization estimate suggests that 100 percent of census tracts possess the potential to create green victimizations from EVAPEs. Since it is possible that some census tracts may be large in terms of geographic area, we cannot conclude that 100 percent of the U.S. population is exposed to EVAPEs. Nevertheless, from these data we can conclude that the likelihood of an EVAPE compared to an NCVS criminal victimization is substantially large.

A more specific and appropriate population-based exposure measure of EVAPE can be created from data collected by the American Lung Association (ALA) in its *State of the Air* report (http://www.stateoftheair.org/, accessed July 2013). The 2009 edition of that study indicates that 60 percent of U.S. residents or 186.1 million people live in an area where air pollution levels are considered elevated— that is, high enough to cause threats to human health and life. Because the ALA study focuses on threats to life and health, these exposures should be compared to violent crime victimizations in the NCVS. As a result, in the section that follows, we compare the American Lung Association's population-based estimates to those for violent crime victimizations in the NCVS.

Comparing Air Exposure Victimizations and NCVS Violent Crime Victimizations

To begin, the American Lung Association study estimated that 60 percent of U.S. citizens were exposed to life and health threatening air pollutants. This population, unlike the NCVS population, includes persons under the age of 12. Thus, to make our comparisons equivalent, we employ the base population data used for the 2007

NCVS, which includes an estimated 252.9 million people over the age of 12 in the U.S. population. The NCVS estimate of violent crime victimizations for this population was 5.117 million. From the ALA data, we can estimate that there were 151.74 million EVAPE victims over the age of 12, or that there were nearly 30 times the number of EVAPE victims compared to NCVS violent crime victims.

The ALA-derived EVAPE estimation, though quite large, counts exposures for each individual *on an annual basis* so that, for example, one person inhaling polluted air for 365 days is equivalent to one victim. In other words, this procedure counts victims but not victimization incidents. In contrast, the NCVS counts victimization incidents, not persons. Thus, to make these data comparable, we need to estimate victimization incidents from the ALA data so that the ALA count and the NCVS count can both be expressed in terms of the number of victimization incidents.

If the equivalent of 151.74 million people over the age of 12 are exposed on an annual basis to EVAPEs, what is the estimated number of annual EVAPE victimization incidents? First, it is necessary to multiply the number of persons victimized by EVAPEs by the number of days in the year (151.74 × 365) which produces a figure of 55,385.1 billion annual EVAPE person victimizations. This figure, though extremely large, still fails to represent the annual number of EVAPE victimization incidents. Why? Because people take more than one breath each day of the year, and each breath of polluted air is a victimization incident. Indeed, the average person takes 18 breaths a minute, or 1080 breaths an hour, or 25,920 breaths a day, or 9,460,800 breaths in a year. To be fair, it is unlikely that every breath a person takes during a day occurs in a contaminated location since people travel to and from different locations such as work or school and so forth. Thus, to be conservative we estimate that people who are exposed to EVAPEs ordinarily spend only *one-third of their day* in a location with excessive levels of air pollution— for example, at work, at home, at school—meaning that the average person will take 3.1 million breaths in a year that produces an EVAPE. Multiplying this by the earlier annual estimate—55,385 billion—we arrive at the following estimate for the annual number of EVAPE victimization incidents: 171,693,810,000,000,000—or about 171.7 quadrillion! This is certainly a very large number, one that is nearly 33.6 *billion times larger* than the number of violent criminal victimizations estimated to occur annually in the United States according to the NCVS.

In short, the number of EVAPEs *far* exceeds the number of violent criminal victimizations in the United States, and makes violent criminal victimizations appear meaningless in the grand scheme of violent crime exposure. While a violent crime or other criminal victimization is, to be sure, potentially more obvious than an EVAPE, and may cause more immediate damage, the consistency of EVAPEs generate a variety of diseases and illnesses, and may also result in death. For example, air pollution exposure has been found to: reduce lung growth in children; increase trips to emergency rooms—estimated as 9,000 additional visits to emergency rooms in California alone; elevate hospital emissions; lead to premature deaths; and produce asthma attacks (Avol et al., 2001; Gauderman et al., 2002; Peters et al., 1999), and heart disease (Peters et al., 2001). Evidence also links air pollution exposure, particularly small particle exposure known as PM-10 and PM-2.5 exposure, to increased lung cancer rates (Pope et al., 2002).[1] Moreover, Pope et al. estimated the effect of this kind of exposure to increase the death rate due to lung cancers by 16 percent. In California alone, it is estimated that improved air quality standards for ozone and small particle matter would prevent nearly 1.3 million illnesses each year (CARB, 2002). California estimates the cost of lost work days to air pollution at $3.5 billion/year (CARB, 2002, 2003), so that it is also evident that EVAPEs have an economic dimension that we will not measure here.

In short, considering just air pollution exposure, we can see that green victimization is much more widespread in the United States than criminal victimization. Our estimate, which is a rough approximation and probably underestimates the extent of air pollution victimization incidents in the United States, indicates that green victimization due to air pollution exposure in the United States is 33.6 billion times more likely than a violent street crime victimization incident. But this estimate only counts one form of environmental victimization, and consequently under-estimates the extent of environmental victimizations in comparison to street crime victimizations.

Water Exposure Victimization

Another essential environmental resource that is widely polluted by industrial toxins is water. For example, 4.3 percent of the U.S. population or 13 million people are exposed to elevated levels of arsenic through public drinking water supplies where the water contains arsenic in excess of the U.S. EPA established level of 10 μg/L for arsenic exposure (Nava-Acien et al., 2008). Arsenic, a toxin, has numerous negative health effects. In addition to persistent, less serious consequences, arsenic exposure may lead to partial paralysis, blindness, type 2-diabetes, and cancers of the bladder, lungs, skin, kidney, nasal passages, liver, and prostate (see Abernathy et al., 1999; Tchounwou, Patlolla, and Centeno, 2003), and death.

Water pollution exposure in the United States is widespread, and results in a variety of negative health effects. Exposure to environmental toxins in drinking water has, for example, been associated with breast cancer (Gallagher et al., 2010). While water sources in urban areas in the United States contain a wide range of contaminants, rural water supplies are also affected, especially by agricultural run-off. Agricultural run-off is, not surprisingly, higher in rural than urban areas, and has been linked to the distribution of cancer mortality in rural areas in the United States (Hendryx, Fedorko, and Halverson, 2010). In addition to agricultural run-off and exposure to toxins in public water supplies, Americans are exposed to

---

1   PM-10 are particles between 2.5 and 10 micrometers—the scientific symbols for which is μ—or particles that are between 9,800ths of an inch to 2,540ths of an inch; and PM-2.5 are particles of less than 2.5 micrometers.

toxins in water through recreational activities in waterways (Wade et al., 2008), through non-public water supplies—about 15 percent of the U.S. population—and mine-drainage and run-off (for example, Hamilton, 2000).

Given the variety of methods of exposure to water pollution, it is more difficult to determine the potential number of people victimized by exposure to polluted water. For example, there are no accurate estimates of the number of people victimized by exposure to water pollution through recreational uses. The extent of victimization through private water supplies is also unknown, and no one has estimated the number of people exposed to mine-drainage run-off or even agricultural run-off that makes its way into private and public water supplies or waters found in recreational areas. Thus, the estimate of victimization for water pollution we offer is considerably less accurate than the one offered for air pollution victimization, and is likely to produce an under-estimate of water-related green victimizations.

To begin, research shows that on average from 2004 to 2009, about 50 million Americans or 20 percent of those served by public drinking water supplies were exposed to public drinking water that violated federal water standards. There is no data on exposure to pollution for the 45 million Americans who obtain water from private sources as these water sources are not regulated by federal law in the same way as the public water supply. If we estimate that the likelihood of exposure to pollution in water supplies is the same for public and private water systems, we can add nine million victims to the count of those exposed to unsafe water. Because private water supplies are unregulated and the potential for exposure of those supplies to a wide variety of environmental pollution run-off is high, this is likely an underestimate of the true extent of water-related green victimizations for private water sources.

As noted, a large number of people are probably exposed to water pollution through recreational use and mine run-off. Because of the popularity of beach-going activities in large coastal cities in the United States, there are probably hundreds of millions of visits to water-based recreational areas each year. Since major beaches are monitored for water quality and closed when water is unsafe, and there is no estimate of exposure to water pollution from these sources, and we omit these forms of victimization from consideration rather than attempt to create what is likely to be a wild estimate of those forms of exposure. It should be noted, however, that in omitting these exposures, we are severely underestimating victimization associated with water pollution exposure.

Given the above, we round off our estimate of water pollution victimization to 60 million individual victims. As with air pollution, these victimizations cause violence, and as we described briefly above, produce a variety of illnesses and diseases. As noted, research also indicates that persistent exposure to water pollution is related to elevated mortality from cancer.

As a base comparison, these 60 million person victimizations far exceed the number of violent victimization incidents (5.117) estimated by the NCVS. Yet, as with air pollution, this comparison is misleading since it compares person incidents for water pollution to victimization incidents from the NCVS. Thus, the number of person incidents for water pollution victimization must be transformed into a comparable unit of victimization.

Water pollution violations occur routinely, yet there are no reliable estimates concerning the number of days any particular person is exposed to water pollution from either private or public water supplies. We can assume, however, that private water supply exposures are likely to last significantly longer than public well exposures given that public water supplies are regulated and that private water consumers have little alternative to local, private supplies. To be conservative in our estimate based on prior research, we assumed that public water supply violations occur on average once per week, or created 52 exposures for each person per year. Thus, for public water supplies there are 2.6 million person exposures annually. For private systems, exposure is likely to be significantly higher, so we double the estimate of exposures. For the 10 million people affected, that produces 1.04 billion person exposures.

These estimates also need to be adjusted for use or ingestion of water in order to produce a measure of water pollution exposure that can be compared to NCVS estimates, since those estimates are incident based. If we conservatively estimate that each person experiences three exposures during a day to a polluted water supply, and there are 3.64 billion person exposures for both public and private water supplies, we arrive at an estimate of 10.92 billion water pollution victimizations in the United States, excluding those from recreational exposure and other sources of exposure we are unable to estimate.

In sum, compared to NCVS violent victimizations, water pollution violent victimizations are 2,134 times more likely. While this is no small difference and clearly Americans face far more extensive threats from their water supply than they do from criminals, the addition of water pollution victimization to air pollution victimizations—though important—is barely noticeable because the volume of air pollution victimization is so extraordinarily large. Nevertheless, water pollution victimization in the United States is extensive, and an issue that should not be ignored. The fact that people are more than 2,100 times as likely to be victimized by water pollution has, however, made no impact on the study of victimization within traditional criminology.

Exposure to Toxic Waste

People are exposed to toxins through a variety of additional pathways. Toxic pollutants are not only in the air we breathe and the water we drink, but in the foods we eat and in the pesticides, herbicides, and fertilizer products that are commonly applied across America. Pollution returns to us in precipitation, and one of the most widespread forms of pollution in the modern era—heat pollution—is changing the planet's climate. Some forms of green victimization associated with polluting the environment are so widespread that they can't be accurately estimated. And sometimes these forms of victimization are so widespread that estimating their extent is a rather meaningless exercise because the entire population is victimized. For example, once heat pollution pushed the ecosystem in a new direction producing heat waves, increased intensity of winter and summer storms, flooding, rising sea levels, and other consequences, it seems rather meaningless to estimate these effects since they impact everyone on the planet at multiple times each year. To illustrate how widespread pollution victimization is compared to street crime victimization, here we explore one last form of victimization—exposure to toxic waste sites.

In 2004, the U.S. EPA projected that there would be an estimated 294,000 waste sites in the United States that would require remediation by 2040 (US EPA, 2004). Typically, researchers don't examine all these waste sites but limit their analysis to the most serious of these sites—that is, to the legally licensed and abandoned waste sites the EPA has recorded and investigated. On this list there are currently:

1. twenty-one permitted hazardous waste landfills in the United States;
2. two thousand EPA permitted Treatment, Storage and Disposal Facilities (TSDFs); and
3. 1,305 of the "worst" hazardous waste sites which have been placed on the National Priority List (Superfund Sites) and designated for remediation.

These are the officially recognized hazardous waste sites in the United States—some 3,326 or far fewer than the estimated 80,000 toxic waste sites acknowledged as existing in the United States by the EPA, and only a fraction of the 294,000 waste sites the EPA estimates need to be remediated.

Not much is known about the harms produced by all hazardous waste sites, and what is known is limited to the 3,326 officially recognized waste sites, which represent only about 4 percent of all waste sites estimated to exist in the United States. Thus, there is limited knowledge with which to estimate violent environmental victimizations associated with hazardous waste sites. For example, we know that 11 million Americans live within one mile of the 1,305 Superfund Sites identified by the U.S. EPA. We don't know how many people live within one mile of the remaining 2,021 known hazardous waste sites, nor how many people live near the estimated 80,000 total waste sites estimated to exist, or the 294,000 sites that will require remediation. Since many of these sites are in urban areas, we can conservatively estimate that at least 10 percent of the urban population, about 24 million people, live in close proximity to those sites. Combined with the estimate of the population living near Superfund Sites, we estimate that about 35 million Americans live near toxic waste sites.

Proximity to hazardous waste sites is important because as medical research indicates, living near a toxic waste site causes a variety of diseases and illnesses, and promotes early morbidity. For example, research by Ala et al. (2006) has linked proximity to toxic waste sites to the rare disease, primary biliary cirrhosis of the liver. Kouznetsova et al. (2007) found that proximity to hazardous waste sites increases hospitalizations for diabetes. In a series of studies, Carpenter and his colleagues have found that proximity to hazardous waste sites increased the likelihood of asthma, infectious respiratory diseases, and chronic obstructive pulmonary disease (Carpenter, Ma, and Lessner, 2008; Ma et al., 2007; Sergeev and Carpenter, 2005, 2010), hospitalization for heart attacks and strokes (Sergeev and Carpenter, 2005, 2010), insulin resistance or metabolic syndrome—known as MetS (Sergeev and Carpenter, 2011), and hypertension (Huanga, Lessner, and Carpenter, 2006).

As before, it is necessary to turn the 35 million person exposures to hazardous waste sites into incidents so that the outcome is comparable with NCVS estimates of violent criminal victimization incidents. It is a much more difficult process, however, to turn proximity to toxic waste sites into victim incidents. To do so we conservatively estimate that populations are proximate to toxic waste sites during one-third of each day, and that even though their exposure to the toxins released by toxic waste sites may be continuous during that time period, we also conservatively estimate that each hour of exposure is equal to one victimization incident. Thus, in a year a person living near a hazardous waste site experienced at least 2,920 exposures to toxic waste, and that for the population of 35 million living near those locations that amounts to 102.2 billion environmental pollution victimization incidents. That figure—which we have conservatively estimated and is likely several times higher than our estimate—is nearly 20,000 times the number of violent crime victimizations estimated by the NCVS.

Again, what we can see when we estimate this form of green victimization is that it far exceeds the volume of violent street crime victimization in the U.S. In our conservative estimate of exposure to toxins from toxic waste sites for proximate populations, the differential in exposure is 20,000—and that is no small difference, and is not one that ought to be ignored. Yet, these billions of green victimizations and the people that suffer from them are ignored by traditional criminology and its approach to studying victimization.

Summarizing Environmental Victimization to Humans

As the data above illustrates, humans are much more likely to be the victims of violent green victimizations than they are to be the victims of criminal acts of violence. The *smallest* difference was found when comparing water pollution environmental violence to NCVS violent crimes. That small difference indicated that water pollution environmental violence is, conservatively estimated and omitting major sources of exposure, more than 2,000 times more likely than criminal violence. Violent green victimization exposures associated with hazardous waste were, for the United States, nearly 20,000 times as likely as NCVS estimated acts of violent victimization incidents. These extremely large differences between environmental violence and NCVS criminal violence incidence, however, are a small fraction of the number of air pollution related environmental violence victimizations which were 33.6 *billion* times more likely than NCVS violent crime victimizations.

The discovery that the average person is either thousands, tens of thousands, or billions of times more likely to suffer from environmentally induced violent victimization compared to acts of street crime violence should startle even green criminologists. With respect to violent victimizations, criminal victimizations, which attract practically all criminological research attention on violent victimizations, comprise such a negligible volume of all violent victimizations that they hardly appear worthy of study. In terms of all victimizations experienced by the population, criminal victimizations of the type criminologists study, are rare events. Yet, these rare events attract the attention of criminologists while the green victimization of the population which is a much more prevalent problem goes unaddressed.

Summarizing this extraordinary level of victimization is difficult. One of the methods criminal social control agencies in the United States have employed to depict the level of criminal violence that occurs is the crime clock. As noted earlier, on the crime clock, about 0.72 acts of criminal violence occur in the United States every second. The green violence crime clock for water pollution would show 1,440 acts of environmental violence per second; 13,752 acts of environmental violence related to hazardous waste exposure per second; and an extraordinary 24 *million* acts of air pollution violent exposures per second in the United States. Given these figures, criminologists must no longer ignore the problem of green victimization. Green victimization is widespread—much more widespread than ordinary acts of violence—and cause much more harm than acts of criminal victimization.

The crime control industry, the media, and even criminologists have built an elaborate mechanism for focusing attention on ordinary crimes. That mechanism has helped stimulate public fear of ordinary crime. The data presented here comparing the volume of green violence to ordinary criminal violence illustrates that the fear of street crime is disproportionate to the role violent crimes play in the overall violent victimization of the general public. The public is much more likely to be victimized by green acts of environmental violence. Yet, these behaviors are largely ignored in the media, by the crime control industry, and by criminologists.

Clearly our estimates, which we again caution probably under-estimate the extent of violent green victimization to humans, should call attention to the problem of green violence. And clearly, because these forms of green violent victimization are so widespread, criminologists should pay much more attention to the issue of environmentally induced violent victimizations.

But, we also caution that while expansive, estimates of human victimization from green violence is just the tip of the iceberg of environmental violence and victimization. The variety of nonhuman species and the ecosystem and its subsystems are also subject to green violence. It is likely much more difficult to estimate how much violence is done to animals, plants, ecosystems, and so on, than humans. Despite this difficultly, the next section discusses some important forms of victimization that we cannot count and which have no comparable criminal statistic comparisons.

The Violent Victimization of Non-Human Species and the Environment

Green criminological interest in violence against non-human animals was stimulated by Piers Beirne's (1999) examination of animal abuse as an appropriate object of criminological study. Subsequent research has employed case study approaches to examine related issues such as poaching (Lemieux and Clark, 2009; Pires and Clarke, 2011), the illegal animal trade (Wyatt, 2011), animal genocide (Hallsworth, 2011) and a variety of forms of animal abuse more generally (Beirne, 2009). These studies provide a measure of the scope of behaviors that count as animal abuse, and have drawn attention to violence against animals as a form of victimization of concern to green criminologists. Generally, those studies have not addressed the volume or number of animal abuse cases that occur. In some cases, it is difficult to produce counts of animal victimization since there may not be any recognized method for doing so. In other cases, however, criminologists can produce some estimate of animal victimization. For example, Lemieux and Clark's (2009) study of elephant poaching provides a rough estimate of poached elephants using herd counts over time. Using the CITES database (Convention on International Trade in Endangered Species and Wild Fauna; http://cites-dashboards.unep-wcmc. org/, accessed July 2013) Lemieux and Clarke estimated losses to elephant herds before and after ivory bans were imposed in African nations. Their data showed that during the 1980s, 900,000 elephants were lost across African nations, while after the ivory ban (1989-2007) only 60,000 elephants were lost. Overall, the population of elephants increased after the ivory ban, and elephant losses were restricted to certain nations—specifically those with unregulated markets. This study indicates that the increase among elephant populations occurred in nations with stronger enforcement mechanisms, and those increases served to more than offset the decline in elephant populations in other nations. This study not only estimates the size of violent green victimization of elephants, but also indicates that laws protecting elephants appear to have some effect.

Nevertheless, the figure that Lemieux and Clarke provides, while useful, is not a direct count of the number of elephants lost to poaching alone since it is an estimate of herd size. But this is one of the problems encountered when attempting to count the number of animals that are victims of green violence. Thus, Lemieux and Clarke are to be applauded for their innovative use of the CITES data as a method for estimating green violence against animals. Because count data on animals harmed as green violence are difficult to discover, however, researchers sometime turn to other estimates such as the number of pets euthanized—which in the United States is estimated to be between 3 to 4 million each year. Some may refer to other measures that are available to indicate the amount of green violence against animals. For instance, data on animals used in laboratories is now more

widely available than it once was, and provides one measure of animal abuse—
though not necessarily green environmental violence in the sense of exposure to
humanly produced, noxious environmental conditions such as pollution. Most
animals used in laboratory experiments are euthanized, and thus the count of
the number of animals used in laboratory experiments can be substituted for the
number of euthanized animals. The British Union for the Abolition of Vivisection
estimated that 10-11 million animals were employed in experiments performed
in the European Union and 3.6 million in the UK alone (http://www.buav.org/
humane-science/statistics, accessed July 2013). These figures exclude animals
killed as surplus, those used for breeding, and those that are not weaned. The
U.S. Department of Agriculture estimates that excluding mice and rats, 1.2
million animals were used in laboratory experiments in the United States (http://
www.aphis.usda.gov/animal_welfare/downloads/awreports/awreport2005.pdf,
accessed September 2013). Since others estimate that mice and rats make up about
90 percent of animals used in laboratory experiments in the United States (http://
www.peta.org/issues/animals-used-for-experimentation/animal-experiments-
overview.aspx, accessed July 2013), we can estimate that the number of animals
killed in U.S. laboratory experiments included an additional 10.8 million rats and
mice, and overall, that the number of animals killed in laboratory experiments in
the United States totaled 12 million.

As an additional example of animal harms, we could include counts of animals
killed for food purposes. The U.S. Department of Agriculture keeps track of
data on animals that are slaughtered for food production. For 2010, the USDA
estimated that 87.395 billion pounds of livestock were slaughtered, or about
10 billion more slaughter pounds than in 1988—about a 13 percent increase in
slaughter pounds (http://quickstats.nass.usda.gov/, accessed July 2013). While
this estimate includes all varieties of livestock slaughtered, we can put this pound
estimate into perspective if we assume that all livestock slaughtered were beef, and
that the average slaughtered animal weighs in at 1,200 pounds. Mathematically,
that produces an estimate of the slaughter of some 73 million animals—assuming
all animals were large (1,200 pound) beef animals. The American Meat Institute
(AMI) estimates that in 2009, average per capita consumption of red meats (beef,
veal, pork, lamb, chicken, turkey, and fish) in the United States was 201.4 pounds
per person. Since the U.S. population totaled 305 million people in 2009, the AMI
data indicate that a smaller volume of meat—about 61.4 billion pounds—was
consumed by the U.S. population. These estimates may be different since some
slaughtered animals are not designated for use as human foods. In contrast to our
estimate, FarmUSA.org (accessed July 2013) estimates that about 10.5 million
animals were slaughtered for food. These different estimates indicate the difficulty
in establishing the exact number of animals harmed in the production of food.

To be sure, the deaths of euthanized pets, livestock, or laboratory animals fits
with Beirne's approach to animal violence and victimization that can be studied in
a green criminological perspective. These estimates, however, do not measure the
number of animals that reside in nature that are killed and harmed by green violence

that occurs through pesticide or pollution exposure, mining or timber harvesting, or other land developments such as filling wetlands, housing development, and the transfer of lands to agricultural production.

It is likely impossible to determine the exact number of animals killed or harmed by activities such as timber harvesting, and information on this subject is difficult to discover. For example, in a 1994 report by Craig Lorimer from the Department of Forestry and Management, University of Wisconsin-Madison, it was estimated that timber harvesting in Wisconsin contributed to the decline of 29 species of birds, while 16 other species of birds showed population increases and 81 showed no change in population (http://forestandwildlifeecology.wisc.edu/ sites/default/files/pdfs/publications/77.PDF, accessed September 2013). Lorimer, however, provides no estimate of the number of individual birds affected (see also, Mitchell el al., 2008).

A number of other green harms cause environmental victimization to animals. Timber clear cutting, for instance, has been shown to have a significant impact on amphibian populations (Semlitsch et al., 2008; Semlitsch et al., 2009). For some amphibian species, the estimated time for a population to recover after timber harvesting exceeds 60 years (Homyack and Haas, 2009). Climate change and logging have been shown to interact and negatively impact species such as the lynx in southeastern Canada and the northeastern United States (Carroll, 2007). Among other species, transformation of woodland by timber harvesting has been shown to have detrimental consequences on endangered species such as caribou (Wittmer et al., 2007).

The loss of biodiversity to human activities is well documented in the scientific literature. Significant impacts on biodiversity have been linked to infrastructural expansion such as road construction. In a meta-analysis of 49 research studies on this issue, Benitez-López, Alkemade, and Verweij (2010) found significant impacts of road construction on the distribution and populations of birds and mammals.

The research studies described above provide evidence of the deleterious effects of environmental harms on various species of animals. These studies illustrate that green harms can produce green violence and victimization for animal species. Nevertheless, these studies do not present estimates of the extent of these harms nor the level of victimization—that is they do not attempt to provide an estimate of the number of animals in a species that are harmed or which may be counted as green environmental victims.

As noted, data on the number of animal victims is difficult to obtain. One source of this kind of data is the U.S. Department of Agriculture which maintains records of the number of animals it kills to protect agriculture and livestock. These data also include estimates of the number of animals trapped and released or relocated, and the method by which animals were killed.

In 2004, the U.S. Department of Agriculture's Wildlife Services reported killing 82,891 large mammals (http://www.bancrueltraps.com/b_pred_killchartFY04.php, accessed July 2013). The number of large mammals killed—for example, bears, wolves, and so on—is a small proportion of the total number of animals killed. In the USDA's 2011 report, a total of 3,752,356 animals were reported killed (http://www.aphis.usda.gov/wildlife_damage/prog_data/2011_prog_data/PDR_G/Basic_Tables_PDR_G/Table%20G_ShortReport.pdf, accessed September 2013). The methods used to kill these animals included: firearms, pyrotechnics, beuthanasia-d (to euthanize canine species), various traps (footholds, neck snares, cages, body grips, suitcase traps, decoys), A/C electrical current, vehicles, drc-1339 (pigeon poison), rejex-it tp-40 (bird poison), gas explosions, m-44 cyanide capsules, dogs, and pneumatic devices. Among the long list of species killed were: anhingas, armadillos*, avocets, badgers, black bears, bobcats, coyote, wolves*, beavers, blackbirds*, bunting*, cardinals, chukars, cormorants*, cowbirds, doves/pigeons*, feral cats, deer/caribou/antelope*, egrets*, feral dogs, feral hogs, frogs/toads*, ducks*, finches*, flickers, foxes*, geese*, grackles*, grebes*, gulls*, hawks*, heron*, ibis*, killdeer, kingbirds*, larks*, magpies, mannikins*, mountain lions, muskrats, opossum*, otters*, owls*, pelicans*, plovers*, prairie dogs*, rabbits*, rats*, raccoons, ring-neck pheasants, ravens, sandhill crane, skunks*, snakes*, sparrows*, squirrels*, starlings, stilts, swallows*, swans*, terns*, turkeys, vultures*, weasels, willets, wolves*, woodpeckers* (* = multiple species).

Moreover, the USDA noted that the vast majority of killings were intentional rather than unintentional, meaning that the killed animals were purposefully targeted and did not die as the result of accidents or efforts to relocate animals. While we have no way of transforming these intentional killings into rates, we note that the number of animals killed by the USDA is about 255 times larger than the number of human homicides that occurred in the United States. And while the number of animals killed is likely to represent a small fraction of all animals—the "animal homicide rate" is probably quite small compared to their numbers in the environment—the number of animals killed by the USDA is substantial and is the only measure by which these forms of harm against wildlife can be measured. Furthermore, the fact that this level of animal killing by the government is deemed acceptable and tolerated—perhaps because they are largely unknown to the general public—illustrates how widely accepted green victimization of wildlife species has become.

The Environment as Victim

Thus far we have discussed green victimization related to humans, comparing this to the level of violent criminal victimizations, and the green victimization of animals. The environment more general or the world's ecology as well as various parts of that ecological system—for example, continents, climate, oceans, or smaller, localized ecosystems—are also victims of green harms.

It is difficult to measure the ways in which the environment is the victim of green harms largely because many of these victimizations have become acceptable and are not measured. The degree to which these behaviors are acceptable to those who make and influence laws is evident in the ways laws that address environmental concerns are constructed. In the United States, for instance, pollution is allowable as long as the polluter has the appropriate permit. In other words, based on the fact that the government issues permits to pollute, it should be clear that this view supports the idea that the environment is either viewed as an appropriate victim, or is not seen as a victim at all. Thus, one way of counting environmental victimization would be to examine permits that allow the environment to be victimized.

For example, in the United States there are 708,662 Resource Conservation and Recovery Act (RCRA) sites permitted by the U.S. EPA. Between 2000 and 2008 these sites violated their permits 48,003 times. Legally, the environment has been victimized 48,003 times during this nine-year period—or on those occasions when permitted facilities violated their permits. On an annual basis, this appears to be a relatively minor problem involving less than 1 percent of permitted sites. But, using the law as an objective standard is likely to provide a misleading picture of environmental violations of this nature since the content of laws related to permits and permit conditions are subject not to an objective, scientific standard, but to a complex mix of scientific research, corporate responses to scientific findings, corporate requests for permit modifications, and perhaps even the influence corporations acquire by donating resources to politicians for their campaigns (Hogan et al., 2006; Long et al., 2007). In addition, the EPA has increasingly turned to self-reporting of violations, which can lead to under-reporting and to modification in charges against violators as a reward for self-reporting (Stretesky, 2006; Stretesky and Lynch, 2009b, 2011a). As a result of the political process employed to set standards for pollution permits, the resulting permit standards are not objective measures of harm, and neither are the resulting violations. Not only are the permit standards questionable, the enforcement of those permits is suspect. For example, in Tampa, Florida there are 1,720 RCRA permitted facilities. The state of Florida employs only 131 environmental enforcement officers for the entire state (http://www.myfwc.com/contact/fwc-law-enforcement/, accessed September 2013) meaning that it is highly unlikely that permit conditions are rigorously enforced. In comparative terms, the city of Tampa employs more than 1,000 sworn enforcement officers to police street crime. As a result, using the activities of environmental enforcement agents as one way of measuring green crimes not only underestimates green crimes and victimizations, but comparing those outcomes to ordinary crimes is likely to severely underestimate environmental violations simply as a result of staffing differences across these agencies.

In addition, when the environment is the victim, we cannot count those victimizations in the same way that we count the victimization of humans or animals. For example, we may be able to estimate how many Americans breathe polluted air, but how does one count a victimization incident to the environment that may be represented by one act of dumping 10,000 pounds of solid waste or 10,000 gallons of waste water? Is this one environmental victimization? Do we need to account for the volume of waste? Its effects? The form of the waste and whether it has spread beyond the area in which it was released or its spread to other environmental media? Because of these issues, the construction of measures of green victimization of the environment is quite different than measures of green victimization of humans or animals where the concept of the victim is itself clearer.

The more general measure of the green victimization of the environment will, as a result, tend to be less comparable to other victimization measures such as those for humans or animal green-victim measures. Consider, for instance, the kind of pollution estimates one normally finds for the environment. Americanrivers. org (accessed July 2013), for example, estimates that 40 percent of U.S. rivers and streams are so polluted that they cannot be used for fishing or recreational purposes. While that figure—40 percent—gives us some indication of the extent of environmental harm, it in no way tells us anything about the additional repercussions of that form of pollution. Are those waterways more likely to be urban areas? If so, given that the U.S. population is concentrated in urban areas, the spillover effects for humans may be quite large. Also missing from that type of estimate is the number of animal and fish affected, or the larger ecological impacts such as the extent of environmental degradation caused by those polluted waterways. How can and should the latter impacts be measured?

Other measures also provide only general indicators of the environmental harm. In Pennsylvania, for example, one-third of streams and rivers fail to meet legal standards contained in the Clean Water Act (http://www.dcnr.state.pa.us/wlhabitat/aquatic/streamqual.aspx, accessed July 2013). Offering a more specific measure, EnvironmentAmerica.org reports that U.S. EPA records indicated that more than 100,000 miles of rivers and streams, 25,000 square miles of lakes, and 2,900 square miles of estuaries in the United States are so polluted by agricultural runoff and pollution that they are unsafe for swimming and fishing—which are conditions that are violations of the Clean Water Act (http://www.environmentamerica.org/home/reports/report-archives/our-rivers-lakes-and-streams/our-rivers-lakes-and-streams/agribusiness-lobby-fights-against-clean-water, accessed July 2013). Moreover, according to this report the number of "dead zones"—ocean areas with low dissolved oxygen incapable of supporting life—off the U.S. coast has increased from 12 in 1960 to approximately 300 today. In addition, this report estimates that mining activities in the Allegheny region alone have caused pollution in 2,390 stream miles. Our point is this: while we possess the ability to summarize some aspect of the environment as a green victim, these measures cannot be compared to the measures of victimization for ordinary street crimes.

Even these estimates of environmental pollution do not tell us how many times the environment has been victimized. How many acts of pollution occur in the estimated 100,000 miles of rivers and streams that are polluted? What we know is that these rivers and streams *are* polluted, not the frequency at which pollution occurs in those locations. Thus, until there are more efficient ways of counting the number of victimization incidents that involve the environment, green criminologists will need to stick with broad measures of environmental victimization.

At this point it is appropriate to provide some additional examples of the issues we have raised about the measurement of environmental victimization. Consider, for instance, the practice of mountaintop removal mining (MTR). In MTR, up to several hundred feet of a mountaintop are removed using explosives and heavy equipment to create access to coal seams which are then mined with surface mining techniques. The resulting rubble from the MTR process is deposited in the valleys between mountains, filling the valley—called a valley fill. How should this kind of victimization, which requires a permit, be measured? Is this one victimization because one mountaintop is involved? Is it two victimizations because the rubble is used to fill a valley? Is there a third victimization because the nature of the local area has been transformed from a mountain area to a plateau? Does the destruction of stream and river headwaters count as part of the scope of environmental victimization? What about the miles of stream filled by the valley fill? How should those be measured? How do we measure the diversion of the stream headwaters to new locations? Is that a single victimization? Are the new areas impacted by the diversion of stream headwaters as the result of human engineering an environmental victimization? What about the displaced species or those killed in the mountaintop blasting? Do we count the number of trees removed and add those to the list? What about the resulting pollution from waste water impoundments or when those waste waters leak into local water supplies? What about the effect of blasting on local human residents? In short, an activity such as MTR creates a wide scope of green victimization both quantitatively and qualitatively. Determining how these victimizations are measured is no small task, and is an area that remains open for further investigation by green criminology. There is no clear or definitive answer to the question: how much environmental victimization is there? Significant work remains to be done on this question.

Conclusion

Beginning in the late 1940s, criminologists began to open space for the discussion of crime victims, and over the past 60 years a significant volume of literature on crime victims has been produced. At the same time, the criminological space that has been opened to examine crime victims remains limited both in comparison to other issues criminologists examine and especially with respect to the issue of recognizing and identifying crime victims who are victimized by crimes committed by persons other than street offenders. These "other" victims include green victims.

For its part, green criminology expands the academic space of victimology by recognizing that green harms/crimes produce green victims. As practiced to date, green criminology has called attention to green victims, but has done so without specifically referencing or creating a green victimology, and without measuring the extent of harm these environmental harms produce. This chapter has outlined the preliminary boundaries of a green victimology and in that process the three broad groups of green victims that can be considered:

1. human victims
2. non-human beings as victims—flora, fauna, insects, and microbes
3. ecosystems and their component parts

In exploring the scope of green victimology, this chapter has also examined ways of counting, assessing, and comparing the extent of green victimization in the United States to street crime victimization. As noted, these comparisons cannot always be made, and sometimes assessments of green victims are required to use measures of victimization that cannot be compared to those that result from street crime. In examining green victimization in the United States, it was not our intention to suggest that this type of study is only possible in the United States, or that green victimization in the United States is more important than its occurrence elsewhere. To be sure, green victimization occurs throughout the world and requires the attention of green criminologists in the world's nations to identify and detail. How widespread is green victimization throughout the world? From various studies written by scientists it appears that this form of victimization is widespread. Is this form of victimization more or less prevalent in certain nations than in others? Such a determination has yet to be made by green criminologists and this remains one of the tasks that lies ahead in the study of green victimology. It is certain, however, that many countries that are engaged in significant levels of production have a significant number of green victims. For example, a report recently released by Hong Kong researchers notes that preventable air pollution in that city is responsible for about 43 in every 100,000 deaths (Chen, 2012).

We view our discussion of green victimology as a preliminary foray into this field of research. As a result, we recognize that the work of others on this issue may well expand the scope of green victimology beyond the scope of issues defined here, and may require modifying the definition we have provided. We welcome additional research on this topic and encourage others to adapt and modify our views on green victimology.

We anticipate that the ideas we have proposed about green victimology will be critically assessed, expanded, and modified. Indeed, we hope that this is the case and that our summary is not the last discussion of this important topic. Moreover, we anticipate resistance to our view from orthodox criminologists who will fail to appreciate our position especially as it relates to non-human and ecosystem victims. We recognize that the general anthropocentric orientation of orthodox criminology has limited the conceptualization of victims to humans, and that our view challenges those assumptions in a way that will promote defense of the more traditional view of victimology. Among our concepts, we imagine that the greatest resistance will be toward recognizing the ecosystem as a green victim. We imagine that many criminologists view ecosystems as inanimate objects and therefore as inappropriate kinds of victims. Despite what criminologists may believe about these victims, however, the scientific literature is replete with references to ecosystems and their components as living biological units and entities. As living entities these victims have definable attributes that can be changed and damaged by human activities. Those human activities are not only a specific form of environmental harm, but can, from the perspective of the living ecosystem, be viewed as crimes. At the same time we remind criminologists that recognizing ecosystems or non-human beings as green victims does not distract attention from other—human—victims. Rather, recognizing other kinds of victims promotes a broader approach to victimology capable of and willing to recognize the variety of ways in which humans create harms.

Chapter 6

Green Behaviorism: The Effects of Environmental Toxins on Criminal Behavior

When green criminologists have examined the problems of environmental exposure to toxic pollutants, they have limited their interpretation of this association by focusing on the negative public and environmental health outcomes related to exposure to toxic wastes. Yet, a significant literature in the medical and biological sciences indicates that exposure to environmental toxins can also change behavior. As criminologists, the implication that exposure to environmental toxins can change behavior can be employed to help explain factors that generate crime and affect its distribution. This chapter takes the suggested association between exposure to environmental toxins and behavioral changes in humans as an area ripe for investigation by green criminology. In order to draw greater attention to that particular issues, this chapter addresses what we call *green behaviorism*, which we define as that branch of green criminology that examines the relationship between exposure to environmental toxins and criminal behavior.[1]

The term "behaviorism" has a long history, primarily associated with psychology. In psychology, the term "behaviorism" has been applied to a number of approaches related to studying human and animal behavior. These approaches include automatic learning (stimulus-response or conditioned response effects; Pavlov, 1927, 1929), associative learning (Thorndike, 1898), radical behaviorism (Skinner, 1965, 1974), and conditioned emotional reactions (Watson and Rayner, 1920) among others. In each of these views the goal is to understand behavior as an outcome determined by a stimulus.

Green behaviorism accepts the most general psychological propositions of behaviorism, namely that:

1. behavior is a response to environmental conditions;
2. that the cause(s) of behavior is external rather than internal—exists outside of the mind; and

---

1   It is plausible that an expanded version of green behaviorism could be applied to issues other than crime, including, for example, the more general category of deviant behavior, mental illness, or other mental health and psychological problems. It should also be noted that there are other responses to environmental toxins such as illness, disease, and death.

3. that behavior is what organisms create and it is that creation that is the proper study of behaviorism.

While we accept these general psychological propositions, it is not our intention to equate green behaviorism with more general forms of behaviorism found in the field of psychology or to reduce human behavior to a psychological response to environmental toxins. One of the significant differences between psychological and green behaviorism is green behaviorism's restriction of the external stimuli that affect behavior to a particular type—exposure to environmental pollution and toxins.

In the case of green behaviorism, the measureable behavioral response— that is, crime—is influenced by the effect of environmental toxins on a subject's physiology or physiological state. In this sense, green behaviorism excludes reference to any specific mental states or processes—for example, operant conditioning, learning—and views these as intervening processes between exposure to environmental contamination, alterations in physiological states and processes, and the end result—behavioral outcomes. The relevance of the intervening psychological processes to green behaviorism isn't their existence and measurement, which is the subject of psychological, psychiatric, and mental health research, but rather that such processes can be affected and set into motion in the first place by exposure to environmental toxins. These intervening processes are relevant to green behaviorism to the extent that scientific studies indicate that exposure to environmental toxins may alter the intervening processes that have been the focus of both psychological and criminological explanations of behavior. These intervening processes include the relationship between learning and crime, the biological basis of learning sequences and processes, and reactions to operant conditioning and conditioned reflexes that may occur when the biological processes associated with learning are disrupted by exposure to environmental toxins. Based on the results of scientific research, it is plausible to assert that exposure to environmental toxins can alter behavior by disrupting biological processes tied to behavior. This may occur when environmental exposure to toxins derails the learning process or causes the disruption of cognate senses, or impacts biologic chemical processes, or leads to the inhibition of mental states related to arousal, frustration, and so forth, or stimulates manifestations of intermediary outcomes such as aggression that may lead to crime.

To make this case, this chapter reviews the overlap between green and psychological behaviorism, the unique features of green behaviorism, and its uses with respect to the study of criminal behavior. To illustrate these points, this discussion also specifically examines the effect of exposure to two specific environmental toxins that have been tied to these processes and leads to behavioral modification: lead (Pb) and endocrine disruptors.

Behaviorism: A Brief Review

Behaviorism has a long history traceable to developments in psychology during the late eighteenth and early nineteenth centuries (O'Donnell, 1985). Unlike other psychological views, behaviorism is held out as the science of behavior rather than as the science of the mind, with the latter view being associated with methodological behaviorism (Day, 1983). Psychological or radical behaviorism holds that behavior can be explained without reference to psychological processes and mental states, and that behavior is instead driven by responses to external stimulus (Staats, 1994). These latter views are also expressed in analytic or logical behaviorism which argues that psychological referents used to explain behavior should be replaced by behavioral categories (Putnam, 1965).

In laying out the position that behavior is a response to external stimuli, behaviorism must reject the assumption, common in other psychological approaches, that there are innate or inherent rules regarding learning processes. Skinner, for example, held that organisms' learning was not based on a precondition that defined the rules of learning. Rather, in Skinner's view organisms create the rules of learning from experience or when confronted with external stimuli and not from some set of expected behavioral rules. Learning, in other words, is an outcome of exposure to stimuli, and the stimuli create a learning response. This view stands in distinction to the idea that innate rules related to learning allow the organism to interpret stimuli because the rules for doing so already pre-exist. Behaviorists interpret the idea that there are preconceived rules for learning as a circular argument which assumes the very behavioral action that results from and explains the behavioral response as a required response to inherent rules about what exists establishes as a tautological explanation.

In the behaviorist view, mental action cannot be separated from behavioral action, and to illustrate this point behaviorists treat mental activities as actions rather than as psychological states. In short, in behaviorism the reference point for explaining behavior isn't other behavior that is part of the behavioral process—mental activity—but rather is an independent, external stimulus that can be separated from the behavioral response process. In doing so, the behaviorist claims to escape the tautology associated with general learning theories. Based on these assumptions, behaviorism stands in stark contrast to more recent developments in cognitive psychology.

Here, we are less concerned with whether learning is innate or external, and whether or not it has cognate references. The primary contribution we adapt from behaviorism is the idea that an organism's behavior is a response to an external stimulus. Further, in the case of environmental toxins the external stimulus is largely an unseen or unknown exposure. As a result, there is little reason to believe that the behavioral response that results from exposure to an environmental toxin is a learned response or one based on recognizing or perceiving a stimulus and reacting to that stimulus based on known rules of behavior. This is true since the organism does not interpret the stimulus as a stimulus, nor does it know from preexisting rules what behavioral effects the stimulus ought to produce. Rather, green behaviorism proceeds from the assumption that the response to an exposure from an environmental toxin is a pre-determined biological reaction set into motion by the chemical processes affected by exposure to toxins. In this view, the biological organism has no control over the chemical processes set into motion by exposure to an environmental toxin, and does not perceive the exposure in a way that affects the organism's response to the exposure. An organism does not need to know what should happen, or what is expected to happen when it is exposed to a toxin in order for the effect to occur; instead, what happens—the biological response—is determined by the chemical basis of the behavioral sequence, and what happens is independent of any psychological state of interpretation on behalf of the organism.

Green Behaviorism

As noted above, there are several varieties of behaviorism. One of the assumptions or features of behaviorism that facilitates its integration into or makes it compatible with green criminology centers on the idea that organisms are biological machines. Why this view is important cannot be neatly summarized, but emerges in the discussion below.

Biological Machinery

In psychology, the "biological machine" assumption allows an analysis of the association between input media or stimulus experienced by an organism and the organism's response to stimulus or its behavioral outputs. In this view, the process through which behavior is produced in response to stimuli occurs at a biological level or through the biological "equipment" or "machinery" within an organism. In some psychological versions of behaviorism, such as B.F. Skinner's, responses are conditioned by prior experience or learning. As medical and psychological research indicates, however, there is a biological basis to learning, and some portion of learning is biological to the extent that the learning involves the translation of stimuli into biological processes and reactions that include electrical impulses in the brain or central nervous system, and chemical reactions that occur biologically that transmit, store, and respond to stimuli and which even encode the behavioral responses chemically and electronically within the brain.

Biological Pathways to Behavior

In the behavioral view, behavioral outcomes are viewed as the organism's response to environmental factors which, in some cases, are modified by prior experience— that is, learning—or even states of conscious activity, and may sometimes involve learning. Not all behavioral responses, however, involve learning or conscious responses by an organism, and some behaviors may be reflexive responses to stimuli. For example, a response to noxious stimuli may elicit an avoidance or aggressive response which is not learned but rather is a reflex action with biological origins. Nevertheless, some response reflexes may also be learned. It is unlikely, however, that biological responses to toxic chemical exposures are learned, but rather are deterministic chemical/biological outcomes. For example, a person does not see polluted air, imagine the effects of being exposed to polluted air, and then in turn develop a mental response to exposure to polluted air such as developing a disease or engaging in aggressive or violent behavior. Rather, whether or not the person even recognizes that they live in a polluted environment, pollution exacts it effect on the individual by altering the individual's biological responses. This biological response to exposure to environmental toxins is not a mental creation, nor can the response be willed away. This outcome can be illustrated, for instance, with reference to the reaction of fetuses or new-born species to environmental toxins. The new born does not possess the cognitive ability to recognize a pollutant, or to know its biological or behavioral effects. Rather, those effects are generated by the biological and chemical interactions of the toxin with the bio-chemistry of the new born.

The Meaning of Environment

The term environment, as used within psychology, must be re-examined to better assert that an organism's behavior reflects environmental stimuli in green criminology. In the psychological view, environment is defined broadly to include a vast array of conditions and essentially includes all conditions external to the organism. This could include, for example, the immediate context of a social interaction such as the nature of the context in which the interaction occurs—for example, for humans, a family context, a friendship network, a social gathering, a formal meeting, an impersonal crowd. For humans, this context may also include the influence of structures that affect the transmission and interpretation of the stimulus such as the nature of communication, the structure of language, or even the broader effects of culture. Green behaviorism, however, omits consideration of these immediate *social* contexts that derive from relationship or relational connections. In green behaviorism, the focus is on the biological nexus that exists between environment and behavior, and green behaviorism draws attention to how the modified natural environment consisting of air, land, and water has been altered by human activities—for example, pollution—in ways that produce exposure to environmentally introduced toxins that interfere with and transform the biological machinery or process associated with behavioral outcomes.

In green behaviorism the environment is not made up of social relations and meanings. The examination of the association between social relations and criminal behavior is, to be sure, a central concern of many criminological approaches, and much criminological literature has attended to interpreting how social relations modify behavior in various ways. In the orthodox view of crime, social, economic, and political relations are viewed as the inputs that impact behavior.

In contrast, green behaviorism focuses attention on chemical exposure effects on behavior, and in that view, the resulting behavioral responses to these environmental conditions are deterministic to the extent that the organism has little ability to intervene in and alter that process through, for example, decision making or sheer will power or a consideration of the social context in which the exposure occurred. An individual exposed to an environmental toxin has been exposed, and its mental state and actions cannot change or eliminate that exposure. Whether the individual is exposed at work, at home, or in an outdoor setting is irrelevant to the effect the exposure produces. That is to say, for instance, the fact that a person is exposed to lead at work, or at home, or in an outdoor setting does not change the effect of the exposure to lead on those individuals. Lead exposure is no more or less serious depending on the location of the exposure, and the location of the exposure has no effect on the outcome unless, of course, the location of the exposure impacts the concentration of lead to which the individual is exposed.

For green behaviorism, the important context consists of the physical qualities of the environment—the chemicals that make up the organism's surroundings and to which it is exposed. In an unmodified or "natural" environment "free" of toxins—to the extent that nature only disperses toxins in limited ways, or in unusual circumstances, through natural disasters such as volcanic eruptions, and so on— and given a healthy or normal organism, the biological process involved in the production of behavior functions in a given, predetermined way. The stimulus is taken in, transmitted chemically and electronically in a specific way and in a certain order under circumstances in which this process is unadulterated—for example, a natural, normal biological reaction. Where the chemical nature of the environment is altered, however, there is the possibility of introducing chemical contaminants or toxins into an organism that affect the normal biological responses of the organism to the stimulus. It is this adulteration of the environment and its modifying effects on behavior through the introduction of chemical contaminants or pollutants into the organism's biological processes that is the concern in green behaviorism.

Consequently, green behaviorism focuses on how toxins or chemical pollutants in the environment affect and alter the normal biological processes involved in the production of behavior—an issue relevant to toxicological approaches reviewed earlier. A significant body of scientific research suggests that exposure to environmental toxins affects behavior by modifying the normal chemical/ electrical biological process that is part of the production of behavior. While the biological processes that affect behavior have been the subject of some research within criminology (Beaver et al., 2009; Roth, 2011), the understanding of this view is appreciably deeper and more nuanced in other disciplines (Preston et al., 2001), and while this topic has been largely examined by biological positivists within criminology, no specific segment of criminology concentrates solely on how exposure to environmental pollutants affects criminal behavior. This role, we suggest, should be filled by green behaviorism.

Unique Assumptions of Green Behaviorism

As described above, in psychological behaviorism the causes of behavior are viewed as external to the organism. In green behaviorism it is the external structural conditions found in both the broader and localized environmental/ ecological systems in which organisms are enmeshed that affects behavior. Of particular importance are local conditions related to industrial pollution, which itself may not be local in origin but may, as described in an earlier chapter, be produced in far off locations.

In addition, what should not be overlooked in this view is the effect and importance of the treadmill of production, which we describe more completely in a green criminological context in a subsequent chapter (see also, Stretesky, Long, and Lynch, 2013). The treadmill of production is a general description of productive and consumptive relationships that adheres in modern systems of capitalist production which appeared following World War II and now dominate the modern world capitalist system of production and consumption. This treadmill approach has been applied at various levels of analysis in an effort to situate both global and local environmental problems within the context of economic production (on global warming see, Baer, 2008; on organic farming see, Obach, 2007; on national ecological footprints see, Jorgenson and Burns, 2007; see generally, Gould, Pellow, and Schnaiberg, 2008).

In taking a green behavioral view it is not our intent to suggest that industrial pollution is *the only* cause of crime, nor even to suggest that it is the most important cause of crime. What we are suggesting, however, is that some portion of crime which at this stage in history and research is unknown, is a function of exposure to the industrial pollutants produced by the treadmill of production. For example, it is known from scientific research that exposure to a variety of pollutants can change human and animal behavior. At the same time, exposure to pollution does not explain all crime; nor does exposure to pollution affect all organisms equally. As a result, behavioral differences due to exposure to pollution across people may be the result of any of the following:

1. the pollution dose
2. the length of exposure to the pollutant(s)
3. the presence of additional pollutants or other chemicals in the environment that may modify the effect of the pollutant in interaction with other pollutants and chemicals
4. genetic differences and thus susceptibilities to environmental pollutants across individuals, some of which have been examined in the scientific literature
5. factors that may affect the metabolism and excretion of specific pollutants including diet, exercise, and the use of vitamin supplements
6. climate conditions which may concentrate or disperse environmental pollutants or affect the biological processing of pollutants

For example, medical, biological, and environmental research has uncovered a number of conditions that impact how environmentally noxious chemicals are processed: allelic variations in genetic structures have been shown to have an effect on the processing of lead (Jaffe et al., 2000); genetic structures have also been related to the impact of various air pollutants on children's lung functions (Breton et al., 2011); research also indicates that oxidative stress-related genes play a role in processing pollutants (Ren et al., 2010); and that genetic make-up affects PCB-induced teratogenic change (Meyer and DiGiulio, 2002). In short, the relationship between environmental pollution and crime is not simple, and is best viewed as involving the likelihood or probability that a behavioral change related to crime may occur.

We must also acknowledge that in taking this view of crime we are engaging in a limited examination of factors that affect one form of crime—street crime. At this point we have little reason to believe that exposure to environmental pollutants is a cause or correlate of crimes committed by the powerful. In our view, the crimes of the powerful are largely a function of economic and political conditions that involve efforts to manage, exercise, control, and accumulate economic and political power. Corporate crimes of violence, for example, are qualitatively different than violent street crimes. These types of crime occur in different situational contexts and milieus, and constitute differential reflections of larger structural forces within the context of class locations and class-related opportunity structures. Thus, while street crimes may reflect the structural parameters associated with non-existent ties to economic and political power and become a projection of those conditions in expressive acts of violence, corporate crimes can hardly be said to emerge from a lack of power nor do they constitute expressive acts of violence. The fact that street crimes and corporate crimes differ in volume and level of harm, in the conditions that force them into existence, or the fact that corporate crimes are not the result of exposure to pollutants does not negate the relevance of pollutants as potential causes of street crime.

One of the primary goals of green behaviorism is to examine the intersection of green criminology and scientific studies on the behavioral effects of environmental pollutants in order to highlight the scientific status of research on pollution exposure-behavioral effects. In taking this view, it is also the intention of green behavior to draw criminological attention to the detrimental consequences of the treadmill of production as the mechanism in modern societies that produces the production and unequal distribution of toxic exposure across populations. As examined elsewhere in this book, treadmill of production explanations explore how contemporary, normalized methods of industrial production and consumption set into motion by elevating the quest for profit above all other potential goals of production creates an inescapable and expanding treadmill of production and consumption that constantly draws resources from the environment and churns out toxic chemical wastes that contribute to ecological disorganization. Those toxic results produce a broad array of negative consequences: the pollution of natural resources; over-consumption; the depletion of natural resources through unsustainable production and consumption patterns; the unequal distribution of environmental harms such as pollution; the creation of unhealthy work and living spaces; and from a criminological perspective, the generation of behavior-modifying pollutants. Green behaviorism calls attention to this treadmill in order both to expose its effects and to seek solutions to its destructive pathway.

Following the description above, green behaviorism must also be seen as one of the elements of a broader critique of capitalism. That is to say that green behaviorism interprets contemporary capitalist production practices—whether in nations with large, fairly unregulated capitalist markets such as the United States, relatively regulated capitalist markets, state capitalism, social market capitalism, corporate capitalism, or welfare capitalism—as a central driver of environmental problems. In capitalist economies, the environment tends to be viewed simply as a warehouse of stored resources (Burkett, 2009; Foster, 2000). The supply of resources is seen as a simple supply and demand problem that is best regulated by market price mechanisms. Because these natural resources are not inventoried as part of the stock of items owned by corporations, but rather are often the result of rent agreements, there is a strong tendency toward super-exploitation of resources (Foster, 2000). Moreover, given these conditions and their short-term focus on profit, corporations in a capitalist economy have no financial interest in the sustainability of natural resources. Likewise, because corporations are profit based and the ramifications of resource depletion have no profit consequences, they have little reason to consider the impacts of either resource depletion or the pollution of nature (Foster, Clark, and York, 2011). As a result, more specific problems such as the effect of pollution on the health and behavior of organisms in the environment have no meaning in the corporate ledger book view of the world. In short, capitalism fosters a situation in which public and environmental health can easily be sacrificed because the costs of those sacrifices are externalized and socialized (Foster, Clark, and York, 2011).

Green Behaviorism and Science

Green behaviorism draws its inspiration from more general forms of behaviorism, but also from the scientific literature which examines the consequences of exposure to pollution on human behavior. The chemical and electrical or biologic processes involved in producing behavior have been the subject of much scientific research. This kind of research has a long history in the natural sciences (Evans and Jacobs, 1981).

It is not the goal of green behaviorism to produce this kind of research on the connection between environmental pollution and human behavior—though in principle, it could—but rather to investigate the importance of this research for understanding one particular behavioral outcome, crime. Scientists, for instance, have discovered that certain kinds of chemical exposure or environmental toxins such as heavy metals can alter behavior by affecting the biological processes involved in learning, or through processes that affect spatial orientations and interpretations, or by stimulating the biological basis of aggression, and increasing hyperactivity (Bao et al., 2009). These various processes may also operate through related conditions such as evidence of decreased brain size in exposed individuals (Cecil et al., 2008). For example, exposure to lead may affect learning and thought processes and produce certain forms of crime; or lead exposure may produce crime by stimulating aggression; or it might function by producing new behavioral responses to new spatial stimuli or to spatial configurations and stimuli that are perceived as if they were new stimuli (see Wright, Boisvert, and Vaske, 2009; Wright et al., 2008). A large class of environmental toxins identified as endocrine disruptors, for instance, act by altering the normal operation of the hormonal system. Endocrine disruptors can change behavior by producing aggressive or passive reactions to stimulus by transforming normal hormonal system functions. Some of the functions may also be linked to learning (see below for elaboration).

Does the biological pathway matter?   It is, for the most part, irrelevant to green behaviorism whether exposure to an environmental toxin alters behavior by affecting learning or the biological basis of reflexive actions. The significance of environmental toxins is that they can and do change behavior, and that part of that change in behavior can produce crime and delinquency (Denno, 1990; Raine, 1993). While the precise pathway of that effect has scientific importance, establishing the pathway's effects is presupposed by green behaviorism—that is, the scientific basis for the effect is established in other disciplines—and its reliance on prior scientific findings related to these outcomes.

Is crime, therefore, biological?   It is not the purpose of green behaviorism to suggest that all crime or even a majority of crime is, so to speak, caused by exposure to environmental toxins, nor that crime is biologically rooted. Rather, the point is to demonstrate that some portion of crime is produced by exposure to environmental toxins and that, consequently, a complete understanding of crime is impossible unless this outcome is considered.

It is also not the purpose of green behaviorism to promote a biological explanation for crime. To be sure, this view does suggest that some crimes may result as a consequence of introducing toxins into environments, and in turn promoting human exposure to those toxins and modifying human biological processes that are connected to the production of behavior. This does not mean, however, that crime is solely a biological process, nor that it can be understood only from this perspective. Nor does it mean that the biological functions involved in this process are of paramount interest. Rather, one of the assumptions of green behaviorism that needs to be made clear is that the actions that produce exposure to environmental toxins capable of altering behavior have a sociologically relevant dimension, and that absent this dimension, there is little need for a green behaviorism of crime. To illustrate this point, consider that while scientists now agree that exposure to many environmental toxins is ubiquitous or found throughout the environment and in all corners of the world, exposure levels and the distribution of these toxins varies both across space and time—that is, levels of toxic chemicals are not always and everywhere the same. Within the United States, for instance, exposure to environmental toxins that can affect behavior varies along with population characteristics, so that generally urban populations, African Americans, and the poor have elevated levels of exposure to environmental toxins. This pattern of relationships mirrors the general geographic pattern of crime and potentially provides some portion of the explanation concerning the variability in crime across these groups and in social space. In addition, exposure to toxins, while geographically distributed and linked to certain population characteristics of sociological relevance, is also conditioned by other relevant sociological phenomena such as access to health care, diet, and so forth. Thus, the effect of exposure to toxins that may impact criminal behavior can also be impacted by the social and economic structure of society. Without the connection between exposure, the biological effects of exposure, and the role social structure plays in mediating this process and potentially the outcomes, green behaviorism fails to contribute to the understanding of the factors that affect the production of crime or its distribution. Indeed, we would suggest that those who see green behaviorism as just another version of biological explanations of crime fail to appreciate its true significance as a social and economic theory of the production of crime.

Green Behaviorism and Policy

It is also important to point out that a key feature of green behaviorism is the kinds of policies it proposes. From the perspective of green behaviorism, crime, if it is the result of exposure to environmental toxins, cannot be eradicated or controlled without also controlling environmental pollution. Thus, the preferred policies that stem from green behaviorism involve those that seek to regulate, limit, and eliminate environmental pollution. This policy focus also connects green behaviorism to the policy positions taken more generally within green criminology—polices aimed at reducing and eliminating environmental pollution to produce a healthier world for all species, not simply humans. Humans are connected to the environment through many pathways—by their consumption of natural resources such as water, air, and land through the natural materials humans consume and through food products harvested from the land. Moreover, humans are connected to other species through consumption. Thus, for instance, policies that limit urban pollution clearly have direct human health and potentially behavioral consequences. The effects of these policies, however, may be limited if they simply shift the distribution of pollution from say urban to rural environments where these pollutants may still affect urban populations through a complex transfer of pollutants through food stuffs, or in the form of long range, air-borne pollution.

In the sections that follow, we review the use of green behaviorism by focusing on some specific examples of toxic pollutants that alter human behavior. The two specific examples we explore are lead pollution and endocrine disrupting chemical pollution.

Example 1: Consequences of Environmental Lead Exposure on Behavior

There is a significantly large scientific literature on the effects of lead (Pb) on learning abilities and the biologic basis of learning that has been produced by studies that employ animal testing. There is also animal testing literature that focuses on the effects of lead on animal behavior including the stimulation of aggression. There is some concern that the results of animal studies, while instructive, cannot be completely transferred to human populations. Unfortunately, the kinds of studies that can be produced by animal research involve forms of true experimentation—for example, exposing subjects to precise doses of an environmental toxin introduced in a controlled setting—that cannot ethically be undertaken with human subjects. Thus, research on the effects of environmental toxins on behavior often begins with such studies in order to establish the feasibility of further research on human populations that might use epidemiological methods.

One of the key concerns in animal experimentation is that animal responses to environmental toxins may not be exactly the same as the responses found in humans. To be sure, this is a legitimate concern. Nevertheless animal studies have provided the basis for extending research on the behavioral effects of environmental toxins to humans.

One of the advantages of animal studies is that the animals used in this research are genetically similar, thus ruling out a variety of competing explanations for the observed effects. In addition, because the experimental conditions for these experiments can be tightly controlled, these experiments have a high degree of validity, and can rule out numerous alternative explanations that cannot be controlled when human populations are examined. Finally, animal studies allow scientists to focus in on specific hypotheses about how environmental toxins affect biological processes, and allow researchers to examine those specific biological processes for important changes.

We appreciate that there is some irony in the discussion of the uses of animal experimentation in a book on green criminology. To be sure, those issues have been widely addressed in the scientific, animal studies and philosophical literatures (Grindon et al., 2006; Hendriksen, 2002; Regan, 2004; Singer, 1990). There are, for example, methods other than animal experimentation that can be employed in the sciences to train biology and medical students (Hakkinen and Green, 2002; Harvey and Salter, 2012; Quentin-Baxter and Dewhurst, 1992) and for drug testing (on cell-testing for drugs, see, Zimmer et al., 2002; on computational toxicology see, Kavlock et al., 2008). Our discussion is not intended to legitimize or endorse animal experimentation (see, Frank and Lynch, 1992 for discussion). Rather, our point is simply that since such evidence exists, it should not be ignored within green criminology despite green criminology's objections to the use and exploitation of animals (Beirne, 1999, 2009; Benton, 1998).

A large number of studies have examined the effect of lead exposure on animal behavior. These studies have various implications for understanding the ways in which environmental exposure to lead impacts human behavior.

Bauter et al. (2003) examined whether post-weaning lead exposure outcomes—specifically enhanced dopamine and blocked N-methyl-D-aspartic acid (DMDA) in nucleus accumben functions (NAC) or the part of the brain related to the perception of rewards—are related to learning impairments in rats. Their results suggest that inhibited glutamatergic DMDA function—a nonessential amino acid that acts as a neurotransmitter that inhibits neural excitement in the central nervous system—affects selective learning impairments related to chronic, low-level lead exposure (for additional confirming results see also, Cohn and Cory-Slechta, 1993; Gilbert and Lasley, 2007). In effect, chronic, low-level lead exposure reduces the ability of the brain's reward receptors to exhibit appropriate or normal chemical "excitement," diminishing the ability of external rewards to promote learning.

Lead has also been identified as reducing learning performance in relation to acquiring information. One specific pathway for this form of learning inhibition is lead's action with respect to AMPA (α-amino-3-hydroxyl-5-methyl-4-isoxazole-propionate) and NMDA (N-methyl-D-aspartic acid) receptors in the synapse (Chen, Ma, and Ho, 2001). Chen, Ma, and Ho found that rats exposed to lead exhibited learning deficiencies related to acquiring information that produces inhibitory avoidance behaviors.

Lead not only appears to disrupt the biological basis of learning, but also long-term memory storage. Vázquez and Peña de Ortiz (2004) report that lead (Pb^{+2}) impairs the brain's long-term memory (LTM) storage abilities by interfering with the learning-induced activation of Ca^{+2}/phospholipid-dependent hippocampal protein kinase C (PKC). In this study, compared to a control group of non-exposed rats, Vázquez and Peña de Ortiz found that rats exposed to Pb^{+2} could learn a spatial task—that is, a maze—but did not retain this information, implying that LTM was disrupted by lead exposure (for supporting results on the effect of lead on repeated multiple learning see Cohn, Cox, and Cory-Slechta, 1993; Cory-Slechta, Garcia-Osuna, and Greenamyre, 1997).

Despite the results of these studies, numerous questions remain concerning the exact biologic processes through which lead exposure impacts the biological roots of learning, and whether this process might also vary across species. Hirsch, Possidente, and Possidente (2009) examined this issue by exploring the effect of lead exposure on hormone regulated traits in the fruit fly (*Drosophila melanogaster*). Their results suggest that lead may affect learning and behavior through two distinct processes: one linked to the direct behavioral effects of lead on neural mechanisms associated with learning, and a second pathway which acts through the endocrine disruptive effects of lead exposure. The first pathway—neural—directly involves disruption of learning processes that impact behavior, while the second pathway—endocrine disruption—appears to involve behavioral outcomes not mediated through learning.

A variety of animal studies suggest that exposure to lead affects behavior independently of biological learning pathways. In an early study, Petit and Alfano (1979) observed that lead-exposed rats demonstrated different behavioral patterns than non-exposed rats in open environments. Open environments are "uncontrolled" or "unregulated" environments where experimental animals can freely interact with the designed environment. These open environments are "uncontrolled" to the extent that they do not involve environmentally constrained environments such as mazes or other specific learning tasks. Petit and Alfano's research indicated that the hippocampus was the major site of lead's activity, and that this activity site played an important role in behavior construction and reactions among rats in open environments. Their research indicated that lead-exposed rats exhibited different behaviors than non-exposed rats in open environments. The researchers suggest that these different behavioral responses appeared to suggest tension and uneasiness with open environments among lead-exposed rats. Uneasiness or over-reaction to open environments among lead-exposed rats was also observed in an earlier study (Winneke, Brockhaus, and Baltissen, 1977). In a more recent study, Malvezzi et al. (2001) report that rat fetuses exposed to lead in the womb demonstrated hyperactivity, decreased exploratory behavior, and impaired learning and memory, indicating multiple pathway effects of lead on rat behavior. In their study Moreira, Vassilieff, and Vassilieff (2001) point out that the level of lead exposure in rat pups that affected behavior would be similar to the level of lead exposure found in children chronically exposed to environmental sources of lead pollution.

More elaborate studies that include observations of the impact of lead exposure on social behaviors among primates support the observations from rat-based studies. Bushnell and Bowman (1979), for example, found that current lead-exposed infant rhesus monkeys as opposed to those previously exposed to lead—measured by high levels of lead tissue burden—demonstrated suppressed play, increased social clinging, and disrupted social behavior when their play environments were altered. These researchers suggested that continuous lead exposure disrupted forms of play development required for adequate socialization, and that lead exposure alters the biological processes involved in interpreting and storing play-related information. Supporting the finding that lead exposure alters behavioral responses to open environments discovered in rats, Levin et al.'s (1988) study of postnatally lead-exposed rhesus monkeys found evidence of decreased "looking behavior" on visual exploration tests and increased arousal and agitation on behavioral assessments.

Lead and Human Behavior

While studies of the effects of lead on the behavior of animals is instructive and provided the impetus for further research exploring this relationship in humans, animal studies alone may not produce sufficient evidence of similar effects in humans. The advantage of animal studies in contrast to human population studies is that animal studies can be carried out as controlled experiments, and thus alternative causal processes may be ruled out as explaining the observed outcomes. Still, animal research may not hold for humans. There are, however, numerous studies of the effects of lead exposure on human behavior (for review of this issue see, Narag, Pizarro, and Gibbs, 2009; Reyes, 2007).

The effects of lead on human behavior and health have long been examined through epidemiological studies. The sheer volume of human lead-health-behavior research studies has produced extensive knowledge concerning the effects of lead on human behavior, and by the mid-1990s numerous behavioral outcomes associated with lead exposure had been discovered and were considered to be valid. These outcomes include the following: impulsivity; delayed reactions and increased reaction times; diminished performance on vigilance tasks; distractibility; shortened attention spans; decreased ability or inability to follow rule sequences; inappropriate problem solving techniques; an inability to alter inappropriate response patterns; deficiencies in reading, spelling, math, and word recognition; and spatial organizational deficits (Rice, 1996).

As noted earlier, lead exposure has been associated with biological changes in human anatomy. For example, lead exposure appears to decrease brain size (Cecil et al., 2008) and gray matter development (Brubaker et al., 2010). A number of studies indicate a possible relationship between brain size and behavior through a variety of pathways. Low-level fetal lead exposure has, for example, been associated with interrupted early life neurobehavioral development (Dietrich et al., 1987). Specific effects of high lead concentrations on children have been noted that involve cognate abilities related to visual-spatial and visual-motor integration (Bellinger et al., 1991). Recent research suggests that lead also appears to act through the inhibition of the N-methyl-d -aspartate receptor (NMDAR) and synaptic functions (Neal and Guilarte, 2009).

The impact of lead on criminal and delinquent behavior has been examined in prior research. These studies lend strong support to the hypothesis that lead exposure has a significant influence on crime and delinquency controlling for a wide range of crime and delinquency correlates.

Rick Nevin has found evidence of an association between lead and crime at various levels of analysis. For example, in a 2007 study, Nevin found an association between measures of preschool blood lead levels and crime across several nations. The data on crime and preschool blood lead levels represent data from the United States, Britain, Canada, West Germany, France, Italy, Australia, Finland, and New Zealand. In Nevin's words, a strong relationship—measured by R^2 and t-values for blood lead—were discovered using lagged models of the association between preschool blood lead levels as a measure of neurobehavioral damage with the index crime rate, burglary, and violent crimes. In a related analysis, Nevin (2000) also found evidence that blood lead levels were related to age-specific arrest rates and incarceration trends. In a final model, Nevin also found evidence that blood lead levels were associated with averaged murder rates across American cities (1985-

1994). Nevin (2000) also found that aggregate trends in lead levels in the environment measured by leaded gasoline use were related to violent crime rates in the United States. (On potentially related issues such as trends in preschool lead exposure and scholastic achievement see, Nevin, 2009 see also, Carpenter and Nevin, 2010.)

In an important study on the effect of lead exposure on crime that demonstrated how early life course lead exposure affects crime later in life, Wright et al. (2008) employed longitudinal data to assess the impact of prenatal and childhood lead exposure on adult criminality. The study examined 250 individuals born in Cincinnati, Ohio between 1979 and 1984. Prenatal blood lead levels were measured during the first trimester or early in the second trimester, while childhood blood lead data were collected quarterly through age six-and-a-half. Data on total arrests and violent arrests were collected from criminal justice records. Their results—covariate-adjusted rate ratios for total arrests and arrests for violent crimes—indicated that prenatal and postnatal blood lead concentrations were associated with both total arrests and violence related arrests.

Herbert Needlman has long been engaged in research examining the effects of lead exposure on human behavior, and was among the first to recognize that low-level lead exposure was a significant health problem that could also promote behavioral changes. In a case control study of the relationship between bone-lead levels and delinquency, Needleman et al. (2002) found that non-delinquent controls had significantly lower bone lead levels than delinquents. Controlling for a range of covariates for delinquency and lead levels, delinquents were four times more likely than controls to have elevated bone lead levels (see also, Needleman et al., 1996). In a related study, Olympio et al. (2010) examined the relationship between lead levels in the surface enamel of teeth and antisocial behavior in a sample of 173 Brazilian youth aged 14-18. Adjusting for covariates of antisocial behavior, these researchers found evidence of an association between lead exposure and antisocial behavior as measured by self-reported delinquency and the childhood behavior checklist.

At the individual level, lead has demonstrated a persistent, significant relationship to measures of crime and delinquency. In order to assess the validity of individual-level study findings based on smaller samples, researchers have also undertaken longitudinal and cross sectional studies. In their longitudinal study, Dietrich et al. (2001) reported that controlling for other covariates, prenatal and postnatal exposure to lead was associated with reported antisocial acts including delinquency later in life. In an attempt to assess whether these micro-level finding hold at the aggregate level, Stretesky and Lynch (2001, 2004) examined the relationship between air lead pollution and crime across U.S. counties. They discovered a cross-sectional association between air lead levels, a measure of lead exposure, and homicide and crime rates across all U.S. counties (on related heavy metals as potential causes of delinquency see also, Haynes et al., 2011).

The research on exposure to environmental sources of lead contamination is only one example of the kind of work consistent with green behaviorism. In the next section we provide a second example that looks at environmental exposure to endocrine disruptors.

Example 2: Endocrine Disruptors

For nearly two decades, scientists have been extremely concerned with the health and behavioral effects of environmental exposure to endocrine disruptors (Colborn, vom Saal, and Soto, 1993), though initial evidence of these impacts have been known to scientists for more than 70 years (Snyder et al., 2004). Endocrine disruptors are named after their role in altering the normal functioning of the endocrine system. Endocrine disruptors are chemicals that act like hormones when introduced into biological species, and which, because of their similar chemical structures when compared to hormones, play the same role as hormones in biological organisms. The endocrine system interacts with the nervous system to coordinate bodily functions by allowing cells to communicate with one another. The endocrine system performs this function by releasing hormones that travel through the bloodstream where they are picked up by receptor/transmitter cells (Molina, 2003).

Endocrine disruptors are essentially environmental pollutants that when taken into the body are treated by the endocrine system as if they were hormones—that is, they act as hormone mimics (Colborn, 2004; Colborn, Dumanoski, and Meyers, 1997). In other words, the pollutants that act as endocrine disruptors are so similar to hormones in their chemical structure that they are mistaken as hormones by the endocrine system and plugged into receptor and transmitter cells where hormones belong. When disrupted in this way, the endocrine system produces cancers, birth defects, and a range of developmental disorders including learning disabilities, attention deficit disorders, and cognate/brain developmental disorders.

The list of endocrine disruptors is currently quite long (see, http://www. ourstolenfuture.org/basics/chemlist.htm, accessed June 2013) and includes about 93 elements, chemicals, and compounds. Some endocrine disruptors are found in common household items such as plastics; others in pesticides, fertilizers, and herbicides. These chemicals include a number of environmental toxins such as PCBs, dioxins, phthalates, alkylphenolic compounds, bisphenol A, some heavy metals (lead, mercury, and cadmium), and many pesticides. Endocrine disruptors may also be classified as persistent organic pollutants (POPs) or a class of chemicals created by humans that biodegrade slowly or resist biodegradation, persist in natural environments for long periods of time, undergo widespread and long-range transport—that is, are distributed long distances by natural processes such as air currents—and bioaccumulate in tissue and biomagnify in the food chain.

The characteristics of endocrine disruptors in the environment—that they resist biodegradation, bioaccumulate, and biomagnify—when coupled with their effects on various species make these chemicals a special concern with respect to their impact on the health and behavior of various species (Colburn, vom Saal, and Soto, 1993). Moreover, because of their special environmental characteristics, endocrine disruptors have become environmentally ubiquitous (Colborn, Dumanoski, and Meyers, 1997). But, endocrine disruptors are a concern not only because of their widespread appearance in the environment, but also because endocrine disruptors have powerful effects at dose levels well below those associated with toxicants that act through other biological processes (Rogan and Ragan, 2003).

Also of special concern is the effect of endocrine disruptors on species' development (Colburn, vom Saal, and Soto, 1993). In humans and other species as well, fetuses, embryos, and the young are particularly susceptible to the effects of endocrine disruptors because they are in stages of development controlled by hormonal systems (Bigsby et al., 1999; Jacobson and Jacobson, 1996). Of particular interest for the present discussion are the effects of endocrine disruptors on sexual identification and behavior (Cacioppo et al., 2000; Palanza et al., 1999), neurodevelopment and motor skills (Nakajima et al., 2006), intellectual impairment (Jacobson and Jacobson, 1996), learning disabilities (Colborn, 2004), and cognitive processes (Schantz and Widholm, 2001). In addition to these effects that can alter behavior, endocrine disruptors are also associated with negative health outcomes such as cancer (Shoulars et al., 2008). These effects are important because recent research indicates that the effect of endocrine disruptors may also be transgenerational or passed on to offspring (Anway and Skinner, 2006) and have important developmental effects (Colborn, 2004).

Researchers have pointed out that many of the factors criminologists have identified as being associated with crime and delinquency—for example, learning disabilities, aggression, developmental delays, low-birth weight, intellectual impairment, and so on—are also associated with exposure to environmental toxins such as lead, which is also an endocrine disrutpor (Stretesky and Lynch, 2001). A similar conclusion can be reached with respect to endocrine disruptors which are also associated with a wide-range a developmental processes as indicated above. Based on the endocrine disruption research produced by scientists, it appears plausible to suggest that the correlates of crime many criminological researchers have discovered in recent years may be the result of, at least in part, exposure to environmental toxins such as endocrine disruptors. In other words, one might expect that correlates of crime and delinquency are correlated with levels of environmental toxins measured in either individuals or environments.

Extant research has not specifically linked endocrine disruptors to crime or delinquency. However, as noted, research indicates that the presence of endocrine disruptors influences biological processes criminologists have linked to crime. Significant research efforts on endocrine disruptors remains to be undertaken, especially with respect to their possible influence on criminal behavior.

Conclusion

To summarize, this chapter has laid out the general parameters for a sub-specialty within green criminology we refer to as green behaviorism. Following the general assumptions of psychological behaviorism, green behaviorism examines the external stimuli that lay behind behavior. In the case of green criminology the behavior under examination is ordinary criminal behavior. The external stimuli addressed by green behaviorism are the various forms of environmental pollution that possess the capability of altering human behavior.

Green behaviorism, unlike psychological behaviorism, also addresses the processes that produce exposure to the stimuli that modify behavior, which in the case of green criminology is environmental pollution. In the context of the world system of capitalist economic relationships, green behaviorism draws attention to the role the treadmill of production and consumption plays in facilitating the production of and exposure to environmental toxins that change behavior.

This chapter also introduced the idea of the treadmill of production. As noted, that treadmill plays an important role in green behaviorism and is a principle force behind environmental exposure to toxins especially, in the case of green behaviorism, for humans. The treadmill of production, however, is also important for understanding exposure to environmental toxins for non-human species and for ecosystems. We explore this issue and the treadmill of production in more detail in Chapter 8.

Chapter 7

The Life Course Trajectories
of Chemical Pollutants

Over the past two decades criminologists have paid increasing attention to criminal life course research and trajectory explanations of criminal behavior. These ideas suggest that the human life course contains defining moments or turning points that shape participation in crime. This shaping process includes specifying the age of onset of crime and desistence from crime, and the analysis of early or late onset and desistence trajectories. Trajectory analysis adds to this approach the observation that the criminal life course can be divided into trajectories or pathways of development that reflect periodic offending, persistent offending, and early and late onset offending patterns among others (Jennings, 2010; Jennings, Maldonado-Molina, and Komro, 2010).

In this chapter we draw from the concepts and perspectives developed in criminological life course analysis related to turning points and trajectories to explore the relevance of this approach for examining the life course of chemical pollutants in the environment as an issue relevant to green criminology. In addition, drawing from observations contained in the toxicological, eco-toxicological, and environmental toxicology, it is clear that chemical pollutants have life courses once released into the environment. These chemical pollution life courses include turning points related to chemical concentrations in the environment and to health standards.

A pollutant's life course also contains trajectories that reflect patterns of chemical accumulation that mark persistent, low-level, and early and late onset chemical pollution trajectories. In our view, these chemical pollution trajectories and turning points can be employed to discuss the relationship between chemical pollution concentrations and accumulation patterns in the environment and the potential for chemical pollution victimization, which have relevance to green victimology, green behaviorism and the study of environmental justice. That is, chemical pollutant turning points and trajectories influence the likelihood and extent of chemical pollution or green victimization, which may also impact the probability of related outcomes such as the spread of illness and disease among species, limiting the ability of the environmental system to reproduce itself, or setting in motion processes that produce criminal behavior. These effects are likely to vary along race and class dimensions of neighborhoods since, as the environmental justice literature illustrates, there is a strong association between pollution exposure and community race and class characteristics.

In short, in this chapter we point out how a pollutant's or chemical emission's life course and life course qualities can be employed to discuss the prevalence and probability that chemical pollutants promote green victimization. In addition, we argue that a pollutant's life course characteristics also affect the likelihood that those pollutants modify human behavior and affect the propensity toward crime.

Pollution in a Life Course Perspective

Pollution and chemical emissions, like criminal behavior or the life of an individual, can be described as following a life course. The life course of a pollutant unfolds as pollutants are added to, accumulate, or decay in the environment and cross thresholds used to demarcate when the level of a chemical pollutant's concentration in the environment has reached a critical stage that may harm the environment or species living in the environment.

The idea that chemical pollutants have a life course reflects concerns that not only relate to the accumulation and concentration of chemicals in the environment, but also to the fate of chemical pollutants in the environment such as their rate of decomposition into either inert compounds or chemicals, or their decay or combination into more serious chemical pollutants. These types of concerns have had a significant impact on the development of sciences devoted to addressing these concerns, such as environmental toxicology and ecotoxicology, as reviewed in an earlier chapter.

Not only is it useful to think of chemicals as possessing life courses and passing through life course turning points in relation to their concentration in the environment, or following pollution trajectories with serious, long-term consequences for the environment, we can also employ the idea of a pollutant's life course to discuss how a pollutant's life course might intersect with human and non-human species, or environmental or ecosystem life courses. For example, when the life course of a pollutant intersects with the life course of living things, the age of the impacted victim may affect the outcome (Gouveia and Fletcher, 2000). This occurs when the chemicals come into contact, for instance, with human individuals of different ages. These effects can be enhanced when the individual who comes into contact with pollutants are in their early life course or developmental phase (Grandjean et al., 2008). But, the life course of pollutants may also have differential effects when they impact people who have compromised life courses that are shaped by poverty or those with compromised immune systems (Johnson et al., 2001). Likewise, we can think of this interaction with respect to its impact on sensitive ecosystem components and subsystems (Catallo, 1993).

The life course of chemical pollutants in the environment, like the life course of an individual, is marked by significant events and turning points. These chemical life courses are also marked by "developmental" patterns related to the accumulation and concentration of chemical pollutants in the environment, and the transition of chemical pollutant from one life course phase to another, or in the age of onset of effects of those pollutants. For example, this may occur at a point in time following the release of or the accumulation of a chemical pollutant in the environment when it reaches a level that causes negative health outcomes that may range from the production of disease, to impacts on learning abilities, and even changes in behavior (see generally, Jorgenson, 2001).

With respect to pollutants, key markers in the life course include:

1. their "birth" or point of generation in the productive process;
2. their introduction or expulsion into the environment;
3. the pathway of their introduction into the environment or route of emission—for example, as air, land, water, or storage site pollutants;
4. their cumulative patterns of emission and accumulation in the environment; and
5. whether they encroach upon or surpass health benchmarks—which we previously described in Chapter 5 as the anthropogenic enrichment factor or AEF—employed to assess the potential of chemical pollutants to produce harm or environmental victimization directly to the environment and its subsystems, or to the environment's various inhabitants (Jorgenson, 2001).

These life course markers and trajectories are useful for understanding when and where the volume of pollution or its introduction into the environment generates problematic outcomes, and why those outcomes persist over time as chemical pollutants accumulate, or decline, or even intensify as chemical pollution decays into other chemical products. Importantly, such information also has relevance to legal standards and regulations (Meyer, 1988). These life course turning points and stages can also be impacted by the treadmill of production, and the phase or stage of the treadmill of production, and the nature of the world system of capitalist production.

These chemical turning points and trajectories can be used to describe the quantitative and qualitative dimensions of pollution in a general sense and also to examine the potential for victimization. For example, the production of a chemical pollutant creates the potential for direct victimization of the environment and secondary victimization of its subsystems and the species living in those environments upon its release. That potential for victimization is dependent upon other life course characteristics of a pollutant including its specific turning points and trajectories in the environment. If, for example, the pollutant is accumulating in the environment, it may reach a turning point where it crosses scientifically established health benchmarks. Following that emission life course, a pollutant may accumulate to such a significant level that its effects will be felt for decades or even centuries as in the case of heat pollutants related to global warming, or persist as in the case of slowly degrading chemicals such as PCBs or the category of chemicals called persistent organic pollutants (POPS; for additional information see the Stockholm Convention website, which reviews the international treaty on POPs, chm.pops.int, accessed July 2013). It is also possible that chemical pollutants follow a trajectory of decay that reduces its health effects, or one which expands its effects by decomposing into more harmful chemical compounds that are more readily absorbed or which interact with other environmental pollutants or naturally occurring chemicals at accelerated rates during the new phase of its life course.

As noted, chemical pollutants may interact with one another or preexisting concentrations of chemicals found in the environment, or decay into more highly reactive chemicals or compounds (Koren and Bisesi, 2003). In such cases, a rather low level of a chemical emission may nevertheless produce a situation where the accumulation of the chemical in the environment poses future health problems and consequences consistent with a late onset life course toxin. Likewise, we also need to keep in mind that a chemical pollutant may have differential effects depending on its life course in different environmental media—for example, in the air, land, or water—and how it spreads or the speed at which it travels through different environmental media (Koren and Bisesi, 2003).

By definition, any chemical pollutant—which we defined in Chapter 5 as any chemical contaminant in the environment that exceeds its natural background level and which, by virtue of its environmental concentration produces harmful consequences—emitted into the environment possesses the potential to produce harm. Some chemicals, however, are not directly emitted into the environment, but, rather, may be placed into storage or treated and processed to prevent harm, at least in the short term. Stored chemical emissions, at least in theory, do not present the same level of immediate threat as a chemical pollutant emitted directly into the environment since chemical pollutants already emitted into the environment may exist in sufficient quantities to produce harm. By virtue of the act of storage, chemical by-products from the production process may possess the potential to create or produce harm, but that potential is, in effect, frozen in time once the chemical is securely stored. Nevertheless, the potential harm of these stored chemical products associated with production may be quite high. And while storage of these chemical by-products distinguishes them from chemical pollutants in the environment, the stored chemical by-products may be released into the environment at any moment by a chemical spill, an accidental chemical release—known as an ACR—or even planned releases. This can occur over time as the storage mechanism fails, or the release can be the result of chemical interactions during improper storage that result in an explosion or fire. In addition, these stored chemicals may reach the environment in the future through their treatment and release into the environment. In this sense, stored chemicals are in a dormant life course phase where they continue to possess their potentially destructive powers. These chemicals, however, may pass into the chemical pollution phase of the chemical life course once released.

Chemical Life Course Phases

Given the general observations described above, once generated, a chemical's life course can be described as fitting into one of the following chemical life course phases or modes:

1. *Low Volume Chemical Emissions* (LVCE). LVCEs include chemicals emitted by the production or consumption process that do not accumulate significantly in the environment. Because their level of emission is low, LVCEs do not surpass the kinds of health benchmarks that are employed to identify them as a pollutant or as a chemical that causes actual environmental harm due to its accumulation above natural background concentrations of the chemical—for example, a chemical's AEF. LVCEs may be periodic or persistent pollutants, but at current emission levels and patterns, cause no harm.

2. *Stored Chemicals or Potential Chemical Pollutants* (PoCP). Potential chemical pollutants (PoCPs) are harmful chemicals generated in the production process that do not pose an immediate harmful consequence because they are not directly released into the environment. This is true because PoCPs are stored in various ways that prevent them from entering the environment. While PoCPs are not immediately harmful in their stored state—assuming they are stored correctly—they possess the potential to cause harm when released. For example, if released in large quantities over a short period of time, PoCPs can cause extensive harm because of their high short-term concentration that may cause death or serious, immediate illness when encountered, or if their accidental emission causes the concentration of chemical emissions in the environment to surpass benchmark criteria—AEF—that would redefine the emission as a pollutant. Through their release into the environment, stored chemicals may enter a life course phase where they become persistent chemical pollutants or where they act as temporary or short-term chemical pollutants so long as their concentration in the environment exceeds their natural background level.

3. *Immediately Harmful Pollution Emissions* (IHPE). Immediately harmful pollution emissions are chemical pollutant emissions that cause harm through their release into the air, land, or water. IHPEs are harmful through one of two pathways. First, their release in the form of an accidental chemical release produces extraordinarily high concentrations of a pollutant that elevate the level of the chemical pollutant above natural background levels—AEF—producing a situation where their harmful consequences for the environment or species living in the environment is instantaneous. These chemicals may be persistent or periodic chemical pollutants. Second, these chemical pollutants may be emitted directly into the environment by industrial processes at concentrations that cause immediate harm. Such emissions may include accidental releases, upset events, or ordinary daily chemical emissions from industrial facilities that cause illnesses or which exacerbate existing medical conditions—for example, asthma. Many chemicals routinely emitted into the environment by industrial facilities possess the potential to cause immediate harm.

4. *Persistently Accumulating Chemical Pollutants* (PACP). Persistently accumulating chemicals include polluting emissions that are routinely emitted into the environment and which over time become more concentrated

in the environment. PACPs can cause immediate harm, but also pose future potential environmental health threats to ecosystems and ecosystem inhabitants. The routine, long-term emission of these pollutants maintains the emitted pollutant at a level of concentration that is persistently above established health benchmarks or background level benchmarks—AEF.

Chemical Life Course Turning Points

In addition to identifying these life course patterns, pathways, or phases of chemical emissions, it is also possible to describe chemical turning points in the life course. As illustrated in the definitions above, sometimes chemicals pass through life course phases, and that change in the life course of a chemical pollutant or emission can be used to identify a chemical life course turning point. We describe these chemical life course turning points as follows:

1. *Type 1 Turning Point.* A chemical enters a type 1 turning point when that chemical moves from an emission level that is "safe" or below its benchmark or natural background criteria to a state near, at, or slightly above its AEF level. In this stage, the chemical emission presents a low likelihood of victimization as long as the emission of this chemical pollutant remains low and does not cause the accumulation of that chemical in the environment at a level that surpasses health benchmarks.

2. *Type 2 Turning Point.* Type 2 turning points exist largely for stored chemical releases, or for potentially harmful chemicals produced in the production process which are neutralized by virtue of their storage. These chemicals can pass into a type 2 turning point phase when they are accidentally or purposefully released into the environment, at which point they shift from being stored, potentially hazardous chemicals to the chemical pollution phase of the chemical life course. The accidental or purposeful release date of these chemicals is, when they are placed into storage, unknown, and thus these potential chemical pollutants have an unpredictable release date that can only be identified once they are released. The transition of a chemical into a type 2 phase cannot, therefore, be predicted with any certainty. Moreover, the type 2 phase is a temporary phase relevant to the period covered by an accidental emission or upset event. Chemicals in the type 2 phase will either move to a higher phase, or a lower life course phase after their release and dispersal in the environment.

3. *Type 3 Turning Point.* Type 3 turning points are used to identify chemicals that upon their release into the environment immediately become chemical pollutants. In terms of the life course models used by criminologists, these chemical pollutants can be described as early on-set chemical pollutants. These chemicals include any chemical emissions that are immediately dangerous to the ecosystem or its inhabitants. Chemical emissions that

exist in the type 3 phase may, over time and through degradation, enter phase 1. Nevertheless, these kinds of chemical emissions are immediately dangerous due to the toxicant properties of the emitted chemical pollutants, or because they already exist at levels in the environment in excess of health benchmarks for AEFs.

4. *Type 4 Turning Point.* A type 4 turning point occurs when a chemical emission that is accumulating in the environment surpasses a benchmark standard—for example, an AEF—and thus becomes a chemical pollutant. The long-term process involved in the accumulation of this chemical in the environment means that this type of chemical pollution can be identified as a late onset chemical pollutant, or as a chemical emission that becomes a chemical pollutant over the span of its life course in the environment as additional volumes of the chemical emission are produced and expelled into the environment. In addition, chemicals may pass through a type 4 turning point when they degrade directly into more reactive and harmful chemical pollutants, or when they degrade into chemicals that interact with other chemicals in the environment, only surpassing a benchmark as a result of this degradation and interaction.

5. *Type 5 Turning Point.* Not all chemicals are constantly emitted into the environment, nor do they necessarily accumulate in ways that cause them to enter a type 4 turning point. Rather, some chemicals may have once been emitted at a high rate or have lived their life as an immediately harmful chemical pollutant or a persistent chemical pollutant (phase 3 or 4). However, over time, as the quantity of the emitted chemical decreases, it is entirely possible that the decomposition rate of the chemical exceeds its accumulation rate and that, therefore, the quantity of the chemical pollutant in the environment recedes to the point where it cross below a benchmark level and becomes a chemical emission rather than a chemical pollutant.

Having described the general nature of chemical turning points in the life course, it is possible to employ these descriptions to link chemical life course turning points to a general discussion of victimization.

Chemical Life Course Turning Points and Green Victimization

As noted in previous chapters, green victimization comes in a variety of forms. These forms include direct and indirect victimization of the environment, its subsystems, and the species that live in those environments. Chemical emissions, as they enter various phases of the chemical life course, reach turning points that define them as chemical pollutants or as emissions capable of causing harm and hence causing victimization at various levels for the ecosystem and various species that inhabit ecosystems.

Chemical life course turning points mark temporal locations in the life course of chemical emissions that can be related to their propensity to, or the probability that exposure to those chemical emissions cause harm or chemical victimization. By identifying these transitional phases in the life course of chemicals, turning points in the life course of chemical emissions can be identified when those emissions become pollutants or conversely, when they cease to become chemical pollutants. These turning points in the chemical life course are important because they also mark the points in time when chemical emissions possess the potential to cause or cease to cause green victimization. Moreover, the existence of these turning points indicate that a chemical emission's effects can and do vary over time, and that the effect of a chemical emission and its relationship to victimization may change.

The chemical turning point types described above can be employed to, for example, mark the initiation of a temporal sequence or phase in the life course of a chemical emission, but also in the life course of chemical pollutant victimization. In other words, there is a strong relationship, one that is largely inseparable, between a chemical's life course's turning point and its victimization potential. These turning points may also signal chemical exposure intensity variations or dose differentials, though these turning points do not constitute explicate measures of exposure or dose except when they exceed health benchmarks in areas where exposure to those pollutants is highly likely.

As noted above, type 1 turning point chemical emissions exist at such a low level that they present little, and in theory, no possibility of victimization. These chemicals have a turning point defined by their low level of emission into the environment. However, since their emission into the environment occurs as such a low rate or level, they do not, at least in theory or with respect to the current ability of science to measure negative health effects, constitute chemical pollutants. Hence these chemicals, while passing a turning point marked by their emission into the environment, do not cause victimization, at least in any scientifically identifiable way—that is, they do not act as chemical pollutants.

Stored chemical emissions or waste products from the production process do not enter the environment directly, nor can they be considered chemical pollutants so long as they are stored. They enter the pollution life course as waste materials, and the first turning point for these chemicals is their entrance into the hazardous waste storage system. These chemicals retain their potential harm qualities, but in their stored state, do not produce victimization unless, of course, the storage condition of those chemicals allows them to be emitted into the environment. In other words, stored chemical waste may, at some later stage in its course, enter a phase where it is released into the environment and causes damage.

Chemicals that demonstrate a type 3 turning point are immediately dangerous upon their release into the environment either because any release of such chemicals surpasses a health benchmark, or because the existing level of those chemicals in the environment has already passed a benchmark or AEF criterion. Chemicals in phase 3, therefore, are immediate causes of chemical victimization and can be described as early onset victim precipitators because they produce harm early in their life course. Chemicals that have passed through the type 1 and/or type 2 chemical turning points may also pass through the type 3 turning point.

Chemicals that pass through the type 4 turning point may be those that accumulate slowly in the environment either because there is a small waste stream of these chemical, or because they breakdown rapidly in nature, slowing their accumulation rate. The harmful consequences of the accumulation of these chemicals in the environment may, therefore, take some time to develop. These chemicals become pollutants late in their life course, and can be considered late onset pollutants. These late onset chemical pollutants are not an immediate threat, however, and the victimization threat they pose emerges over time or late in the chemical's life course. Moreover, some chemicals emitted into the environment become pollutants as they degrade or as they degrade and interact with other chemicals in the environment (Koren and Bisesi, 2003). These chemicals become pollutants over time, and thus pass a late onset marker as this process unfolds.

Chemicals that pass through turning point 5 may have also passed through any or all of the above turning points. These chemicals have, once they pass turning point 5, changed from chemical pollutants into chemicals emissions relative to the harm they produce. That is, these chemicals may once have caused extensive, long-term, or periodic, short-term health consequences. However, at their current rate of decomposition and concentration, they no long pose a victimization threat, having passed below a relevant health benchmark. It is also possible that some chemical pollutants move into phase 5 following a site remediation—that is, a cleanup effort designed to reduce the concentration of a chemical in a particular location.

These various turning points, as noted, demarcate phases in the life course when a chemical pollutant may cause harm, or a phase where the chemical as an emission does not cause harm. These turning points do not address the scope of victimization in any terms—for example, geographically or with respect to dose/exposure levels. These turning points, therefore, simply provide a means of assessing the ways in which chemical emissions may become harmful and produce victimization for the environment and species that live in affected environments. This is not to say, however, that these chemical emissions once they become pollutants cannot have wide-ranging effects. Take, for example, carbon dioxide, which already exists in the environment at a level above its AEF benchmark with respect to its effects on climate change. In this case, every release of carbon dioxide counts as a chemical pollution emission, and thus causes harm and victimization. In the case of carbon dioxide we can infer that the form of victimization is widespread and unlimited in a geographic sense since these emissions are associated with the process of global warming.

Chemical Pollution Trajectories

In addition to turning points, the life course of chemical pollutants can also be described with respect to a chemical pollutant's trajectory. Chemical pollutant trajectories include both the long- and short-term patterns of a chemical pollutant's accumulation in the environment. That accumulation pattern has, as already noted above, something to do with a chemical pollutant's turning point, as a chemical's accumulation trajectory can be used to establish the point in time where a pollutant might/will become problematic with respect to exposure, or the point in time where it has already become problematic.

As noted, a chemical's turning point in its life course demarcates the point at which a chemical emission becomes a chemical pollutant. In contrast, the chemical's accumulation trajectory not only can be employed to mark turning points in a chemical's life course, but can also be used to discuss that chemical's potential effect on the environment and the host of species occupying environments into which chemicals are emitted.

To illustrate these points, let us employ an example of toxic chemical releases reported in the EPA's Toxic Release Inventory (TRI) for the state of Pennsylvania. These data are displayed in Table 7.1. That Table shows the pounds of TRI releases per year from 1988 to 2010, and the aggregate total pounds of releases from 1988 onward.

The trend in releases varies over time, snaking up and down over this time period. There is some question about the significant decrease shown in the early part of the series, especially from 1990 to 1995, which, given emission levels in other years, may indicate a data quality problem. Nevertheless, the average annual emission of TRI chemical appears to be around 118 million pounds per year, and in the aggregate for the entire 23-year period, amount to a total release of more than 2.7 billion pounds of regulated toxic waste. Total toxic waste releases for this time period are likely larger than these data suggest given that TRI release reports are self-reports and likely underestimate actual emission levels. Moreover, since some facilities that release toxic waste are not required to report under the TRI, these data should not be considered absolute measures of toxic releases to the environment. Despite that caution, these data still have utility for the purpose of examining the trends in the life course of toxic releases.

There are two life course trajectory trends apparent in these data. The first relates to annual releases and the second to aggregated releases. Annual release levels fluctuate, while the aggregate releases grow steadily. To illustrate the magnitude of the release of TRI emissions, consider that in 1988 and in 2008, about the same volume of TRI chemicals were released in Pennsylvania, and that in Pennsylvania those releases total about 3,100 pounds per square mile of land and water. Over the entire time period or for the aggregate total TRI emission for this time period, TRI releases amounted to nearly 61,000 pounds per square mile. This is because once released, these pollutants accumulate. To be sure, not all these pollutants stay within the borders of Pennsylvania since some are released to the air and may travel significant distances and cross into other states.

The point here is that annual releases, while certainly large—averaging around 118 million pounds—measure only one aspect of a chemical pollutant's life course. As in this case, the annual emission data indicates that the volume of these pollutants emitted changes annually. Hidden by those annual changes, however, is the fact that annual emissions accumulate in the environment, generating an accumulation burden for the environment and the species that live in those environments. Thus, while annual emission levels are certainly a concern, so is the long term accumulation of pollutants in the environment. In the case of Pennsylvania, for example, nearly 2.73 billion pounds of TRI chemicals accumulated in the environment in this 23-year time period. Without needing to think about that number too hard, it should be quite clear that this total represents *a lot* of toxic pollution. That volume of waste is represented by the chemical pollutant's annual emission trajectory and its total accumulation trajectory.

Table 7.1   Total environmental releases, Pennsylvania, Toxic Release Inventory Data, 1988-2010, in pounds

	(1)	(2)
Year	**Releases**	**Aggregate Releases**
1988	144,238,989	0,144,238,989
1989	108,178,468	0,252,417,457
1990	096,067,888	0,348,485,345
1991	078,654,040	0,427,139,385
1992	071,125,366	0,498,246,751
1993	055,279,844	0,553,554,595
1994	053,300,850	0,606,855,445
1995	054,260,053	0,661,115,498
1996	066,730,493	0,727,845,991
1997	079,885,141	0,807,731,132
1998	155,972,576	0,963,703,708
1999	171,659,971	1,135,363,679
2000	154,946,464	1,290,310,143
2001	119,278,546	1,409,588,689
2002	110,987,443	1,520,576,132
2003	168,087,478	1,688,663,610
2004	164,714,507	1,853,378,117
2005	161,222,047	2,014,600,164
2006	157,235,817	2,171,835,981
2007	164,027,298	2,235,863,279
2008	151,458,598	2,487,321,877
2009	125,169,056	2,612,490,933
2010	116,446,353	2,728,937,286

We must keep in mind that there are sub-trajectories within these data related to specific pollutants that comprise TRI emissions. TRI data tracks more than 600 chemical pollutants. We could also chart the trajectories of each of these chemicals. The reason for doing so is that those individual trajectories can be employed to determine when and if the release of any specific TRI pollutant reaches a life course turning point. That is, the emissions of any specific pollutant may, at some point in time, surpass a health and safety or concentration benchmark which indicates that the chemical under examination has reached a turning point and has entered a phase in its life course that will cause an escalation in the damage associated with that chemical pollutant.

In tracking these chemical trajectories and sub-trajectories, it is necessary to keep in mind the distinction between annual and accumulated emissions. It is entirely possible, for example, for the annual emission level of a pollutant to be below a level considered to be a health threat. At the same time, it is entirely possible for the accumulated level of that pollutant in the environment to surpass a toxicity threshold that produces environmental damage.

Chemical Pollution Trajectories and Environmental Justice

It is important to acknowledge that the trajectory of chemical pollutants, which we illustrated above employing aggregate data for Pennsylvania, can be disaggregated to lower levels of analysis. The disaggregation of the chemical pollutant trajectory has important implications for assessing the distribution of chemical pollutants, which vary geographically, and the variation in the life course of pollution relative to the characteristics of populations that inhabit different geographic locations. These geographic variations in chemical pollutant trajectories across space and time have relevance to a related area of interest to green criminologists— environmental justice.

Environmental justice research examines the distribution of and exposure to chemical pollutants and hazards, and variations in responses to chemical pollution patterns in relation to the class, race, and ethnic characteristics of populations in different geographic locations. The question environmental justice research raises is whether class, race, and ethnicity characteristics of an area affect the distribution of chemical harms such as chemical pollution, and the quality of justice and social control applied across areas experiencing chemical pollution exposure.

Combining the idea of chemical trajectories and environmental justice, we can ask whether the chemical trajectory patterns apparent across geographic locations provide evidence of the existence of environmental injustice. In other words, the aggregate chemical trajectory, as illustrated above, is a concern in itself because it contains information about the emission and accumulation pattern of chemical pollutants in a large environmental space. In addition, we noted that hidden within those trajectories are indicators of a turning point when a chemical pollutant poses more significant public health harms. But, since chemical emissions are not uniform across geographic space, we can disaggregate these emissions and examine their trajectories to determine if their distribution over space is unequal and has a greater negative impact on some areas that is related to the class, racial, and ethnic composition of those areas.

To illustrate a pattern that may emerge related to race, class, and ethnicity, Table 7.2 displays projected future emission based on reported 2010 emissions—or where missing, the nearest date—for four zip codes in the city of Pittsburgh: 15201, 15222, 15225, and 15232. Table 7.2 displays the basic characteristics of each area including mean income, black population percentage, TRI released reported in pounds for 2010, and projected aggregate releases for 2015, 2020, and 2025 in millions of pounds.

Table 7.2   TRI releases for 2010 in pounds, and projected aggregate releases, 2015-2025 in millions of pounds, for four Pittsburgh zip codes

Zip Code	Mean Income	% Black	TRI Releases Pounds	Projected TRI Releases 2015	2020	2025
15201	$20,142	29.9	88,428	0.44	0.88	1.36
15222	$42,027	17.4	1,207	0.00	0.01	0.02
15225	$30,625	53.1	673,987	3.37	6.74	10.11
15232	$95,713	6.1	0	0.00	0.00	0.00

The zip codes included in this limited analysis were selected based on income and race distributions. The few zip codes examined here illustrate the association between race, income and TRI emissions.

In this small sample, both class and race effects are evident. A large class effect is seen as income declines. That effect peaks is found for the 15225 zip code, which is not the zip code with the lowest income mean, and declines for the lowest income zip code. Nevertheless, the effect for the lowest income zip code is substantially greater than for the two highest income zip codes. The relationship is, however, non-linear, and as the race relationship illustrates, may reflect a race-income interaction. In terms of income alone, however, only the two zip codes with the lowest mean income show evidence of significant accumulation of pollution, and a potential chemical life course trajectory that will produce health effects on local populations that may also be classified as evidence of a possible environmental justice effect.

The race effect in this small sample is much more linear. The zip code with the highest black population percentage is also the zip code with the highest pollution emission rate, while the zip code with the lowest black population percentage has the lowest pollution emission level. The remaining zip codes fall in the expected order. With respect to race, on average a 1 percent increase in black population percentage across these zip codes is associated with a mean increase in pollution emissions of 14,340 pounds. Thus, the nearly 50 percent increase in black population percentage between the zip code with the lowest and that with the highest black population produces an extremely large emission difference.

This small sample illustrates the general relationships expected between race, class, and TRI emissions. For areas with a high concentration of black and low-income residents, this relationship indicates the existence of environmental injustice or unequal exposure to TRI emissions, and the potential for a chemical emission life course associated with race and class characteristics of zip codes. Moreover, as the TRI emission trajectory indicates, zip codes with the highest black population percentages and the lowest incomes are exposed to pollution trajectory patterns likely to produce negative health consequences. Given the selectivity of these data, these results cannot be generalized, but are useful for illustrating how chemical life course and environmental justice issues may intersect and be studied as disaggregated levels of analysis.

Health and the Life Course

Epidemiological literature, like criminological literature, has made reference to the effect of the life course on outcomes of interest to each discipline (Lynch and Smith, 2005). Epidemiological literature suggests that the life course of chronic disease and health is clearly impacted by socio-economic characteristics (Lynch and Smith, 2005).

This literature also notes that the economic and social factors related to a disease's life course pattern in the population may be related to additional factors such as exposure to environmental toxins and pollutants (Bartley, Blane, and Montgomery, 1997). Moreover, the life course perspective on disease argues that childhood exposure to pollutants or exposure to pollutants early in the life course is an important dimension of health inequalities seen in adult populations (Chaix et al., 2006; Wadsworth, 1997). Even in egalitarian countries like Sweden with little variation in race, and with low levels of income inequality, the interaction of environmental justice effects of early life course exposure to pollution can be seen (Chaix et al., 2006).

Some studies show that the effects of life course in relation to socioeconomic status have long-term health consequences. These effects are particularly relevant, some research finds, in relation to variations in the life course of pollutants. For example, in Rome, variation in the emission of particle matter (PM-10), one of the characteristics of certain forms of air pollution related to, for instance, traffic patterns, were found to be influenced by socioeconomic characteristics of effected populations with respect to mortality rates (Forastiere et al., 2006).

These health studies that relate to life course are an important tool for connecting chemical life courses and trajectories to negative health outcomes for human populations, especially in urban areas. That is, the life course of pollution and the life course of individuals intersect to produce disease patterns, and those disease patterns may also be related to socioeconomic characteristics such as race and class at both the individual and community levels. These observations can be assessed by green criminologists in a variety of ways by employing empirical data on chemical emissions and disease patterns across communities or within communities over time. There remains much work to be done on this issue, and green criminologists can contribute to the development of this literature using insights from the chemical life course models discussed above.

Conclusion

This chapter has offered a brief examination of the life course perspective as one way of using a green criminological frame of reference to understand how chemical emission trajectories and turning points can influence public health, especially in urban environments. What we have illustrated here is how green criminology and its environmental frame of reference can be employed to broaden the idea of a life course so that it applies to chemical pollutants and their emission and accumulation in the environment. In taking this view, we have been able to demonstrate the intersection of human and chemical life courses, and how the intersection of these distinct life course processes affect the distribution of diseases not only in the life course, but across areas inhabited by persons of different economic and racial backgrounds.

This view has important implications for the study of environmental justice from a green criminological perspective. Moreover, this examination exemplifies how green criminology can take existing orthodox criminological concepts and expand their use and importance in promoting a green criminological revolution.

Chapter 8

Green Criminology and the Treadmill of Production: A Political Economy of Environmental Harm

As described in Chapter 2, green crimes are not a series of isolated environmental problems. Instead, green crimes are patterned, and those patterns can be identified in reference to local and global political economies. In this chapter we expand upon the notion that green crimes are produced by humans and the way human societies are organized to carry out production. The idea that productive forces are related to crime is not new to criminology. For example, the main assumption of Marxist criminology is that class structure and formation explains the shape of criminal laws, policing, courts, corrections, and the causes of various types of crime and deviance (Lynch and Michalowski, 2006). The way we produce things not only shapes the definition of crime, but also creates harm and produces chemically-induced violence. Considered from this perspective, production is central to the etiology of green crimes. In addition, the type of production a society engages in helps to explain patterns of green victimization and the types of green offenders and offenses that exist.

To explore that idea, this chapter examines treadmill of production theory. The term "treadmill of production" is often used to describe how environmental problems in society are increasing in relation to the expansion of production (Schnaiberg, 1980). As we demonstrate, treadmill of production theory is useful for explaining the political economy of environmental crime and lends important insights into explaining green behaviorism, the chemical life course, green offenders, and victims.

Background

People often assume that economic growth, or the increase in goods and services, is essential if societies are to advance. One only need listen to politicians talk about economic growth to understand the importance they place on production. U.S. Treasury Secretary, Timothy Geithner, recently commented that production is so important that "policy makers [must] continue to work to get the economy growing fast in the short term and not shift prematurely to fiscal restraint" (Reuters, 2012). As a result, government and firms of various sizes constantly seek to increase their level of production in an effort to expand their market share through consumption and exports of goods and services to other countries to gain footholds in new markets.

Treadmill of production theorists, however, question the belief that economic growth is always a desirable outcome—similar arguments can be found in some of the sustainable development literature as well. Drawing on insights from political economic explanations of economic systems and the destructive impacts economic development has on ecological systems, treadmill theory suggests that the environmental harms associated with constant economic expansion threatens the health of the ecosystem and its ability to maintain the conditions for life for the species that inhabit the earth. Examples of the types of green harms that can result from production were reviewed in Chapter 3 and include some of the most pressing environmental problems facing the world today.

Schnaiberg (1980) first described the harm associated with the treadmill of production in his work *The Environment: From Surplus to Scarcity*. Schnaiberg developed treadmill of production theory to explain an outcome he calls "ecological disorganization." We will examine the concept of ecological disorganization in more detail in Chapter 9. For the time being it is sufficient to point out that we create products and environments to "organize" human life according to the social and economic values associated with capitalism. At the same time, however, producing these socially and economically valued commodities simultaneously creates ecological disorganization by taking natural resources and converting them into products. The mass production techniques used in that process destroys—disorganizes—the environment through three processes. First, through the mass harvesting and extraction of natural resources, which sometimes is accomplished with extraction technologies that cause extensive environmental harm to the environment surrounding natural resource locations—for example, mountaintop removal mining; hydraulic fracturing—in addition to the harms that can result from resource extraction—for example, the effect of timber clear-cutting methods on the integrity of forests. Second, in modern commodity production, manufacturing processes often employ large quantities of fossil fuels including oil and coal to turn raw materials into commodities, which leads to the production of heat pollution and the expansion of entropy. Third, modern techniques of production often rely on the use of chemically assisted production technologies that create vast chemical waste streams that are then emitted into the environment in the form of pollution and chemical wastes.

Treadmill of production theory draws attention to several production-related processes that create environmental disorganization. First, as noted in previous chapters, the extraction of resources can impact ecosystems by disrupting the equilibrium of the ecosystem and limiting its ability to reproduce itself. For example, when a forest is clear-cut to obtain timber, the process of clear-cutting or deforestation impacts the local forest ecosystem. Studies indicate that it may take at least one to two centuries for clear-cut areas to recover (Bonnell, Reyna-Hurtado, and Chapman, 2011; Chai and Tanner, 2011; Duffy and Meier, 2003) and as much as four thousand years to recover when measures of species diversity are included (Liebsch, Marques, and Goldenberg, 2008). In addition, clear-cutting impedes the ability of forests to regulate the climate and process carbon dioxide (Houghton, 1991), and where deforestation promotes forest fragmentation, these negative ecological conditions as well as related ecological conditions may accelerate (Laurance and Williamson, 2001). Second, the manufacturing of products also generates toxic waste that is disposed of in ways that disrupt ecosystems and causes harm.

In addition, treadmill of production theory specifically draws attention to the adverse ecological impacts generated by one particular form of organizing economic production—capitalism. For example, as Paul Burkett (2009) and John Bellamy Foster (2000) have argued, the inherent expansionary tendencies of capitalism, and hence its constant need to expand the consumption of raw materials to expand production and accumulate profit, force capitalism and nature into an antagonistic relationship. Capitalism must consume nature to expand, and expand its consumption of nature continuously. In so doing, capitalism constantly expands ecological disorganization through consuming and extracting resources in ways that damage the environment, and by the ways in which productive wastes are disposed or by adding pollution to the ecosystem. In short, treadmill of production theory suggests that capitalism's effort to organize social and economic life in ways that are consistent with capitalist values drives ecological disorganization.

As Schnaiberg (1980) noted, the drive to expand production and consumption forces a constant expansion in ecological disorganization over time. This increase in ecological disorganization became most apparent following World War II when capitalists made a concerted effort to expand sales and markets by investing in chemical technologies that increased productive capacity by increasing the "efficiency" of resource withdrawals and the processing of raw materials into commodities (Gould, Pellow, and Schnaiberg 2008). Since World War II, the reliance on these chemical technologies of production has continued to accelerate, an observation that even industries acknowledge. For example, the American Chemistry Council (2011: 2) reports that

> Chemistry transforms raw materials into the products and processes that make modern life possible. America's chemical industry relies on energy derived from natural gas not only to heat and power our facilities, but also as a raw material, or "feedstock," to develop the thousands of products that make American lives better, healthier, and safer.

The investments in chemical technology following World War II appeared to have paid off in terms of production. In the United States, for example, gross domestic product (GDP) has increased every decade since the end of World War II. Schnaiberg (1980) notes that capitalists make investments in chemical technology and are repaid when a firm increases its profits as those chemical technology investments improve the efficiency of production.

Schnaiberg uses the term treadmill of production to indicate the interconnection between the constant expansion of capitalist production, its increased reliance on chemically assisted extraction and production technologies, and the constant expansion of ecological disorganization and damage that system produces. That is to say, the system operates as if it were on a treadmill. In this view, the political economic system or treadmill of production is characterized by the continued expansion of "industrial production, economic development as well as increasing consumption" (Gould, Schnaiberg, and Weinberg, 1996: 5). This tradeoff between investments in technology, increases in production, and ecological disorganization forms the treadmill of production. This system is driven forward not only by the accumulation tendencies of capitalism, but by class relations and the intersection of the interests of capital, labor, and the government, as well as the ideological belief that expanded production will advance public welfare. The expansion of capital through the use of chemical technology has, however, resulted in a major social problem that impacts traditional crimes as well as green crimes associated with two major types of environmental behaviors: natural resource withdrawals and additions (Schnaiberg, 1980). We first examine the way that chemical investments lead to community disorganization and then examine the crimes associated with ecological withdrawals and additions.

Toxic Chemicals and Community Disorganization

In an effort to increase production, limit the use of and intensify human labor, and produce more commodities and economic values, following World War II, capitalists increasingly turned to the use of chemical technology and chemical labor—including fossil fuels. These technologies reduced the quantity of human labor needed in the production process, and increasingly removed workers from the production process while increasing the quantity of value each worker produced by substituting chemical labor for human labor. In short, advances in chemical technology led to increased production with fewer workers. This change in production promoted long-term unemployment and changed the nature of the relationship between workers and capital. This is, perhaps, best observed in agriculture as Rifkin (1995: 30) warns:

> The rapid elimination of work opportunities resulting from technical innovation and corporate globalisation is causing men and women everywhere to be worried about their future. The young are beginning to vent their frustration and rage in increasingly antisocial behaviour. Older workers, caught between a prosperous past and a bleak future, seem resigned, feeling increasingly trapped by social forces over which they have little or no control. In Europe, fear over rising unemployment is leading to widespread social unrest and the emergence of neofascist political movements. In Japan, rising concern over unemployment is forcing the major political parties to address the jobs issue for the first time

in decades. Throughout the world there is a sense of momentous change taking place – change so vast in scale that we are barely able to fathom its ultimate impact.

Workers that do not lose their jobs as the economy shifts to the forms of toxic technology and mechanization characteristic of the treadmill of production are often put at risk through exposure to dangerous chemicals used in the production process. For example, Apple, which produces millions of iPhones for U.S. consumers, has recently been accused of poisoning many of its workers in Suzhou, China with n-hexane (Kan, 2011). The story in China is not unusual and it has been revealed that workers in a variety of industries have been poisoned by their employers (Rosner and Markowitz, 1989). To be sure workers have faced oppressive conditions throughout history, but the shift in production from labor-intensive and machinery-based technology to increasingly toxic chemical production technology has introduced a new type of risk—one that is less overt and more invisible, but very harmful. As workers have been displaced by toxic technology they have found themselves unemployed—and perhaps some even eventually become part of the criminal or delinquent class of society—or working in low-paying service sector jobs (Harrison and Bluestone, 1988). As noted in Chapter 9, this situation has also led to social disorganization in cities where high levels of unemployment have produced communities that suffer from concentrated poverty. Thus, labor has often sided with the state to loosen environmental restrictions and increase production in order to employ more people. This push by labor to produce more through advancements in chemical technology is one of the major ironies of the treadmill of production.

As production increases to compensate investors, capitalists must also find ways to extract more natural resources from the environment. The extraction of natural resources from the environment is described by treadmill of production theorists in terms of "ecological withdrawals" (Schnaiberg, 1980). The extraction of natural resources from the environment has caused major ecological disruption as capitalism extracts resources produced and organized by nature to perform ecological labor, and coverts them into products and pollution that promote ecological disorganization.

Crimes of Ecological Withdrawals

Natural resources are needed for production. Nature uses its labor to create those natural resources, and continually reproduces resources required for the functioning of an efficient, life-supporting ecological system. As Burkett (2009) argues, one of the contradictions of capitalism is its basic need for the raw materials provided by nature, and at the same time capitalism's basic tendency to disrupt and destroy ecosystems, ensuring declining supplies of raw materials and rising raw material prices. Moreover, because capitalism is based on the generation of short-term profit, contemporary production decisions related to the ecological destruction caused by the use of machine and chemical extraction technologies are of no concern to the current generation of capitalists. Take, for example, the numerous long-term consequences of mass timber harvesting that supplies capitalism with an expanding raw material base from around the world. In the first place, those extraction technologies cause extensive damage to local ecological systems and the world ecosystem. Processes such as clear-cutting of old growth forests not only damages the local rainforest ecosystem and leads to ecosystem recovery times of anywhere between 100 to 1,000 years, as noted earlier, but also damages the climate regulating capacity of the ecosystem, facilitating the process of climate change. In local ecologies, the extraction of timber has been linked to flooding in many parts of the world and has also led to the extinction of plants, animals, and human communities (Bell, 2004). Currently there is an intense and ongoing debate in the academic literature concerning whether deforestation is related to flooding and the loss of lives (Bradshaw et al., 2007). If conservation biologists are correct, then logging-linked flooding may be directly related to the deaths of many people across the globe. In either case, activities such as mass timber harvesting causes extensive, long-term ecological damage that not only undermines the health of the ecosystem, but which illustrates that capitalism and nature cannot coexist (Foster, 2002).

Ecological Withdrawal and Underdeveloped and Developing Nations

Consistent with economic expectations, Marxist economic theory and the motivating drives behind capitalism, resource extraction rates and locations—or the geography of resource extraction—changes over time. Consistent with those expectations and observations of capitalism, treadmill theory points out that rates of natural resource extraction have decreased in developed countries because the cost of natural resources in developed countries accelerates as the cost of living and wages rise in developed nations. At the same time, in the contemporary world labor market, the unequal distribution of wages entices capital to use that wage differential to its advantage, and to shift resource extraction to developing and underdeveloped nations. As a result, the ecological damage associated with natural resource extraction occurs at higher rates in both underdeveloped and developing countries, and those nations become the targets of multinational companies that are attempting to "find deals" on natural resources that can be used in production. For example, the chief economist of the World Bank, Joseph Stiglitz, suggests that "it is not hard for a country rich in natural resources to find investors abroad willing to exploit those resources, especially if the price is right" (Mabey and McNally, 1999: 27). Property rights, social opposition to mass resource extraction, and environmental regulations are generally relaxed in developing and underdeveloped countries, and in those locations natural resources may not only be cheaper to extract, but can also be more easily accessed due to political instability (Asiedu, 2006), which in turn enhances the ability to bribe government officials (Bulte and Damania, 2008). In some instances, governments, militaries, and rebel groups are willing to help facilitate natural resource extraction at rates well below the value of those resources in order to raise money to maintain their power and fund violent conflicts (Global Witness, 2002). For example, Global Witness, a non-governmental organization, reports that conflict timber is usually harvested illegally and is used to help support corrupt governments such as those in Cambodia, Liberia, Burma, and Indonesia (Global Witness, 2002). Gould, Pellow, and Schnaiberg (2008: 34) note that "the globalizing of capital flowing from investors from industrial countries has been guided by cheap natural resources and weak environmental regulations." Much of this resource extraction has been described in terms of environmental crimes because resources are often stolen from the commons (—that is, these are resources owned by the population of the targeted nation and held in common rather than as private property—by corrupt governments and corporations. In other instances, the ecological disorganization caused by environmental withdrawals may be legal under state laws even though, as noted in previous chapters, the harm associated with those withdrawals may be significant.

Promoting Green Criminological Research on Ecological Withdrawal

Green criminological research must be oriented in a way that examines these crimes of withdrawals and their consequences. For instance, green criminologists can examine the ways in which laws that govern natural resource extraction favor actors that are part of the treadmill of production. In an effort to take advantage of the international market place for raw materials, governments may offer incentives to attract foreign investment and in the process facilitate harmful and often criminal ecological withdrawals (Gould, Pellow, and Schnaiberg, 2008; O'Connor, 1973). There are many other examples of how green criminology may be relevant to resource extraction.

Hydraulic fracturing   Recent evidence suggests that new methods of hydraulic fracturing are releasing harmful chemicals into the environment. Hydraulic fracturing, also known as "fracking," is a process that uses massive amounts of water, sand, and chemicals to create pressure far below the surface to create cracks in shale substructures so that the gas in the shale can be released into the well and be collected for energy use. Until recently in the United States, the chemical composition of fracking fluids were treated as trade secrets (Associated Press, 2012), and companies were not required to notify the government of the contents of their fracking fluids. As a result, it was unclear to environmental regulators if the chemicals used posed any immediate or long-term health threats, or what potential crimes were being committed through the fracking process (Associated Press, 2012). However, recent scientific studies suggest that there are indeed adverse health effects associated with fracking, and that one of the chemicals used in this process, benzene, is a significant health concern for residents living within half a mile of fracking operations, increasing their likelihood of contracting cancer (McKenzie et al., 2012).

Coal extraction   Coal extraction provides another example of the types of harms—many of which may also be defined as crimes—that may occur as a result of ecological resource withdrawals. Coal is increasingly extracted through strip mining and mountaintop removal mining. Those techniques cause extensive ecological disorganization and harm humans and facilitate the commission of environmental crimes of violence. As Stretesky and Lynch (2011b) observed, coal mining is often a deviant and criminal industry and there is a long history of coal companies ignoring safety regulations and using force against workers. Their study of environmental violations by 110 U.S. coal strip mines suggests an association between regulatory inspections and crime. Capital's desire to increase coal production as one of the fuels that runs the treadmill of production has led to the widespread adoption of coal strip mining, a practice that is much more environmentally harmful than underground mining. This trend toward the increased use of strip mining is consistent with the notion of the treadmill of production because a strip miner produces 2.66 times more coal than an underground miner (Energy Information Administration, 2006). Likewise, consistent with the expectations of treadmill of production theory, over the past 30 years the shift from underground to strip mining has led to a 45 percent reduction in the coal miner labor force and an 84 percent increase in the amount of coal produced (Stretesky and Lynch, 2011b).

Coal strip mining has significantly expanded the use of chemicals and explosives in the strip mining process, causing significant ecological damage in order to reduce coal extraction costs (Bell and York, 2010). In addition, the coal industry has used its power to lobby the state for access to natural resources and to weaken environmental regulations related to strip mining and the protection of lands surrounding strip mines. Gould, Schnaiberg, and Weinberg (1996) note, for example, that lobbying and political donations have important effects on regulations that facilitate the kinds of productive practices that can be used and which in turn impact environmental withdrawals and additions. Gould, Schnaiberg and Weinberg's observations are consistent with empirical evidence produced from studies of the coal industry. For instance, Long et al. (2011) found evidence that coal corporations increased their donations to politicians prior to being adjudicated for environmental violations. Long et al. found that the odds of an environmental violation increased by a factor of 6.25 with each $100,000 donation made by a coal company.

The coal industry has also been able to carry out production within a political climate that has encouraged expanded coal production and coal generated electricity (Lynch, Burns, and Stretesky, 2010). As a result crimes that may be discovered in the process of strip mining may not receive priority by federal agencies designed to regulate environmental crimes in the coal extraction sector (Kennedy, 2005). In fact, many behaviors that could be treated as crimes under existing environmental laws are turned down by the Department of Justice for prosecution.

Despite the fact that potential coal strip mining violations have not been pursued as crimes or can be carried out legally with the proper permits, strip mining has been documented as destructive to the basic ecology and social fabric of an area (Reece, 2006). For instance, Goodell (2006) estimates that the overburden—the rubble from blasting mountaintops that includes earth, rock, trees, and so forth—from mountaintop removal operations have been used to fill 1,200 miles of streams and headwaters in the eastern United States (see also Bell and York, 2010; Stretesky and Lynch, 2011b). The impact of these fills causes ecological disorganization, adversely impacting the natural ecology by altering water flow patterns, reducing water quality (Parker, 2007; Reece, 2006), causing a decline in important micro-organism populations (Pond et al., 2008), and promoting flooding and soil erosion. In some cases, entire towns have been flooded following mountaintop removal (Reece, 2006). Related crimes and harms emerge from the storage of toxic wastes associated with strip miming and the preparation of coal for use. These impacts include pollution of waterways by coal sludge (Hudson-Edwards, 2003) and from coal ash spills (Ruhl et al., 2009). In December of 2008, the coal ash spill at the Tennessee Valley Authority's Kingston facility released an estimated 1.1 *billion* gallons of coal ash waste into the environment, covering 300 acres with toxic coal ash waste. That coal waste contained high levels of arsenic, mercury, and radioactive materials (Ruhl et al., 2009). Currently, it has been estimated that only 3 percent of that spill has been cleaned up, and that the clean-up costs could run as high as $1 billion. The toxins contained in coal ash dumps and retention ponds are so hazardous that the U.S. Department of Homeland Security prevented Senator Barbara Baxter of California from releasing the location of the 44 most hazardous of these sites to the public in the interest of protecting national security. Despite these restrictions, the U.S. EPA released the 26 locations that contain 45 sites that pose the greatest environmental risks: seven are in North Carolina; five in Ohio; four in Kentucky; three in West Virginia; two each in Illinois and Utah; and one each in Georgia, Pennsylvania, Montana, and Indiana. Sourcewatch has posted a list of 350 such sites (http://www.sourcewatch.org/index.php/Category:Coal_ waste, accessed October 2013).

In exploring environmental crimes, green criminologists have neglected the way that environmental regulations are created and whose interests these laws serve. Formal enforcement efforts have also been reduced with the new emphasis on "self-regulation" (Stretesky, 2006). Under self-regulation principles companies can police themselves, and report and correct violations that they discover to the proper regulators in order to avoid prosecution or in exchange for less severe penalties (Stretesky and Lynch, 2009b, 2011a).

In short, despite the role toxic technology plays in enhancing productivity and profit and converting human labor and natural value into surplus value, increased production promotes less efficient use of natural resources resulting in expanded ecological disorganization. In terms of extraction, the constant push to produce more creates unsustainable and increasing levels of natural resource depletion. This natural resource engine of ecological disorganization drives the treadmill of production (Bell and York, 2010).

Crimes of Ecological Additions

Increased production not only disrupts the environment and produces green crimes and green victims through the extraction of natural resources, it also generates additional pollution that threatens the ecosystem through the chemical life course reviewed in the previous chapter. As noted below, this destruction occurs despite advances in technology.

Chemically intensive production technology increases the release of harmful chemicals into the environment. This can occur for two reasons. First, in the process of production, polluting chemicals are released into the environment as part of the production and resource extraction processes. Second, driven by capitalism's expansionary tendencies, production continually increases and accelerates the release of chemical pollutants into the environment. As noted in Chapter 4 and earlier in this chapter, the globalization of production has shifted production and pollution from the United States to other parts of the world system of capitalism (Stretesky and Lynch, 2009a). For example, many of the goods consumed in the United States are produced elsewhere in the world, and thus U.S. consumption patterns are linked to chemical releases associated with production in foreign countries (Stretesky and Lynch, 2009a). Thus, U.S. consumption patterns can be traced back to production processes that result in chemical releases in developing countries. In some cases, the forms of production and the pollution created by those forms of production that occur overseas, which would be illegal in the United States, add significant quantities of pollutants to under-developed nations, promoting ecological disorganization in those locations and globally (Stretesky and Lynch, 2009a).

The shift of production from developed to developing and underdeveloped nations transfers productions from nations with more restrictive to less restrictive environmental laws and regulations. In that context, environmentally destructive behaviors that might be regulated and treated as crimes in developed nations are overlooked when they occur in underdeveloped and developing nations. For example, production may lead to the occurrence of "chemical accidents." These accidents are treated differently in developed and developing nations (for example, see, Lynch, Nalla, and Miller, 1989), although even in developed nations like the United States, "accidental" chemical releases are often overlooked by the regulatory system (Jarrell and Ozymy, 2010; Ozymy and Jarrell, 2011, 2012). For example, the World Health Organization notes that "chemical production and use is increasing worldwide ... particularly in developing countries and those with economies in transition where chemical production, processing and use is closely tied to economic development" (United Nations, 2009). The report lists several releases that have occurred in 2008 and 2009 in developing countries. For example, in Angola, sodium bromide releases poisoned 467 people, and in Senegal 18 children died when they were contaminated with lead from battery recycling. The World Health Organization suggests that these chemical events are widespread and severe (United Nations, 2009). The worst of these disasters occurred in Bhopal, India in December 1984 when Union Carbide of India Limited released a deadly combination of gasses that killed nearly 10,000 people in the short term (Lynch, Nalla, and Miller, 1989; Pearce and Tombs, 1993).

Green criminologists should not overlook more routine forms of pollution. Of special concern is the effect of air pollution on disease, illness, and death rates in developing countries. Cohen et al. (2006) estimated that worldwide, fine particle air pollution (PM 2.5) causes 800,000 deaths a year in children under age 5 alone. In 2002, the World Health Organization (2002) estimated that worldwide, air pollution leads to 3 million premature deaths each year. Even in developed nations like the United States, fine particle pollution has a significant effect on cardiopulmonary and lung cancer mortality (Pope et al., 2002). The American Lung Association's report, *State of the Air, 2012*, indicates that 127 million residents in America's top ten cities with the highest levels of air pollution—in rank order, Bakersfield, CA; Hanford/Concordia, CA; Los Angeles/Long Beach/River Side, CA; Visalia/ Porterville, CA; Fresno/Madera, CA; Pittsburgh/New Castle, PA; Phoenix/Mesa/ Glendale, AZ; Cincinnati, OH-Middletown, KY-Wilmington, IN; Louisville/ Elizabethtown, KY; Philadelphia, PA—face air pollution concentration high enough to making breathing dangerous. These 127 million people who routinely suffer green victimizations associated with ecological additions generated by the treadmill of production have not received significant attention from green criminologists.

In addressing these kinds of issues, green criminologists should not overlook the other impacts of the diverse array of pollution found in the contemporary world, or its effects on people in developing and underdeveloped nations. In China, half a billion people live in the Yangtze River Basin, where the Chinese Ministry of Environmental Protection estimates more than 400,000 polluting facilities also exist, which are estimated to dump *34 billion pounds* of toxic waste into the Yangtze *annually*. New Delhi, India and Beijing, China are recognized as having the highest levels of air pollution among the most populated cities in the world. Between those two cities, 36 million people are exposed to dangerous levels of air pollution. These polluting outcomes illustrate the extent of harm caused by the capitalist treadmill of production across the nations of the world. They also illustrate why green criminologists ought to pay greater attention to these forms of green victimization.

Green Criminology and Ecological Additions

Criminologists in general as well as green criminologists have not given much consideration to crimes associated with environmental additions such as the illegal dumping and release of hazardous chemicals into the environment (except see Pellow, 2004; Situ 1997; Szasz 1986; for criminological studies see, for example, Lynch, Stretesky, and Burns, 2004a, 2004b; Stretesky and Lynch, 1999, 2011a). Some of these releases are defined as violations of law, and it is possible to examine the enforcement of such crimes (Long et al., 2012; Lynch, Stretesky, and Burns, 2004a, 2004b; Stretesky and Lynch, 2011b) and their relationship to the treadmill of production. Other ecological disorganizing activities of the treadmill of production, however, are ignored by law, yet still produce forms of ecological disorganization that green criminologists can address (Lynch, Burns, and Stretesky, 2010).

The connection between the production of commodities and ecological additions—toxic waste—may not seem to be relevant to criminology at first glance, especially if we consider the tendency of orthodox criminology to focus its attention on street crimes of the powerless. However, nothing could be further from the truth. For example, Pellow's (2004) recent case study of illegal dumping in Chicago offers an interesting application of treadmill theory that helps explain why such behavior is relevant to green criminology.

During the 1990s Chicago experienced a rapid increase in construction that helped bolster the city's economy. Increases in natural resource extraction that created the products used in construction such as steel beams, lumber, siding, paint, wire, and plastic provided the components for the construction boom. The expansion of the construction industry provided needed jobs and was essential to the economic health of the city. However, as Chicago's construction industry expanded, it created a growing quantity of waste. On the surface the urban reorganization associated with new construction was producing considerable visible ecological disorganization and crime. But there were significant volumes of unrecorded crime that were also occurring related to the construction boom.

As Pellow (2004) notes, the construction boom created large quantities of waste, and the construction industry needed to dispose of those large quantities of waste. Significant portions of that waste were disposed illegally. In Chicago, the result was widespread illegal dumping across many poor neighborhoods. This problem was initially ignored, however, because the social and economic forces that connected corporate interests and political institutions promoted a situation where the illegal dumping of construction waste was overlooked by enforcement agencies. Companies that disposed of waste were often allowed to operate without permits under the guise that materials were being "recycled." Moreover, one company, KrisJohn operated dozens of illegal dumping sites within the city of Chicago. That company used its economic power to bribe politicians and citizens to allow the illegal dumping in their communities. This illegal construction-related waste stream caused significant health problems for residents living near the illegal dumps. At the same time, city and state law enforcement agencies and even the EPA failed to take action until the level of political corruption became widespread. At that point the Federal Bureau of Investigation started to document the construction-related waste corruption and made a significant number of arrests that lead to several prosecutions and convictions, including the president of KrisJohn. In short, the waste generated by the construction boom in Chicago created a significant number of green victims and caused significant levels of ecological disorganization.

In many instances ecological additions have become so widespread that they seem acceptable, and society fails to question them and in many instances regulations that are supposed to prevent such behavior are ignored. Thus, harmful corporate behavior seems ordinary and is often described as the "price of progress." As a result of the normalization of these chemical crimes of ecological addition, more than 41 million Americans live within four miles of 1,134 Superfund waste sites—and millions more live near unlisted waste sites (Burns, Lynch, and Stretesky, 2008). This is true despite the fact that the health hazards associated with exposure to chemicals found in these waste sites have been widely studied, and the human risks associated with these waste streams are well known. For example, a study of 593 sites in 339 U.S. counties with hazardous waste ground water contamination revealed increased levels of lung, stomach, intestinal, bladder, and rectum cancer (Griffin et al., 1989; Osborne, Shy, and Kaplan, 1990). In short, as a society, we have come to accept the creation of toxic waste as necessary for production and are often reluctant to treat ecological additions as crimes. Because criminologists are also part of society, our views on ecological additions are also shaped by this ideology of indifference toward the toxic wastes associated with production. Consequently, most criminologists ignore crimes of ecological addition, and view these outcomes as necessary evils that do not require criminological attention. The creation of green criminology helps to reveal these contradictions and focuses criminological attention on the study of ecological additions as crime by employing evidence of harm such as the type discussed in Chapter 6.

Greenwashing

Corporations that cause significant harm while engaging in ecological withdrawals and additions often attempt to cover up and/or hide their behaviors. Many times corporations argue that they are using environmentally friendly technology that is helping the environment and reducing environmental harm (Lynch and Stretesky, 2003). Thus, companies engage in claims-making which suggests that they are improving their production practices and their products so that they are more environmentally friendly. The term "greenwashing," first used by biologist Jay Westerveld in 1986 to describe the hotel cards that ask guests to refrain from washing towels to save the environment while at the same time engaging in other more serious forms of ecological disruption, has been used to describe these practices (Motavalli, 2011). Greenwashing is simply a form of corporate deception that occurs when corporations use the term "green" to advertise small changes in environmental efficiency without changing production in ways that actually improves environmental performance in any meaningful way (Greer and Bruno, 1996).

There are many examples of greenwashing among corporations. For example, the automobile industry claims it is becoming environmentally friendly. And, on average automobile gas mileage has improved over the years in the United States. The industry notes that environmental performance is improved because cars and trucks use less gasoline. Unfortunately, vehicle efficiency is offset by increases in vehicle miles driven and additional vehicle technology that requires the use of more gasoline (Difiglio and Fulton, 2000). Moreover, some of the green technologies used to improve vehicle efficiency are still environmentally destructive. For example, lightweight vehicles, which use less gasoline, are created from special alloys that take an incredible amount of energy to mine and are often mined in environmentally destructive ways (Cáceres, 2007). Thus, in the case of automobile fuel efficiency, using technology to reduce carbon pollution may be offset by the reorganization and expansion of the treadmill of production with respect to productive practices and in terms of its expansion into national territories with the required natural resource stores and low labor costs. Consequently, while green technology may sometimes decrease pollution per unit produced, it does not necessarily decrease environmental pollution since the number of units produced increases or other detrimental environmental consequences follow (Gould, Pellow, and Schnaiberg, 2008). This is especially true when production increases to offset any advances in technology.

Unfortunately, greenwashing efforts are often accepted by the public, who believe that improvements in technology can solve environmental problems. Greenwashing has become so pervasive among corporations today that it is often used to promote environmentally destructive practices and has itself been treated as a criminal act. For example, in California the Attorney General brought an action against several companies that were claiming that their plastic bottles were good for the environment because they were biodegradable and recyclable. The bottles the company created, however, were produced in a way that prevented them from being reasonably recycled and they were not biodegradable as stated. Because these bottles are placing a heavy burden on state and local governments in terms of disposal, the state Attorney General filed a complaint for injunction and civil penalties in 2011 (*People of the State of California ex rel. Kamala D. Harris, vs. Enso Plastic; Aquamantra, Inc.; Balance Water Company*). Other companies that create significant amounts of environmental harm also use greenwashing techniques to hide their destructive behavior (Greer and Bruno, 1996). In the end, greenwashing techniques allow corporations to continue their ecological withdrawals and additions in a business as usual fashion.

Treadmill, Enforcement, and Environmental Justice

Race and class inequality are characteristics of U.S. society and both have important implications for the treadmill of production. As we suggested in Chapter 7, environmental injustice occurs when race and class influence the location and production of environmental hazards. Environmental justice is the struggle against environmental injustice, and those involved in the environmental justice movement advocate for equal protection of the laws, equal access to decision-making, and an equal say in how things are produced (Pellow, 2000). As we have already observed, evidence of environmental injustice suggests minorities and the poor are not only more likely to live near environmental hazards, but are also more likely to suffer from adverse health consequences associated with production. In short, ecological disorganization in the form of ecological additions and withdrawals has the greatest negative impact on those members of society who are the most socially and economically disadvantaged.

At the local level, the racial and economic make-up of communities impacts residential quality of life. That is, residents living in predominately black and/ or poor communities are more likely to live near environmental hazards, and are less likely to have a voice in the types of production that take place in their communities. Residents living in communities with few economic resources are more likely to suffer from the results of under enforcement of environmental laws (Stretesky and Lynch, 2011b). The balance of power between treadmill institutions and local residents, especially marginalized communities, favors corporate interests (see Gould, Schnaiberg, and Weinberg, 1996; Pellow 2004). As a result the political economic forces that maintain the treadmill of production penetrate local communities. The issue of environmental regulatory practices—especially in relation to race and class—are important issues for green criminologists to address in their research. To be sure, criminologists are concerned with and have addressed issues of race and class inequality in traditional criminal justice research (Lynch, Patterson, and Childs, 2008). However, studies of race and class inequality in environmental enforcement have yet to garner sufficient attention among green criminologists (for exceptions see, Lynch, Stretesky, and Burns, 2004a, 2004b; Stretesky and Lynch, 1999, 2003).

To achieve environmental justice, treadmill theorists emphasize production-related solutions and point out that environmental hazards must be reduced and eliminated through sustainable and nonpolluting production practices. In short, to achieve environmental justice the treadmill must be stopped and reversed. Thus, treadmill of production theory recognizes that decreasing production and changing the mode and relations of production are major factors in achieving environmental justice (Gould, Pellow, and Schnaiberg, 2008). Treadmill of production theory also recognizes that the unequal distribution of environmental violations is a result of political economic forces, and that race and class relations and neighborhood composition determines where and how ecological withdrawals and additions occur, and whether those environmental crimes will be met with diligent enforcement efforts. Green criminologists, like treadmill of production theorists, suggest that production practices are harmful and the most marginalized segments of society are the ones who suffer the consequences and receive the least amount of protection from the treadmill of production.

The Warren County (North Carolina) protests that occurred during the early 1980s provide one of the best examples of environmental injustice in the enforcement of environmental laws (Stretesky, 2006). The protests were a response to criminal violations of the Toxic Substances Control Act (TSCA) by the Ward Transformer Company. Ward sold electrical transformers that contained dangerous chemicals known as Polychlorinated Biphenyls (PCBs) that aid in the manufacturing process and sometimes in products by dissipating heat and therefore increasing production efficiency. Prior to the 1970s PCBs were used in a variety of commercial products because of their desirable chemical properties.

PCBs were a product of capital investment in chemical technologies consistent with the expansion of the treadmill of production, and were supposed to make life safer and more convenient. However, worldwide evidence suggested that PCBs are extremely harmful chemicals, and these effects have long been known to the scientific community (Cordle et al., 1978; Drinker, Warren, and Bennett, 1937; Kimbrough, 1987; Kimbrough et al., 1978). PCBs, for example, acts as endocrine disruptors (Brouwer et al., 1999), meaning they impact the ability of the body's hormone system to operate efficiently or as it should. Case studies of populations exposed to PCBs, such as the residents of Yucheng, Taiwan, show the effects of PCBs on those prenatally exposed to this chemical (Guo et al., 2004; on developmental effects, see also, Colborn, vom Saal, and Soto, 1993; for further discussion see Chapter 6). Summarizing the available evidence, the U.S. EPA reports:

> PCBs have been demonstrated to cause a variety of adverse health effects. PCBs have been shown to cause cancer in animals. PCBs have also been shown to cause a number of serious non-cancer health effects in animals, including effects on the immune system, reproductive system, nervous system, endocrine system and other health effects. Studies in humans provide supportive evidence for potential carcinogenic and non-carcinogenic effects of PCBs. The different health effects of PCBs may be interrelated, as alterations in one system may have significant implications for the other systems of the body (http://www.epa. gov/osw/hazard/tsd/pcbs/pubs/effects.htm, accessed October 2013).

Given the dangers they present, in 1979 the U.S. Congress eventually banned these chemicals in the United States—Japan was the first to ban PCBs in 1972. The PCB ban created a situation where large quantities of PCBs needed to be disposed of in accordance with the law. Ecological additions of PCBs to the environment up to that point occurred through events such as leaky transformers and the disposal of commercial products that contained the substance. However, the ban internalized the cost of PCB exposure through environmental regulations, and led corporations to innovate illegal means of disposing of PCBs.

Some companies paid these new disposal costs. However, some PCBs were also illegally disposed. Ward Transformer decided that the proper disposal of PCBs would impact company profits beyond an acceptable level. Thus, Ward Transformer decided to dispose of the regulated waste stream illegally and the president of the company hired Robert Burns and his sons to dispose of the chemicals. Burns created a specially modified truck with a concealed hose that could release the chemicals under the truck as it drove along the highway. The under-truck spray device was operated from the passenger's seat. Burns then employed the vehicle to secretly dump PCB waste along 243 miles of North Carolina roads (Stretesky, 2006).

The PCB-contaminated soil along the roadside was eventually discovered and removed for disposal. These PCB-contaminated soils were unwelcome in all communities, and were finally shipped to a specially designated and newly created landfill in Warren County. The community where the landfill was located was largely African American and poor. Thus, the waste stream that had been created through chemical technology and illegally disposed of along the roads of North Carolina found its way into one of the most marginalized communities in the South through the path of least political resistance. Citizen groups within the community protested using political and direct action tactics, but in the end the landfill was sited in Warren County (Bullard, 1990).

The Warren County landfill is typically cited as an example of environmental injustice. We would argue that it is also an example of the treadmill of production in action, and how that treadmill operates to disadvantage minority and low-income communities. In the case of the Warren County landfill, the investment in chemical technology produced dangerous chemical by-products that required disposal. In the first instance, the public health rules that should be in place to protect the public were lax, and were irregularly enforced, promoting noncompliance with those rules and regulations. Once these illegal disposal methods were discovered, the federal government attempted to remediate the problem, but did so in ways that promoted environmental injustice by selecting a disposal site for the PCB waste stream that was proximate to a low-income, African American community.

To be sure, the lack of enforcement that leads to the disposal of waste in marginalized communities in the United States and is illustrated by the Warren County case also occurs globally (Anyiman, 1991; Brownell, 2011). For instance, when the United States ships waste overseas, residents in developing countries often become the victims of those disposal practices. U.S. consumers who believe that they are properly disposing of computer equipment through green recycling programs are unaware that their computers are being shipped to dumps in poor countries where they can be sifted through by the poor—often children who can easily climb the garbage piles—in search of the valuable metals and components inside the machines. Unfortunately computer equipment is also hazardous and children are unprotected and therefore exposed to lead and other hazards when they sift through the products in search of parts they can recover (Flynn, 2005). Recognizing the role of unequal enforcement and the resulting green victimizations that occur when enforcement fails is an important role of green criminology.

While the lack of enforcement may lead to green victimization of the disadvantaged, there is also evidence which suggests that criminal and civil enforcement are unequally distributed by race and class. Lavelle and Coyle (1992) found that race and class biases existed in the distribution of monetary penalties for environmental regulations. The researchers ranked each penalty according to race and income in the zip code where the violation occurred and when they calculated average fines they revealed that the average environmental monetary penalty in white neighborhoods was $153,067 while the average monetary penalty in black neighborhoods was $105,028. This was also the case for income; green offenders in high-income neighborhoods received fines that averaged $146.993 or 35 percent more than those who violated environmental laws in low-income zip codes. Lavelle and Coyle's findings are consistent with observations concerning the treadmill of production, and demonstrate the political economic interpretation of the operation of environmental law (Boyce, 2002). In short, industry's economic interests appear to supersede public interest in health and safety—especially when those impacted by the law are social and economically disadvantaged.

Summary

To examine the relationship between the treadmill of crime and green criminology we organized this chapter according to crimes associated with ecological withdrawals and ecological additions. Corporations that engage in such crimes often try to cover up their crimes through the technique of greenwashing. As we have noted, the withdrawal of natural resources from the ecosystem is necessary for production to exist. The challenge for green criminology is to examine these crimes of ecological withdrawal. In the case of ecological additions, we noted that environmental injustice is especially problematic. While we are all threatened by the disposal of toxic chemicals into the ecosystem, those residents who live in socially and economically marginalized neighborhoods or countries are less likely to have adequate enforcement and more likely to become green victims. Because treadmill impacts are most likely to be felt by the most marginalized, organizations have formed which frame their struggle in terms of environmental justice. In short, environmental justice movements and organizations attempt to remake environmental law and social control in order to reduce ecological disorganization. In the next chapter we examine the concept of ecological disorganization in more detail, observing how chemicals can cause this type of disorganization.

Chapter 9
A Green Criminological Approach to Social Disorganization

Social disorganization has long been held up as an explanation for crime, both with respect to the causes of crime as well with respect to the formal and informal social control of crime. As a cause of crime, social disorganization may operate in any number of ways: in the Durkheimian sense by facilitating anomie or strain; following Sampson and Groves' (1989) arguments, this may occur in relation to the promotion of ineffective social bonds and poorly integrated local social institutions at the neighborhood level; others frame this view with respect to urban patterns of ecological development linked to social mobility and immobility as well as the dispersion of economic organization and influences, in relation to the concentration of disadvantage, as a consequence of the differential distribution of norms and values, in relation to rapid social change, family disruption, and urban decay, and in terms of relative deprivation. In this sense, social disorganization can produce a variety of effects that in themselves are also considered independent causes of crime that have been examined both within the social disorganization perspective and outside of that tradition. The connection between social disorganization and other explanations of crime also indicates that social disorganization appears to be an effective mechanism for integrating research findings on crime into a broader and more general theory of crime.

Social disorganization has not yet been applied to the study of green crimes. Green crimes and harms come in a variety of forms, and each of those forms may be amenable to explanations linked to the emergence of social disorganization. The most relevant of these crimes would appear to be those related to the distribution of ecological hazards that promote differential exposure to environmental toxins and pollutants. This particular issue is relevant to green criminology's focus on the relationship between political economy and green victimization, the more general analysis of urban patterns of exposure to environmental toxins and pollutants, and green criminology's examination of patterns and issues related to environmental justice. This chapter explores these links in order to promote a green criminological interpretation of crime linked to social disorganization. In that view, the focus isn't on social disorganization, but rather on urban ecological disorganization, or how the economic and social structure produces zones and patterns of ecological/environmental disruption within urban areas. Moreover, in that view, urban ecological disorganization has the potential to generate social disorganization.

Background

An initial point of intersection between green criminology and the social disorganization perspective begins with the view both approaches take with respect to the importance of an ecological frame of reference. As noted in this work, green criminology recognizes the ecological frame of reference by situating discussions of crime and justice in an eco-centric framework to promote the analysis of green harms that directly affect environmental quality and conditions. In turn, direct ecological or green harms produce the secondary victimization of species within those environments. In this sense, green crimes or harms are not the product of social disorganization but rather produce ecological disorganization, an argument that reflects observations found within the treadmill of production approach to environmental hazards. This, in turn, means that it is the organizational features and forces of political economic relations that produce the urban forms of ecological disorganization associated with the process of production, and that these influences can also be related to the treadmill of production and the production of ecological disorganization.

The Chicago School version of social disorganization also grew from ecologically based assumptions which viewed urban ecology in relation to processes of natural ecology and the depiction of urban ecology as a living entity (Park, Burgess, and McKenzie 1925: 1, 4). In addition, Park and Burgess recognized that the ecological space of urban areas was shaped by the process of competition, an idea that reflected Darwinian interpretations of the effects of competition on species and the structure of ecosystems. That idea of competition in the urban ecological model included competition for resources, and recognized that the city was "not ... merely a geographical and ecological unit; it is at the same time an economic unit" (Park, Burgess, and McKenzie, 1925: 2).

Park, Burgess, and McKenzie's elaborate description of urban ecological units is informative and theoretical rich. It describes urban environments and life in those environments and is clearly an important advance in the understanding and analysis of urban life. However, their theory falls short of depicting urban environments outside of the ecological boundaries of human organization within the city. That is, Park, Burgess, and McKenzie exclude the natural ecology from their vision of the ecological system. As a result, despite recognizing and borrowing concepts from the natural sciences on ecology, Park, Burgess, and McKenzie failed to develop a broad view of ecology, and limited their analysis to the ecological fragment of the world built and inhabited by humans, ignoring natural ecology and its connection to human ecology. In sum, like other social science perspectives, Park, Burgess, and McKenzie's view suffers from a limited anthropocentric view of ecology. That anthropocentric orientation, as the term social disorganization implies, limits the idea of disorganization to human ecological units or the ecological world humans create(d).

This anthropocentric view and orientation has important consequences for the kinds of analysis social disorganization theory undertakes. In discussing and describing the humanly constructed aspects of social ecology and its organization and disorganization, the Chicago School theorists as well as contemporary social disorganization theorists overlook the effect of human organization on the ecological organization and functioning of the natural world. This is particularly true with respect to the widespread forms of natural ecological disorganization human communities produce related to problems such as the production and disposal of pollution and toxic waste. To be sure, these are large issues in urban environments, and a significant volume of the world's pollution and toxic waste problems are produced within urbanized areas to facilitate human urban lifestyles.

To be fair, at the time Park, Burgess, and McKenzie were analyzing social disorganization in urban areas, pollution and toxic waste issues had not been accorded the same priority they received from the 1950s onward. Yet, at the same time there were well known descriptions of urban areas both in the academic literature and novels that described urban ecological disorganization, such as the smoky and brown haze of urban life in industrial cities. Indeed, in locations such as London, smog had become so extreme as to cause mass deaths on at least three occasions during the 1880s and 1890s. Moreover, pollution was enough of a concern in the late 1800s and early 1900s that social movements aimed at controlling pollution were not uncommon. In the city of Chicago where Park, Burgess, and McKenzie developed their ideas of social disorganization, for example, businessmen had organized a movement against industrial pollution (Rosen, 1995). Indeed, in response to its air pollution problems, Chicago became the first American city to pass an air pollution law in 1881. Nevertheless, despite the problems presented by urban pollution, its clear physical manifestations, and the borrowed ecological frame of reference that informed social disorganization theory, that approach omitted an examination of the problem of pollution and the impact of pollution on residents, and ignored the general problem of urban ecological disorganization.

This omission of the relationship between human and natural ecology and the effect of cities on the ecological organization of nature is at best, some might say, simply a curiosity. After all, this argument might suggest, the goal of the social disorganization theorists was to examine how the social organization of the urban ecology constructed by humans produced both positive and negative consequences. Still, in identifying the negative consequences of human organizational strategies, social disorganization theory has left out a significant and widespread problem— pollution and toxic waste exposure—that affects not only urban residents, but possesses the potential to affect the entire worldwide functioning of the ecological system. Thus, it seems fair to ask the following question: Why has the social disorganization approach in criminology ignored the production and distribution of hazardous/toxic waste and pollution, the forms of crime and social control related to the control of these noxious outcomes, and the effects of humans on the natural ecology in favor of a focus on street offending and deviance? While it is not our intention to provide a complete answer to this question, the neglect of pollution, toxic waste, and their effect on the natural ecology and humans would appear to be a consequence of social disorganization anthropocentric orientation. But, this cannot be the entire answer.

Clearly, the forms of social disorganization that attracted the attention of social disorganization researchers primarily addressed lower-class crime and deviance, and this implies that a form of class bias also influenced the interpretation of social disorganization put forth in this view. Thus, despite recognizing the influence of the economy on the social organization of cities, and despite viewing urban ecology as a living organism that reflected natural science descriptions of the natural ecological system, criminological versions of social disorganization have been unable to conceptualize social disorganization and economic organization in relation to their negative ecological consequences for the natural environment or as a source of green victimization, crime, and injustice.

In the social disorganization view, what clearly matters are the human aspects of ecological organization and disorganization as these appear within cities as isolated, human environments. That frame of reference leads to a focus on human ecological units of analysis relevant to urban environments such as neighborhoods, and their aggregation into districts and zones that share similarities in that human frame of reference. Omitted from that urban ecological, anthropocentric frame of reference is a broader understanding and interpretation of ecology that includes nature and the intersection of nature's and humans' ecological systems. This view, as a consequence, ignores the ways in which human social ecology produces natural ecological disorganization. It is this latter link that green criminology provides, and which in doing so changes how social disorganization can be examined.

Green Social Disorganization or Urban Ecological Disorganization

In a green perspective, cities are not only viewed as "independent" or separate ecological units constructed by humans. They must, at the same time, be viewed in their interconnection to nature's ecology and organization and to nature as a living system (Hough, 1995). Cities are, in short, enmeshed within the organizational network of the natural ecology. Indeed, cities cannot be otherwise, and are shaped by a wide variety of nature's forms and structures such as waterways, mountains, and the availability of natural resources. That is, in designing cities, humans structure the urban ecology to take advantage of natural resources, but can also not build urban ecological units that ignore the structuring effects of nature. A city, for instance, may be built on two sides of a river—but it cannot be built by ignoring the river's structuring influence on the scope of urban designs that are possible.

The city, then, is not a unit that is completely independent from nature. The tendency to view cities as independent, human ecological units isolated from their web of interdependency within nature creates an abstract, human-centered understanding of the city and its connection to and effect on the natural ecology (Benton-Short and Short, 2008). This theoretical abstraction means that the intimate intersection of the urban and natural ecology will be overlooked in describing the city and laying out theories that attempt to capture urban ecology.

Green criminology's attachment to an eco-centric frame of reference erases this artificial distinction between the urban ecology and the natural ecology. And in erasing that distinction, green criminology forces a reconceptualization of the dimensions of social disorganization that criminologists ought to address. By erasing the urban-ecological split, green criminology forces a more holistic interpretation of the city within its broader ecological frame of reference.

By erasing the artificial distinction between urban and ecological systems, green criminology promotes a reconsideration of the city as a space within the broader ecological system. That reorientation produces a reconceptualization of the city's impact on the natural ecology. For example, in the green criminological view, it is important to consider the history of the intersection of urban and ecological spaces. Since the industrial revolution, or for more than two centuries—and in some views, such as world system's theory, for a much longer period dating back to the fifteenth century—the city as a form of human organization has done extensive damage to the natural world. Cities take up and convert natural space, and have broad impacts on the immediate and proximate environment or ecosystem structures. But the ecological effects of cities are not simply those that occur within the proximate range of the city's grasp. Modern cities, for example, import products from around the world, and have a global reach, affecting the ecology of far off lands, and in some cases—such as through the extraction, refining, and use of fossil fuels—can impact the entire structure of nature.

As an example of the far-reaching effects of production, consider a recent U.S. federal government raid on the Gibson Guitar Company. This was the second such raid on Gibson since 2009. In the most recent raid, the federal government seized shipments and stores of what it claims were raw wood materials illegal imported from Madagascar in violation of the Lacy Act. By either importing or possessing illegal wood materials, the Gibson Company has potentially engaged in acts that endanger the ecosystem in Madagascar, and the ability of that ecosystem to support rare wildlife and to perform its role in maintaining both the local and worldwide ecological system. Gibson Guitars agreed to pay a $300,000 fine to settle this claim, which implies that the Gibson Guitar Company, located in Nashville, Tennessee, has impacted the local ecosystem halfway around the world.

Contemporary cities do not, of course, have an isolated impact on one ecosystem in a far off land. Their effects are widespread, and may include the ecological impacts of using natural resources as well as manufactured products from Middle Eastern, African, South American, and Asian nations among others. This is particularly relevant to modern cities in the "Western" portion of the world, because of the high consumption in those locations and the historical processes that have occurred in those locations which consumed vast quantities of local resources forcing urban areas to seek out raw materials from other locations (Stretesky and Lynch, 2009a)—an issue related to the expansion of the treadmill of production described in the previous chapter. In many areas of the world, modern cities have used up local resources, and depend on raw material as well as finished goods supplied by less developed nations. This international supply chain and its environmental effects is one of the neglected dimensions of ecological disorganization caused by extensive urbanization, and an issue that has been largely neglected within green criminology.

As a result of being unable to recognize or situate the intersection of urban and natural ecology within its frame of reference, the anthropocentric, urban-based social ecological approach taken in criminology by social disorganization theory is incapable of producing an analytic perspective that captures the full range of ecological disorganization promoted by modern cities. There is thus much disorganization that is omitted from the social disorganization view.

To be sure, the large populations that inhabit urban areas are a source of environmental strain and disorganization for the global ecological system and for localized ecosystems both in proximity to urban areas and in other nations (Rees, 1997). In making this point, however, it is not our intention to overlook the local ecological effects of the modern city on its residents. These ecological effects occur through the effects of polluting local, urban environments, and as we have detailed earlier, these pollution outcomes impact millions of residents in the United States alone, causing trillions of green victimization incidents.

Toxic Waste in Urban Environments

One of the overlooked dimensions of ecological disorganization in cities is the direct effect of the production and distribution of toxic waste and pollution on environmental quality and, as an indirect result, on human health, lifestyles, and organization. In large cities in the United States, for example, tens of millions of tons of toxic waste may be produced. Some of that waste is emitted into the air; some is injected underground; some goes to the landfill; some is emptied into waterways; and other portions of that waste are stored in "secure" waste facilities or burned. These various activities may occur in compliance with or in violation of the law, but in either case this dispersion of toxic waste in the environment has detrimental health consequences for the local inhabitants of cities by impacting and changing local natural ecology, including the quality of air and water systems.

As noted in earlier chapters, the emission of toxic waste into the environment can produce direct harm to the environment and indirect harm to the species that inhabit locations near those emissions. Sometimes those emissions can have an extraordinary geographic range and effect. For instance, industrial pollutants have been found far away from where they are produced—in Siberia, the North and South Poles, and throughout the world's oceans, including pollution hotspots such as the Pacific Ocean Garbage Patch. And while these far-off effects are important, here we focus attention on the effects felt in local urban environments.

In the local urban environment, toxins abound and are ubiquitous (on water pollution see, Ellis, 2006; Lapens et al., 2008; on air pollution see; Li et al., 1996;

Marshall et al., 2005; Tsapakis and Stephanou, 2005), and permeate the land, water, and air. Urban residents are, as a result, likely to come into contact with a wide range of environmental pollutants in urban areas that reach them through different environmental media every day, and within any given day, numerous times (see Chapter 5 on green victimology, for examples). In some urban locations the exposure to toxins may be nearly constant. And, while pollution is widespread in urban areas, there are locations in urban areas where toxins are highly concentrated and form pollution hotspots (on pollution hotspots see, for example, Marshall, Nethery, and Brauer, 2008). In other words, there is variability in exposure to toxins within urban areas that are also related to the life course of chemical pollution. But that exposure range is unlikely to include areas where exposure is limited. Nevertheless, while exposure is widespread, the concentration of chemicals to which differentially located populations are exposed may vary.

Pollution hotspots are important concerns because they can change the ecology of urban areas in multiple ways. First, in extreme cases, and where these hotspots are officially identified and recognized, agencies in charge of public health may prohibit people from inhabiting hotspot areas and even nearby locations. When a hotspot such as a Superfund site is discovered, the federal government may move people from their homes, causing community disintegration and migration away from that location and into other areas within a city. If social disorganization theory is correct, that movement can facilitate the weakening of interstitial bonds, produce the decline of local community connections and social control, and contribute to the loss of bonds between neighbors and relatives. That is to say, pollution hotspots may produce the disorganization process that has been identified as being related to crime in the social disorganization literature.

Before an area becomes an official toxic hotspot, its negative characteristics such as foul odors, an abundance of smoke-belching stacks, the expansion of industry, and the general appearance of deterioration associated with the process of chemical pollution over its life-course may drive stable and upwardly mobile residents away from those locations (Camagni, Gibelli, and Rigamonti, 2002). In addition, those environmental conditions may prevent others who seek stable residence from moving into emerging hotspot areas—the reverse situation can also been seen when environmental hotspots are cleaned up (Gamper-Rabindran and Timmins, 2011). In these environmentally transitional urban areas that are becoming more environmentally unstable or which display visible signs of environmental decay, residential property values are likely to fall, facilitating continued outward migration—outcomes long known to researchers (Ridker and Henning, 1967; Smith and Huang, 1993). Declining property values are likely to attract less stable residents, and the increased number of abandon buildings left behind by population movement or the abandonment of these area by industry as well may become targets for vandalism and shelters for poor migrants and the homeless.

It should be clear from this brief description of the impact of toxic hotspots and their distribution within urban areas, that these hotspots have the potential to alter the urban landscape and to produce the kinds of social disorganization Chicago School theorists pointed toward as problematic. But, these forms of social disorganization linked to green harms such as hotspots within urban ecological zones are only the most visible signs of extraordinary urban decay that can be linked to the destruction of urban ecology. "Ordinary" or more typical instances of environmental decay linked to the expansion of ecological degradation and the life-course of chemical pollution may be less apparent.

For the majority of residents, urban ecological disorganization may not be extensive enough to force them out of their neighborhoods or to change their lifestyles in any apparent ways. Indeed, most residents of urban areas must endure the consequences of urban ecological disorganization on a daily basis. These consequences include elevated levels of diseases caused by exposure to pollution and toxins, which are higher in urban areas than elsewhere (Eiguren-Fernandez et al., 2004; McDonnell et al., 1997). In some locations, pollution may be so concentrated that many residents suffer similar illnesses, and while their lives may become disorganized as a result, they are bonded together by their diseases and their inability to escape the ecological disorganization of their urban homes.

Pollution and toxins do not have equivalent effects across a population of residents. Because pollution levels and measures of toxicity are quite often calculated with reference to adult males (Rodricks, 2007), people of smaller stature and lower body weights such as women, children, and some ethnic populations, are the first to show the signs of pollution's effects. Children are especially vulnerable (Wargo, 1996), and many suffer consequences from urban ecological disorganization when these effects may not be apparent in adults. These ecological effects related to pollution can be seen in elevated rates of asthma and other lung diseases in urban children (Kramer et al., 2000; van der Zee et al., 1999), increased rates of childhood cancer (Raaschou-Nielson et al., 2001; Reynolds et al., 2003, 2004), and as some studies show, elevated rates of attention deficit disorder (Mill and Petronas, 2008) and learning disabilities (Margai and Henry, 2003), elevated rates of lead poisoning (Centers for Disease Control and Prevention, 1997), and poor school performance (Needleman et al., 1979). Thus, among all urban residents, children are the most likely to be the victims of the kinds of green harms associated with urban ecological disorganization.

In sum, pollution and toxic waste disorganizes the urban ecology in several ways by producing green harms, especially where pollution hotspots are a concern. In some ecological zones and neighborhoods, the presence of toxic waste forces residents and businesses to move because of its high concentration. That movement or migration away from a given area impairs residential stability, and can alter residents' perceptions of neighborhoods (Gould, 1997). It can also facilitate the outward migration of capital both in economic and social terms. Economically, capital migration may be so great as to cause disinvestment not only in the affected area, but in nearby areas as well, which is related not only to current, but to past pollution and the presence of factors such as brownfields (Bjelland, 2004) related to the life-course of chemical pollution. The same may happen at the level of social capital.

Residents in proximity to an affected neighborhood may also move, impacting residential stability in nearby communities and extending the impact of the pollution hotspot with respect to social disorganization (Ridker and Henning, 1967). In such a neighborhood, it is likely that patterns of disease and illness have emerged, and the potential forced migration of residents enforced by public health agents may move them far away from the medical resources they employ. Pollution hotspots may have long-term effects and cause identified areas to remain uninhabited for decades because of the high, unabatable levels of pollution—for example, Love Canal, NY. In less serious cases, the concentration of pollution can also cause the long-term disintegration of neighborhoods and make those locations undesirable urban spaces. The impact of pollution may be disorganizing to the extent that pollution and toxic waste spread from an affected area into nearby communities through the air and waterways. This kind of toxic migration may cause extreme environmental conditions in some locations as toxins spread into water supplies, or as in the case of the Cuyahoga River fire produce extensive, short-term disorganization for patterns of daily life, or in cases of heavy smog, the deaths of urban residents (Wilkins, 1954; Popkin, 1986). At a more general level, this association between green harms and ecological disorganization has been examined by Pellow (2004) with respect to Chicago's "garbage wars."

These are just some of the forms of ecological disorganization related to the green harms that affect urban areas. It is also important to recognize that these effects, because of their local intensity and placement, may not have an equal impact across urban areas or across populations, an issue we address in the following section.

Environmental Justice and Green Harms that Produce Urban Ecological Disorganization

In the early 1990s, Massey and Denton (1993) published their widely recognized work on segregation in American cities. They argued that modern cities remained racially segregated. Other researchers have pointed out that urban space is also segregated along class lines. These forms of residential segregation are important concerns with respect to the green harms produced by urban ecological disorganization that result from the distribution of toxic waste. Why? Because if cities are segregated along race and class lines, then the effects of urban ecological disorganization can be expected to fall disproportionately on minorities and the poor.

The association between the location of toxic and hazardous waste sites and other polluting facilities and the racial, ethnic, and class composition of neighborhoods is the core issue in the study of environmental justice. That is, the environmental justice literature examines whether there is a discernible pattern of inequality in the distribution of environmental harms and exposure to environmental pollution and toxins. Green criminology has shown considerable interest in the issue of environmental justice and the political and economic relationships that promote environmental injustice as a form of green harm.

Concern with the problem of environmental injustice emerged in the late 1970s, and the study of environmental injustice is now more than 30 years old. There is now a significant body of literature which indicates that toxic/hazardous waste and polluting facilities are not evenly distributed within urban landscapes, and that these hazards are more likely to be found in or proximate to communities with high minority populations and higher concentrations of low-income individuals and families (Liu, 2001), and that these race and class effects extend to children (Powell and Stewart, 2001), and for the most serious disease, cancer (Morello-Frosch and Jesdale, 2005). This association means that minority populations and low-income groups are more likely to be impacted by green harms associated with urban ecological disorganization.

As noted in a previous chapter, green criminological concern with environmental injustice addresses the empirical evidence of this form of injustice, the causes of environmental injustice, and addresses the particular race and class manifestations of injustice and solutions to those problems. With respect to urban ecological disorganization, the issue of environmental injustice is important with respect to the differential effects of urban ecological disorganization across neighborhoods in relation to their racial and class composition, with respect to variability in social justice across neighborhoods, and even with respect to the distribution of factors that may produce crime. It is also likely that these forms of environmental injustice have their own unique life-course patterns, and issue that has not been explored.

Given the results from the extensive literature on environmental injustice, it is clear that pollution, toxic hazards, and waste are unevenly distributed within urban ecologies. In this sense, toxic waste and pollution are distributed in a definite, observable pattern with identifiable neighborhood, zip code, census tract, zonal, and buffer dimensions. In other words, these ecological patterns have a distribution, and that distribution reflects one aspect of urban ecological disorganization. More specifically, we can say that the prevailing pattern of urban ecological disorganization displayed by pollutants and toxins reflects ecological patterns in the distribution of races and classes within urban areas as well as the effect of productive forces, such as the treadmill of production, on how pollution is distributed and how ecological media that are impacted.

It should be quite clear that if urban ecological disorganization is strongly influenced by race and class characteristics of communities—or one could say that urban ecological disorganization is organized along race and class lines—then environmental injustice exists. This simply means that urban ecological disorganization associated with environmental injustice is likely to be prevalent in lower-class and minority communities. As a result, the negative effects of proximity to toxic hazards and ecological disorganization within urban areas are more likely to be experienced by minorities and the lower classes.

The observation that urban ecological disorganization is spatially distributed in ways that have a greater adverse consequence for minorities and the lower classes coincides with observations concerning neighborhood race and class characteristics made by social disorganization theory with respect to the distribution of crime and social control (Krivo and Peterson, 1996; Nielsen, Lee, and Martinez, 2005). Thus, there is nothing particularly startling in the green perspective on urban ecological disorganization from the perspective of social disorganization theory, at least with respect to expected outcomes. The difference between these views is not their inclusion of race or class as determinants of specific forms of disorganization, or an expectation related to race and racial variation, but is found in the fact that social disorganization approaches have omitted discussion of the negative environmental aspects related to the intersection of urban ecological disorganization and racial, ethnic, and class segregation. Moreover, in omitting those negative connections, social disorganization theory has neither paid close attention to nor addressed the additional forms of victimization minority and lower-class residents of cities face where green crimes are concerned; nor has it addressed the disruption of social control that occurs when formal social control agencies accept unequal impacts associated with the distribution of ecological disorganization within urban areas. In other words, by omitting the natural ecology, social disorganization omits analyzing the forms of crime and justice relevant to a broader interpretation of ecology and ecological disorganization. Even if social disorganization theorists are only interested in the anthropocentric dimensions of those relations—for example, human victimization—this escapes the focus of disorganization theory when it is focused solely on its human ecological dimensions.

Above we noted that pollution and toxic waste disorganizes the urban ecology, produces green victimization, pollution hotspots, migration away from ecologically disorganized zones or neighborhoods, impairs residential stability, alters residents perceptions of neighborhoods, facilitates the outward migration of economic and social capital from affected areas, reduces residential stability, and establishes disease and illness patterns related to exposure to toxic waste and pollution. In addition, the persistence of urban ecological disorganization can promote the long-term disintegration of neighborhoods and lead to the identification of certain neighborhoods as undesirable residential or even business locations. The effects described above may not be limited to hotspots or highly polluted areas, but may extend to nearby communities. While it is possible for these kinds of urban ecological disorganization effects to be found in any neighborhood within an urban area, environmental justice research indicates that these conditions are more likely to be found in minority and lower-class communities. Thus, the impact of urban ecological disorganization is unequal. Not only is it unequal, it has an obvious structural dimension that is unrelated to the characteristics of the kinds of individuals who live in an area outside of their identification with particular racial, ethnic, or class groups. That is, urban ecological disorganization is not caused by persons who are minorities or from the lower classes. Rather, urban ecological disorganization is a symptom of the way in which toxic production and disposal are organized and carried out within urban areas, and which are promoted by the economic forces of production and relate to the life-course of chemical pollution in urban locations. With respect to discussions in prior chapters, we can say that urban ecological disorganization is related to the form the treadmill of production acquires, the kinds of pollutants being emitted, and the life course of those pollutants as well. Combined, these factors produce forms of environmental injustice that also impact the nature of green victimization in urban areas.

Given that urban ecological disorganization results from economic organization, it can be suggested that not only does the economic structure in the United States produce ecological disorganization—both urban and rural—it has a strong influence on the disproportionate impact of urban ecological disorganization on minorities and the lower classes. This means that urban ecological disorganization and its class and race effects must be examined within the context of an ecological theory that provides a connection to economic production.

Urban Ecological Disorganization and Capitalism

As noted in Chapter 8, the economic forces and organization of capitalism play a significant role in creating toxic hazards, affecting their scope, and influencing their distribution. In the United States, for example, the majority of toxins produced have a rather clear connection to the economics of production and consumption or to the treadmill of production. In the first place, as noted in an earlier chapter, U.S. industries produce an extraordinary volume of toxic waste. Once produced, that toxic waste must be placed somewhere—and often that somewhere is back into the environment as an environmental hazard—and in locations that tend to be proximate to lower-class and minority neighborhoods. This is part of the life-course of chemical pollution associated with the capitalist treadmill of production.

Second, because capitalism is based in mass production and consumption, among other structuring influences, the decisions made about production, how it is carried out, the kinds of raw materials it employs, and the chemical processes it entails, affect not only the waste stream, but the kinds of toxic hazards that are produced. Capital is constantly in search of cheaper, more efficient ways to produce products, and many of those efficient techniques of production pose risks to the environment and to consumers. In recent years, evidence of this association has been produced in relation to the invention of new plastics implicated as endocrine disruptors examined in an earlier chapter.

Third, the use of mass produced products designed and engineered by corporations involves marketing products that cause harm. An example is the automobile, which is an especially relevant example in American society and in urban areas. Historically, automobile manufacturers have engaged in activities that have shaped the urban landscape and its level of pollution by organizing against public transportation and in support of state and federal road ways and systems. These efforts have a strong impact on the structure of cities and on urban ecological disorganization.

With respect to waste production and disposal, capitalists seek the least expensive alternatives, and prefer solutions that externalize the costs of production. This argument was a central point in the work of James O'Connor (1973) who explored the ways in which capitalists influence state functions in order to externalize the costs of economic reproduction so that those costs shift from corporations to the state and hence to individual tax papers. In recent decades, that process has been facilitated by shifts in the tax structure, which have lowered tax rates for corporations, for capital gains, and for the wealthiest income earners, which in turn shapes the location for the production and disposal of toxic wastes.

In addition, the costs of activities such as industrial pollution are externalized through a variety of processes. One of those processes is federal and state permitting procedures related to the production, emission, handling, disposal, and storage of hazardous waste. The elaborate federal system that tracks waste is an example of this externalization of costs.

Systems of environmental permitting also lend legitimacy to the production and disposal of hazardous wastes. Corporations must apply for permits, and when they receive a permit, that permitting process suggests that the conditions specified in the permit ensure minimal harm to the environment and the various species that inhabit affected environments. Thus, for instance, when a permit is granted to a facility that pollutes local waterways or the air in a minority community, the federal (or state) permitting system makes it appear that there are no substantial issues related to where those facilities are being placed, and whether they cause unequal harms.

Capital has often been absolved of its responsibilities for environmental contamination and the unequal distribution of toxic production and disposal through one of several arguments. One argument suggests that toxic waste and production techniques are the price for modern conveniences. This argument, however, is highly questionable, and numerous production and disposal techniques, some of which enhance rather than destroy environmental quality, exist (McDonough and Braungart, 2002a, 2002b).

Another argument suggests that corporations are not responsible for the differential effects of hazardous waste across race and class groups, because it is the process and events that occur following the placement of hazards that produce unequal exposure, an issue examined in the chapter on environmental justice (Stretesky and Hogan, 1998). This argument suggests that once established, the presence of toxic production and disposal alters property values and perceptions of neighborhoods. In the face of declining prices, those with the economic means to move do so, while those with restricted economic means choose to move into neighborhoods where toxic facilities are located. Not only does this argument ignore differentials in the initial placement of toxic facilities, it also ignores how this process plays out in locations where populations have "no choices" at their disposal. It is in these latter areas that we can potentially better evaluate these claims. For instance, in rural locations where populations affected by extraction activities such as underground or surface mining accomplished via mountaintop removal practices, or in the many areas now affected by the extraction practice of "fracking"—which has produced a widespread social movement—populations exist that have no residential choices to make. That is, affected populations cannot simply move to another part of the mountain because, first, there may be no housing elsewhere on the mountain, and secondly, because all areas of the mountain is equally impacted by mountaintop removal mining. A similar argument applies to children, who do not possess either the intellectual capability to recognize the ecological harms they face, or the financial resources or even the legal right to move to safer locations.

At the heart of urban social disorganization are economic processes that shape the city's landscape, and in our view, are related to the nature of capitalism itself, the conflict between nature and capital, and the nature of the treadmill of production. Capital's decisions about where toxic manufacturing will occur and where it will be disposed, and where it has historically produced and disposed of hazards, shapes the urban landscape and the concentration of pollutants that impact the exposure of ecosystems and the human inhabitants of cities to toxic waste and pollution. Clear examples are brownfields or abandoned former manufacturing sites, and abandoned toxic waste disposal facilities. When abandoning one of these sites, corporations do not first clean the site—they leave it as is, in an extreme state of ecological disorganization. If one were, for example, to pull up a map of Niagara Falls, New York on Google Maps, finding Love Canal along the Niagara River, now an abandoned brownfield, would not be difficult.

Love Canal has a long history that produced its state of ecological disorganization and its current uninhabitable condition. Originally conceived as a water-way short cut around Niagara Falls, its builder went bankrupt. The property on which the large canal had been dug but not completed was purchased by Hooker Chemicals and used as a toxic waste disposal site. The site, because it was an effort to build a canal, backs up to the Niagara River, and thus the choice of this location as a disposal site threatened the quality of water in the river. After filling the canal with toxic waste and covering the site, Hooker sold the site to real estate developers and the City of Niagara Falls School Board. The portion of the site purchased by the School Board was sold for $1. Over the next 20 years, the site was developed, and residents moved into the new Love Canal neighborhood. Soon thereafter, health problems began to emerge among the population, and especially among children. Lois Gibbs, now well known for her environmental activism and her legal reform efforts that changed American environmental laws and regulations, was a housewife and mother in Love Canal, and this became the site of her first battle with the government and corporations over the creation of and response to hazardous waste sites. Eventually, the government paid to relocate Love Canal residents, and much of the site remains closed today, more than 35 years after its discovery. This short story plays out across America in numerous large and small cities, affecting the ecological disorganization of urban areas—not to mention rural areas as well—areas for future green criminological investigation, though some literature on mountaintop removal in green criminology and hog farming has already addressed these forms of rural ecological disorganizations (for example, see, Stretesky, Johnston, and Arney, 2003).

Our point is that economic organization and the capitalist treadmill of production lies behind environmental problems, whether those problems are social disorganization or urban ecological disorganization, or even more far-reaching consequences and related environmental issues. Whatever the environmental issue, green criminology ought to attack the problem from an eco-centric frame of reference, and append to that frame of reference a political economic approach in which the problem can be analyzed and dissected. To be sure, there are problems that green criminologists have addressed, such as non-human animal abuse, which could benefit from the insights gained by employing political economic analysis.

Conclusion

There are a wide variety of criminological perspectives that can be modified by and benefit from the insights from green criminology. In this chapter, we have illustrated this point by drawing on one of the oldest and most important criminological approaches to crime in urban areas—social disorganization theory—to make our point. In earlier chapters we have explored how green criminology can be used to remake a select sample of the criminological literature—victimology, life course, and behaviorism. We have undertaken this discussion to point the way toward a green criminological revolution in how criminologists can think about the extensive array of problems that face the contemporary world and make criminology more relevant to those circumstances.

Chapter 10

The End of Crime, or the End of Old-fashioned Criminology?

Criminologists have devoted considerable attention to understanding crime, its causes, distribution, and control since the first study of criminal statistics by Adolphe Quetelet in 1831 (Hagan, 2011: 105-7). A wide range of explanations for crime have been produced in an effort to understand and explain crime and to suggest why some people commit crime. These explanations are extraordinarily diverse in nature and content, and include biological, psychological, small-group interaction, self-control, social control, learning, and social disorganization perspectives among many others (Hagan, 2011). In some cases, these approaches include reference to the content of law, law making, and the role of law enforcement agencies. Other views refer to broad concepts such as culture, to the postmodern conditions of life, and to more specific and narrow issues such as the role of immigration. The vast majority of these explanations produce rather weak results with respect to the accurate prediction of crime, and in statistical terms, one is often better off flipping a coin than relying on the prediction produced by empirical assessments of criminological explanations of crime. Among approaches that eschew empirical analysis in favor of qualitative examinations, the lack of any form of standardized measurement means that the contribution of these theories to our knowledge of crime cannot be assessed in any rational manner, and whether or not one finds these approaches useful is merely a matter of opinion (see Sherman, 2005).

Criminologists have also devoted significant attention to counting street crime and the victims of street crime, and when not counting those kinds of crimes, engaging in qualitative work on street offending or with victims of street crimes. In doing so, criminologists continually contribute to the stereotypical image of crime as the work of the poor and powerless (Reiman, 2006). Largely omitted from this work on crime, whether it is produced by conservative criminological theories that use small group, psychological, or other forms of individual explanation, or "progressive" approaches that employ qualitative approaches to study the culture of crime, are the vast array of harms that are related to the environment.[1]

In our view, many criminologists that we have reviewed in this book have helped to establish a field of green criminology. They have employed their significant talents and abilities to explore one of the most widespread and harmful

---

1   We note that this condition is changing and there are several criminologists who are now paying much more attention to environmental harm even if they still make up a very small proportion of criminologists.

forms of crime, green crime. Nevertheless we believe that relative to the harm created, there is a shortage of such work. By ignoring green harms and crimes, criminologists—except as noted—have largely left the examination of this social problem to other disciplines. Instead, criminology continues to be dominated by routine forms of harms committed by the powerless. This condition is not surprising since, historically, criminology has done a very poor job of explaining the crimes of the poweful, and the vast majority of models of street offending prove to be poor predictors of those outcomes—they fail to explain an adequate amount of variance in the dependent outcome, thus producing statistically significant effect outcomes in underestimated models (for general discussion of this problem see, Yong, 2012). We believe that the exertion of significant time, effort, and resources that has been devoted to explaining street crime has severely limited the quantity of time criminologists devote to green crime, and the volume of space it occupies in the criminological literature. This heavy emphasis on mainstream issues allows green crimes to be examined only at the margins of the discipline. To be sure, in the modern era—an era of global warming, wetland destruction, the removal of mountains to unearth coal seams, the highly unsafe and unhealthy practices of drilling for oil in oceans and seas, or the use of controversial and understudied mining techniques such as hydrofracturing—ignoring the ways in which the powerful continue to drive a political economic network of environmental destruction forward for the sake of instantaneous profits, misses the most harmful crimes of our times, and, one could say, given the extraordinary extent and volume of those crimes, and the various forms of destruction they bring, *the biggest crimes in the history of the world.* No other crimes have threatened the existence of the entire planet.

The Distracted Criminologist

As noted above, criminologists, as an aggregate, spend the vast majority of their time examining street crime. Evidence for this statement can be produced in different ways. For example, one could take the leading criminologists of the time and examine their publications. One is unlikely to find that they have produced any literature on any forms of crimes committed by the powerful.

Criminologists spend significant time and resources studying crime, producing little useful knowledge along the way. Consider, for example, that in 1992 in the United States, the rate of crime began to decline. That crime decline has shown up in many nations. This crime decline has continued, unabated for two decades. Despite its breadth of research, criminologists did not possess the kind of knowledge necessary to predict the crime decline or its extensive life course, nor have they found sufficient explanation for the crime drop or its persistence. Moreover, the crime drop was not the result of any policy about crime derived by a criminologist. Critical criminologists should not be let off the hook here either, as they hardly seem to notice that a crime drop occurred, and their attention to postmodern and cultural theories are of no help on this issue (for an exception see, Lynch, 2013).

We draw attention here to the inadequacies in criminological theory, criminology's neglect of the crimes of the powerful in general, and criminology's weak explanations of crime drop to support our argument for reforming criminology, for creating a criminological revolution that would allow criminologists to address issues of contemporary importance—green crimes. Over its 180-year history—if Quetelet is the starting point—criminology has often fared poorly when it comes to explaining its topic of interest—crime. For the majority of its history, orthodox criminology's main interest has been the behavior of the "typical" or "average" offender, which in criminological terms has been defined as the street offender.

Corporate, white collar, state crime, and green research suggest that the street offender is not the typical offender. Moreover, that research suggests that the average street offender and the average street crime is hardly the most significant form of harm we face today. In addition, the street offender and the street crime is hardly a threat to our way of life or our existence, unlike green crimes that disorganize and undermine the ability of nature to do its work. Throughout its long history, crime has never caused the decline of society, shaken it to its core, and damaged it to the extent that it has caused the ruination of a nation. At the same time, we can no longer make that same claim about the kinds of crime that have been the focus of this book—green crimes.

Green crimes are currently extraordinarily widespread, so widespread that they threaten the existence not only of individuals within given locations within particular societies, but the nature of life as we know it. Yet green crimes expand, and the more they come to play a role in the contemporary world, we are shocked by the quite limited attention these crimes and behaviors, and the forms of regulation and control directed at them, have attracted from criminologists. If one were to read the criminological literature, they would not conclude at the end of their studies that green crimes were a problem, that toxic waste was widespread and caused extensive victimization, that there was an issue called global warming. Criminology is and has been written as if these adverse events, these green crimes and injustices, do not exist. This is not the case, however, *outside* of criminology.

Green Harms Beyond Criminology

Referring more generally to the problem of environmental destruction, for example, a quite different conclusion about the importance of green crimes and harms and the extent of green victimization would be reached from reading the scientific literature. In that literature, environmental problems are a significant concern, and scientists of all varieties have devoted significant attention to the study of environmental destruction. The list of disciplines that address environmental destruction includes, but is not limited to medical sciences, epidemiology, physics, chemistry, biology, toxicology and its branches, and newer branches of science such as green chemistry. Scientists in these areas have made significant contributions to our knowledge of the modern world and its physical nature and operations. These scientists include, for example: James Lovelock, knighted by the Queen of England for his scientific contribution to Gaia theory and global warming research; Rachel Carson, whose book *Silent Spring* ushered in the environmental movement in the United States and brought worldwide attention to the problem of pesticides in the environment; National Academy of Science member and a consultant to various Presidents, Devra Davis and her work on pollution; Sandra Steingraber and her influential work on the link between pollution and cancer; or the influence of those in the activism community such as Lois Gibbs and Ralph Nader that relate to environmental protection and health; or the effort of NASA scientist, James Hanson, outspoken critic of government and industry in his stance on global warming; or the ecological writings of Bill McKibben, including his now classic book, *The End of Nature*. To this list we could easily add hundreds of names to identify people who have taken up the challenge of investigating the contemporary problems the world faces from environmental destruction.

These works, and many, many others, describe the changing nature of the world around us—a changing world that humans have produced by harming the environment through over-consumption, over-production, re-engineering nature, filling in wetlands, mining coal and drilling for oil and natural gas, and via the massive level of pollution humans have created all over the world in the process. Criminology has ignored the changing nature of the world around us, and has become less and less relevant to the problems found in the contemporary world. It is time for criminologists to wake up.

The New Eaarth

In his recent book, *Eaarth: Making a Life on a Tough New Planet*, Bill McKibben lays out the evidence for the fact that planet earth has entered a new environmental era. McKibben, and many scientists and environmentalists who came before him, have long recognized the emergence of this serious problem.

As McKibben poignantly noted in a previous work, "we are no longer able to think of ourselves as a species tossed about by larger forces [of nature]—now we are the larger forces" (2007: xviii). As McKibben goes on to argue, this contention can be supposed by an array of specific examples:

> by changing the very temperature of the planet, we inexorably affect its flora, its fauna, its rainfall and evaporation, the decomposition of its soil. Every inch of the planet is different … The by-products—the pollutants—of one species have become the most powerful force for change on the planet. This change in quantity is so large that it becomes a change in quality (2007: xix).

In addition, we should consider and keep in mind that as McKibben goes on to point out, and as many natural scientists have acknowledged, the world's ecosystem has now crossed a threshold, a temperature-sensitive threshold. In crossing that threshold human behavior is driving the earth toward conditions that will no longer be able to support human life as we know it. That problem and addressing the behaviors that contribute to that outcome, ought to weigh more heavily than assessing the causes of crime, and ought to cause those who wish to contribute to solving the contemporary problems of our times to assess the role they can play in that process, and how they may need to actively get involved in changing not only what they do, but in changing the contents of a discipline that does not contribute toward those ends.

The world around us has changed dramatically and continues forward on its course of change, moving closer and closer to becoming an uninhabitable place—at least for humans. As long as humans continue to stress the environment, the world's ecological system will continue down this path (Lovelock, 2007).

We raise this point to note that despite these vast environmental changes that have altered the very nature of the world around us; despite the importance of these changes in the world around us; despite how these changes have impacted national and global policies and politics; despite the apparent threat we face as species within a changing global environmental system; despite the recognition of these problems by scientists and world leaders; despite the increased appearance of these issues in academic literatures across disciplines; despite all of this change and the extraordinary level of harm these changes produce, criminology has built an intellectual wall that has for the most part prevented criminology and criminologists from recognizing and discussing the green harms involved in this process, from examining their scope and importance, and has insulated criminology from the need to respond to these very real world conditions as they change around us. While the world has changed quite radically, criminology has refused to change, clinging to an old conceptualization of the problem of crime and victimization; to old and dated views on law and social control as forces that are only relevant to the control of street crime; to the idea that the only victims that matter are the victims of street crimes.

As criminologists ourselves, we are disturbed by the general failure of the criminological community to take green crimes and harms seriously. To be sure, there are some who have taken green crime, harms, law, social control, and green victimization seriously, but they are few in number. They see the ways in which criminology can be relevant to the study of green crimes, harms, laws, social control, and green victimization. But the majority of criminologists do not, and continue to investigate crime in very traditional ways, in relation to a very traditional understanding of crime, and in relation to social and psychological relationships that have much less relevance than criminologists can imagine.

Greening Criminology

As we have demonstrated in this work, there is no shortage of ways in which criminology can address the problem of the green harms. These green harms and the problems that produce them have been the subject of this book and the topic for the handful of criminologists who have attempted to modernize criminology so that it can addresses the important topic of our times—green harms. There is no need to produce a list of the names of these criminologists who have dedicated themselves to address green harms, crimes, and justice; those who are making criminology relevant to the major social and environmental issues of our era. Many are referenced throughout this work. They are not engaged in these activities to draw attention to themselves or their work: they are engaged in this work to make the world a better, healthier place and to reduce suffering and victimization.

In this book we have attempted to expand the scope of green criminology using a variety of examples that connect green criminology to the kinds of work criminologists perform and the orthodox theories criminology has preferred. In employing examples from orthodox criminology and remaking these approaches in a way that is consistent with a green frame of reference, we have attempted to make green criminology more relevant to criminology, and to make criminology more relevant to the changing world around us. At the same time it is necessary for us to point out that the different positions we have taken in this work are insufficient when they are not connected to the political economy of the world system, a system we see as driving the green issues we have examined in this book through its emphasis on profit making, production, and consumption about other values and aspects of living life.

We are not the first, nor do we believe we will be the last to make these kinds of observations about the connection between political economy and the deterioration of ecosystems and the world environment. Numerous economists have worked on addressing this connection, and we have been influenced in our view by, among others, the works of James O'Connor, Paul Burkett, John Bellamy Foster, James Boyce, Herman Daly, James Hanson, and Barry Commoner. These are a few of the many economists, scientists, ecologists, toxicologists, biologists, and physicists who have influenced our interpretation of green criminology and its relationship to political economy and environmental destruction.

Like those named above, we believe that the contemporary political economic system must be remade in order to address the broad scope of environmental harms around us. That is no small task. We have also drawn inspiration, but do not necessarily agree with those who argue that capitalism can be remade so that it addresses environmental problems simply by changing the ethic of capitalism (Hawken, Lovins, and Lovins, 2008; McDonough and Braungart, 2002a, 2002b; for discussion see Wallis, 2010). The kinds of changes suggested in this "green capitalism" literature have not been widely applied or accepted within capitalism or by its leaders (Rogers, 2010). Consequently we see green capitalism's claims as equally unlikely as a call for replacing capitalism with a new view on the purpose of economic systems. Nevertheless, we admit that we are willing both to listen to these views on green capitalism and to determine if there is sufficient evidence that this approach can deliver what it claims, since in some cases this alternative view of capitalism has indeed been implemented, even if on a limited scale—although on this point we must admit that our tendency is to side with the ecological Marxists like Foster and Burkett and their discussions of the inherent contradiction between capitalism and nature.

In our view, green criminology isn't simply a series of conjectures about possibilities, about the metaphysical nature of the world, or a means for describing the natural order of things with respect to species hierarchies and interactions. For green criminology to be practiced seriously, it must have a goal in mind that leads to the reduction of harms humans commit against nature. And, since the harms humans regularly and persistently commit against nature are organized by their economic purposes and functions, the analysis and discussion of green harms, law and justice must always be undertaken with reference to political economic explanation. The attachment of green criminology to political economic understanding and explanation is where Lynch (1990) began the effort to develop green criminology, and that was done precisely to create a different ways of seeing harms against the environment and to help end destructive practices.

In the last two decades, much has changed about the work criminologists undertake under the heading green criminology. A large number of harms, policies, laws, and justice issues have now been examined from a variety of perspectives. In our view, this vast expansion is unfortunate to the extent that it undermines the original intent of green criminology which was to continually return to political economic groundings to understand environmental harm. Rather than reinforce that view, much green criminology ignores that connection to political economy (except see Ruggiero and South, 2013: Walters, 2006; White, 2002 to name a few), fashioning instead a tapestry of green approaches, causing green criminology to more and more resemble orthodox criminology in terms of its proliferation of explanations of crimes and harms, and in its ability and tendency to ignore political economy.

We can, of course, only suggest where we think green criminology and criminology more generally ought to focus its efforts. Whether or not criminology joins in the fight against environmental destruction or continues to turn its back on that struggle and the important implications of environmental destruction remains to be seen. Given the nature of criminology we are not optimistic in this regard, because we see criminology mostly as a science developed for controlling and oppressing the marginalized and the lower classes (Lynch, 2000). Doing otherwise would require a complete transformation of the vision of the purpose of criminology, a vision that criminologists seem rather incapable of entertaining.

Criminologists have long used the legal definition of crime as if it were an objective definition of harm disassociated from influence and interest, to guide the study of crime and criminals. In doing so, they have directed their attention toward offenses most likely to be committed by the most marginalized members of society. There is indeed some level of harm associated with these behaviors. At the same time, these are not the behaviors that harm any given society or the world the most. Moreover, there is now an elaborate bureaucratic mechanism for controlling street crime, and society has built up strong mechanisms for resisting, discovering, and punishing the crimes of the powerless.

The same cannot be said about green harms. As we have illustrated, green harms are far more widespread and cause significantly more harm than street crimes. And if it is the intent of criminology to protect the victimized from harm—and there would not appear to be another reason to explain crime other than to control it unless the effort to explain crime is simply idle curiosity—there is a greater need for and a potential for doing so by adopting a green criminological position.

Historically, criminology has been built on an elaborate framework that has created a disciplinary focus on the lower classes and minorities. That focus has served the goals of the political economic structure, by devising theories that apply to the lower classes, by pointing to "them" as problematic, by legitimizing their control, and by engaging in the support of corrective policies that expand the quantity and quality of social control applied to the marginalized. In this way, criminology's disciplinary thrust has reinforced the inherently unequal power relations of capitalism. In doing so and endeavoring to present itself as the scientific study of crime and criminals, but at the same time uncritically accepting the legal definition of crime as an objective statement about criminology's anchoring point, criminologists have constructed—perhaps unwittingly—the scientific basis for oppressing and contributing to the oppression of the lowest social classes and serving on the side of capital in the class struggle and in the effort to dominate and exploit rather than respect the environment.

In taking up this position in the study of crime and to construct criminology, criminologists have also sided with—again, perhaps unwittingly—those who oppress and exploit not only in the class war, but in the economic war against nature. In the historically defined battle of humans against nature, criminologists have sided with humans *against* nature, failing to see that humans and nature are joined together rather than antagonistic entities. And in taking up the human side, criminology has joined with capital to justify and rationalize the exploitation of nature by ignoring harms against nature, by legitimizing ignorance of those offenses, by constructing a discipline in which the green harms of capital are hidden.

In the End …

This particular depiction of criminology we have described above may appear to many to be harsh, one-sided, misguided, and exaggerated—too harsh. To those who hold that view, our perspective on green criminology certainly provides a challenge, a challenge that requires criminologists to defend themselves against our argument. As we have shown, there is considerable scientific evidence supporting our argument about the extent of green harms and victimization—and we believe it is the scientific evidence on this point that ought to concern and be persuasive to criminologists who, after all, often claim that their field is a scientific endeavor. Moreover, as we have illustrated, there is sufficient evidence to support the argument that green crimes and harms are far more widely distributed than street crimes, cause more victimization and harm than street crimes, and are more serious in terms of outcomes. The extent of death, disease and financial loss are far more prevalent with respect to green crimes than street crime. In the face of that evidence as well as the evidence produced by scientists about environmental harm, it is difficult to accept the traditional criminological focus on street offenders.

Disciplines do not change overnight. And when they do change, the literature on these subjects suggests that the change is the result of a scientific revolution. With respect to recognizing environmental harm and addressing that issue, that revolution has emerged in a number of disciplines. That revolution in the way humans conceive of the environment and their relationship to it which in turn affects the perception of human ability to change the environment in very detrimental ways—that revolution in thinking—has been resisted by criminology. And thus, while other disciplines respond to and respect this new scientific understanding of human-environment interactions in the age of environmental destruction, criminology sleeps and dreams its long dream as if the world was not in crisis and the old routines practiced by criminology were sufficient. Whether or not criminology wakes to the call for a green revolution, we can not say. But given its historical tendency we doubt it will. For our part, we have left the dream behind and welcome others who wish to do the same.

Appendix: A Manifesto for Green Criminology

In the summer of 2011, we presented a Green Manifesto to the members of the International Green Criminology Working Group. We reproduce that Manifesto here in slightly modified form as a general description of the goals and scope of green criminology.

Introduction

Environmental harms and their consequences have been widely ignored by criminologists. In this statement, we propose a green manifesto that describes the extent of environmental harms and why criminologists must take action, paying greater attention to environmental harms, their causes and consequences, and why green criminologists ought to become involved in solutions to the problems identified below.

The State of the World

Contemporary science makes it clear that the most significant problems facing the world today are environmental problems in their various forms. These environmental problems include, but are not limited to the following major issues that impact the health of the planet and the species that exist in that planetary environment:

1. global warming/climate change;
2. the ubiquitous nature of industrial pollution;
3. environmental sustainability;
4. health and survival concerns for human and non-human species, and the natural state of the environment;
5. deforestation;
6. the rate of species extinction;
7. the destruction of local eco-systems, their continuity and function as affected through practices such as mountaintop mining, hydrofracturing, and chemical mining for minerals and precious metals;
8. the effects of over-population on the environment;

9. air pollution associated with automobiles, trucks, and buses;
10. the abuse of the world's oceans, including its populations;
11. the unequal exposure to pollution and toxins or environmental injustice;
12. the effects of chemical pollutants on the behavior of various species;
13. the destruction of wetlands; and
14. the consequences of over-production and over-consumptions in relation to these negative environmental outcomes.

Environmental Problems and Orthodox Criminology

The world faces a serious challenge from these environmental problems. Traditionally, outside of green criminology, these concerns have not been afforded a significant or valued place within criminology, and the criminological literature generally fails to recognize these important issues, the dimensions of crime these behaviors include, and the forms of injustice and harm these green crimes produce. Orthodox criminology justifies this oversight by relying on the traditions established within criminology that focus on crimes of the powerless and interpersonal harms and the violent victimization that result from interpersonal violence. These are certainly serious social problems that deserve some attention, but which do not require the attention of an entire discipline.

The orthodox criminological tradition with its focus on street crimes and street offenders excludes consideration of forms of environmental or green victimization that harm the wide variety of non-human species and living ecological systems, and the secondary effects of environmental harms committed against ecological systems on humans. Given the severity of these environmental concerns, the extent of green victimization, and the problems they present with respect to maintaining an environmental system capable of reproducing itself, we call upon criminologists to reconsider the content and purpose of the discipline of criminology, and to incorporate and respect the effort to take these issues seriously through the practice of green criminology.

The handful of major issues briefly listed above produce extensive levels of violent harm in and across societies, and affect a variety of species—humans, non-humans, the ecological system and its components, and even non-human-non-animal species. These violent harms which include exposure to toxins and pollutants, the destruction of the environment, compromising the reproductive ability of the ecosystem, and so on, produce far more harm than the kinds of criminal violence orthodox criminologists have tended to study and to which they devote the majority of their attention. Again, while criminal harms are serious, there is a greater need to acknowledge and study environmental harms, and to pay much more attention to these issues because they cause such extraordinary damage. This vast level of green harm can no longer be ignored by a discipline devoted to the study of harms and victims, and to the understanding and prevention of harm.

As a discipline, criminology has lagged behind other disciplines in its failure to acknowledge and take environmental harm seriously. The current level of environmental harm is so extraordinary that the task of studying these harms, their effects, and mechanisms for controlling those harms cannot be left to a handful of criminologists from around the world. Moreover, these harms cannot be left to those in other disciplines to study, since criminology has much to offer to the study of environmental harms. There is a need for a concerted effort by criminologists to do their part to address the legal and criminal aspects of these harms, the rights of the variety of victims of these harms, and the forms of social control that can be applied to address these harms. In order for this to happen, not only must individual criminologists recognize and address these problems, they must help remake their discipline to provide greater space for the examination of green crimes, harms, and victimization. Pedagogically, for example, criminological departments must add courses that educate students about these matters, preparing the next generation of criminologists who will be more capable of taking on the responsibility of addressing environmental harms.

Reorientation

In addressing green harms and crimes, criminologists must be willing to recognize that the driving force behind the crimes and harms humans commit against the ecological system are crimes of exploitation and appropriation driven by the ways in which humans organize their societies around political economic systems. Thus, solving the problem of green crimes requires addressing the role of political economy and policies that reorganize political economic relations and goals.

We stand at the edge of an era that has been coming into being for decades, but has largely gone unnoticed by criminologists. In that era, the world has and will continue to change. There is much in that world that requires the work of criminologists to expose, understand, and address.

There is a great urgency in doing so now. The environmental problems facing the world are vast, and a criminology that avoids these issues abandons its basic mission as one of the disciplines that addresses victimization.

Bibliography

Abernathy, C.O., Y.P. Liu, D. Longfellow, H.V. Aposhian, B. Beck, B. Fowler, R. Goyer, R. Menzer, T. Rossman, C. Thompson, and M. Waalkes. (1999). "Arsenic: Health Effects, Mechanisms of Action and Research Issues." *Environmental Health Perspectives* 107,7: 593-7.

Agnew, R. (2012). "Dire Forecast: A Theoretical Model of the Impact of Climate Change on Crime." *Theoretical Criminology* 16,1: 21-42.

Ala, A., C.M. Stanca, M. Bu-Ghanim, I. Ahmado, A.D. Branch, T.D. Schiano, J.A. Odin and N. Bach. (2006). "Increased Prevalence of Primary Biliary Cirrhosis near Superfund Toxic Waste Sites." *Hepatology* 43,3: 525-31.

Allen, T.F.H., J.A. Tainter, J.C. Pires, and T.W. Hoekstra. (2001). "Dragnet Ecology-'Just the Facts, Ma'am': The Privilege of Science in a Postmodern World." *BioScience* 51,6: 475-85.

American Chemistry Council. (2011). "Shale Gas and New Pretrochemicals Investment: Benefits for the Economy, Jobs, and US Manufacturing." *Economics and Statistics American Chemistry Council*. Available at: http://www.americanchemistry.com/ACC-Shale-Report (accessed April 2013).

Anastas, P. and J. Warner. (1998). *Green Chemistry: Theory and Practice*. New York, NY: Oxford University Press.

Anderson, S., W. Sadinski, L. Shugart, P. Brussard, M. Depledge, T. Ford, J. Hose, J. Stegeman, W. Suk, I. Wirgin, and G. Wogan. (1994). "Genetic and Molecular Ecotoxicology: A Research Framework." *Environmental Health Perspectives* 102: Supp. 12: 3-8.

Anway, M.D. and M.K. Skinner. (2006). "Epigenetic Transgenerational Actions of Endocrine Disruptors." *Endocrinology* 147,6: s43-s49.

Anyiman, C.A. (1991). "Transboundary Movements of Hazardous Waste: The Case of Toxic Waste Dumping in Africa." *International Journal of Health Services* 21,4: 759-77.

Aono, S., S. Tanabe, Y. Fujise, H, Kato, and R. Tatsukawa. (1997). "Persistent Organochlorines in Minke Whale and Their Prey Species from the Antarctic and the North Pacific." *Environmental Pollution* 98,1: 81-99.

Asakawa, A., M. Toyoshima, M. Fujimiya, K. Harada, K. Ataka, K. Inoue, and A. Koizumi. (2008). "The Ubiquitous Environmental Pollutant Perfluorooctanoicacid Inhibits Feeding Behavior via Peroxisome Proliferator-activated Receptor-Alpha." *International Journal of Molecular Medicine* 21,4: 439-45.

Asiedu, E. (2006). "Foreign Direct Investment in Africa: The Role of Natural Resources, Market Size, Government Policy, Institutions and Political Instability." *The World Economy* 29,1: 63-77.

Associated Press. (2012). "Gov't Audit: Safety Risks Tied to Gas Pipelines Used in Fracking Process Need Federal Scrutiny." *The Washington Post Online.* Posted March 23, 2012. Available at: http://www.washingtonpost.com/ business/industries/govt-audit-safety-risks-tied-to-gas-pipelines-used-in-fracking-process-need-federal-scrutiny/2012/03/23/gIQAPPxCVS_story.html (accessed April 2013).

Atedhor, G., P. Odjugo, and A. Uriri. (2011). Changing Rainfall and Anthropogenic-induced Flooding: Impacts and Adaptation Strategies in Benin City, Nigeria. *Journal of Geography and Regional Planning* 4,1: 42-52.

Avol, E.L., W.J. Gauderman, S.M. Tan, S.J. London, and J.M. Peters. (2001). "Respiratory Effects of Relocating to Areas of Differing Air Pollution Levels." *American Journal of Respiratory and Critical Care Management* 164: 2067-71.

Baer, H. (2008). "Global Warming as a By-Product of the Capitalist Treadmill of Production and Consumption." *The Australian Journal of Anthropology* 19,1: 58-62.

Bao, Q-S., C-Y. Lu, H. Song, M. Wang, W. Ling, W-Q. Chen, X-Q. Deng, Y-T. Hao, and S. Rao. (2009). "Behavioural Development of School-aged Children Who Live around a Multi-metal Sulphide Mine in Guangdong Province, China: A Cross-sectional Study." *BMC Public Health* 9: 217.

Bargagli, R. (2000). "Trace Metals in Antarctica Related to Climate Change and Increasing Human Impact." *Reviews of Environmental Contamination and Toxicology* 166: 129-73.

Barnett, H.C. (1999). "The Land Ethic and Environmental Crime." *Criminal Justice Policy Review* 10,2: 161-91.

Bartley, M., D. Blane, and S. Montgomery. (1997). "Socioeconomic Determinants of Health: Health and the Life Course—Why Safety Nets Matter." *British Medical Journal* 314: 1194-6.

Bauter, M.R., B.J. Brockel, D.E. Pankevich, M.B. Virgolini, and D.A. Cory-Slechta. (2003). "Glutamate and Dopamine in Nucleus Accumbens Core and Shell: Sequence Learning Versus Performance." *Neurotoxicology* 24,2: 227-43.

Bazerman, C. and R.A. De los Santos. (2005). "Measuring Incommensurability: Are Toxicology and Ecotoxicology Blind to What the Other Sees?" In R.A. Harris (ed.), *Rhetoric and Incommensurability*. Lafayette, IN: Parlor Press, 424-63.

BBC News. (2010). "Haiti Quake Death Toll Rises to 230,000." Available at: http://news.bbc.co.uk/2/hi/americas/8507531.stm (accessed July 10, 2012).

Beaver, K., M. DeLisi, J.P. Wright, and M.G. Vaughn. (2009). "Gene-Environment Interplay and Delinquency Involvement: Evidence of Direct, Indirect and Interactive Effects." *Journal of Adolescent Research* 24,2: 147-68.

Beirne, P. (1993). *Inventing Criminology: Essays on the Rise of "Homo Criminalis."* Albany, NY: State University of New York Press.

——. (1997). "Rethinking Bestiality: Towards a Concept of Interspecies Assault." *Theoretical Criminology* 1,3: 317-40.

——. (1999). "For a Nonspeciesist Criminology: Animal Abuse as an Object of Study." *Criminology* 37,1: 117-48.

——. (2002). "Criminology and Animal Studies: A Sociological View." *Society and Animals* 10,4: 381-86.

——. (2007). "Animal Rights, Animal Abuse and Green Criminology." In P. Beirne and N. South (eds), *Issues in Green Criminology*. Cullompton: Willan, 55-83.

——. (2009). *Confronting Animal Abuse: Law, Criminology and Human-Animal Relationships*. Lanham, MD: Rowman & Littlefield.

Beirne, P. and N. South (eds). (2006). *Green Criminology*. Aldershot: Ashgate.

——. (eds). (2007). *Issues in Green Criminology: Confronting Harms Against Environments, Other Animals and Humanity*. Cullompton: Willan.

Bell, M. (2004). *An Invitation to Environmental Sociology*. Thousand Oaks, CA: Pine Forage Press.

Bell, S.E. and R. York. (2010). "Community Economic Identity: The Coal Industry and Ideology Construction in West Virginia." *Rural Sociology* 75: 111-43.

Bellinger, D., A. Leviton, J. Sloman, M. Rabinowitz, H.L. Needleman, and C. Waternaux. (1991). "Low-Level Lead Exposure and Children's Cognitive Function in the Preschool Years." *Pediatrics* 87,2: 219-27.

Benítez-López, A., R. Alkemade, and P.A. Verweij. (2010). "The Impacts of Roads and Other Infrastructure on Mammal and Bird Populations: A Meta-analysis." *Biological Conservation* 143,6: 1307-16.

Benton, T. (1998). "Rights and Justice on a Shared Planet: More Rights or New Relations?" *Theoretical Criminology* 2: 149-75.

——. (2007). "Ecology, Community and Justice: The Meaning of Green." In P. Beirne and N. South (eds), *Issues in Green Criminology*. Cullompton: Willan, 3-31.

Benton-Short, L. and J.R. Short. (2008). *Cities and Nature*. London: Routledge.

Berdyugina, S.V. and I.G. Usoskin. (2003). "Active Longitudes in Sunspot Activity: Century Scale Perspective." *Astronomy and Astrophysics* 405,3: 1121-8.

Bigsby, R., R.E. Chapin, G.P. Daston, B.J. Davis, J. Gorski, L.E. Gray, K.L. Howdeshell, R.T. Zoeller, and F.S. vom Saal. (1999). "Evaluating the Effects of Endocrine Disruptors on Endocrine Function during Development." *Environmental Health Perspectives* 107,4: 613-18.

Bisschop, L. (2012). "Is It All Going to Waste? Illegal Transports of E-waste in a European Trade Hub." *Crime, Law and Social Change* 58,3: 221-49.

Bjelland, M.D. (2004). "Brownfield Sites in Minneapolis-St. Paul: The Interwoven Geographies of Industrial Disinvestment and Environmental Contamination." *Urban Geography* 25,7: 631-57.

Bonnell, T.R., R. Reyna-Hurtado, and C.A. Chapman. (2011). "Post-Logging Recovery is Longer than Expected in an East African Tropical Forest." *Forest Ecology and Management* 261,4: 855-64.

Boyce, J.K. (2002). *The Political Economy of the Environment*. Cheltenham: Edward Elgar.

Bradshaw, C.J.A., N.S. Sodi, K.S.H. Peh, and B.W. Brook. (2007). "Global Evidence that Deforestation Amplifies Flood Risk and Severity in the Developing World." *Global Change Biology* 13, 2379-95.

Breton, C.V., M.T. Salam, H. Vora, W.J. Gauderman, and F.D. Gilliland. (2011). "Genetic Variation in the Glutathione Synthesis Pathway, Air Pollution, and Children's Lung Function Growth." *American Journal of Respiratory and Critical Care Medicine* 183,2: 243-48.

Brouwer, A., M.P. Longnecker, L.S. Birnbaum, J. Cogliano, P. Kostyniak, J. Moore, S. Schantz, and G. Winneke. (1999). "Characterization of Potential Endocrine-related Health Effects at Low-dose Levels of Exposure to PCBs." *Environmental Health Perspectives* 107,4: 639-49.

Brown, L.R. (2008). *Plan B, 3.0: Mobilizing to Save Civilization*. New York, NY: W.W. Norton.

Brownell, E. (2011). "Negotiating the New Economic Order of Waste." *Environemntal History* 16,2: 262-89.

Brownstein, J.S., T.R. Holford, and D. Fish. (2005). "Effect of Climate Change on Lyme Disease Risk in North America." *EcoHealth* 2,1: 38-46.

Brubaker, C.J., K.N. Dietrich, B.P. Lanphear, and K.M. Cecil. (2010). "The Influence of Age of Lead Exposure on Adult Gray Matter Volume." *Neuro-Toxicology* 31,3: 259-66.

Bullard, R.D. (1990). *Dumping in Dixie: Race, Class, and Environmental Quality*. Boulder, CO: Westview Press.

Bulte, E. and R. Damania. (2008). "Resources for Sale: Corruption, Democracy and the Natural Resource Curse." *The B.E. Journal of Economic Policy and Analysis* 8,1: 1935-68.

Burkett, P. (2009). *Marxism and Ecological Economics: Toward a Red Green Political Economy*. Chicago, IL: Haymarket Books.

Burns, R.G. and M.J. Lynch. (2004). *Environmental Crime: A Sourcebook*. New York, NY: LFB Scholarly.

Burns, R.G., M.J. Lynch, and P.B. Stretesky. (2008). *Environmental Law, Crime and Justice*. New York, NY: LFB Scholarly.

Bushnell, P.J. and R.E. Bowman. (1979). "Effects of Chronic Lead Ingestion on Social Development in Infant Rhesus Monkeys." *Neurobehavioral Toxicology* 1,3: 207-19.

Butler, G.C. (1984). "Developments in Ecotoxicology." *Ecological Bulletins* 36: 9-12.

Cáceres, C. (2007). "Economical and Environmental Factors in Light Alloys Automotive Applications." *Metallurgical and Materials Transactions A* 38,7: 1649-62.

Cacioppo, J.T., G.G. Berntson, J.F. Sheridan, and M.K. McClintock. (2000). "Multilevel Integrative Analyses of Human Behavior: Social Neuroscience and the Complementing Nature of Social and Biological Approaches." *Psychological Bulletin* 126,6: 829-43.

Camagni, R., M.C. Gibelli, and P. Rigamonti. (2002). "Urban Mobility and Urban Form: The Social and Environmental Costs of Different Patterns of Urban Expansion." *Ecological Economics* 40,2: 199-216.

CARB (California Air Resources Board). (2002). *Staff Report: Public Hearing to Consider Amendments to the Ambient Air Quality Standards for Particulate Matter and Sulfates*. California Air Resources Board and Office of Environmental Health Hazard Assessment. Available at: http://www.arb.ca.gov/research/aaqs/std-rs/pm-final/pm-final.htm (accessed April 2013).

——. (2003). *The Economic Value of Respiratory and Cardiovascular Hospitalizations*. California Air Resources Board and California Environmental Protection Agency. Available at: http://www.arb.ca.gov/research/apr/past/99-329.pdf (accessed April 2013).

Carpenter, D.O., J. Ma, and L. Lessner. (2008). "Asthma and Infectious Respiratory Disease in Relation to Residence near Hazardous Waste Sites." *Annals of the New York Academy of Science* 1140: 201-8.

Carpenter, D.O. and R. Nevin. (2010). "Environmental Causes of Violence." *Physiology and Behavior* 99,2: 260-68.

Carrabine, E., P. Cox, M. Lee, K. Plummer, and N. South. (2008). *Criminology: A Sociological Introduction*. London: Routledge.

Carroll, C. (2007). "Interacting Effects of Climate Change, Landscape Conversion, and Harvest on Carnivore Populations at the Range Margin: Marten and Lynx in the Northern Appalachians." *Conservation Biology* 21,4: 1092-1104.

Carson, R. (2002 [1962]). *Silent Spring*. Boston, MA: Mariner Books.

Catallo, W.J. (1993). "Ecotoxicology and Wetland Ecosystems: Current Understanding and Future Needs." *Environmental Toxicology and Chemistry* 12,12: 2209-24.

Cecil, K.M., C.J. Brubaker, C.M. Adler, K.N. Dietrich, M. Altaye, J.C. Egelhoff, S. Wessell, I. Elangovan, R. Hornung, K. Jarvis, and B.P. Lanphear. (2008). "Decreased Brain Volume in Adults with Childhood Lead Exposure." *PLoS Medicine* 5,5: e112.

Centers for Disease Control and Prevention. (1997). *Screening Young Children for Lead Poisoning: Guidance for State and Local Public Health Officials*. Atlanta, GA: CDC.

Chai, S-L. and E.V.J. Tanner. (2011). "150 Year Legacy of Land Use on Tree Species Composition in Old-Secondary Forests of Jamaica." *Journal of Ecology* 99,1: 113-21.

Chaix, B., S. Gustafsson, M. Jerrett, H. Kristersson, T. Lithman, A. Boalt, and J. Merlo. (2006). "Children's Exposure to Nitrogen Dioxide in Sweden: Investigating Environmental Injustice in an Egalitarian Country." *Journal of Epidemiology and Community Health* 60: 234-41.

Chapman, P.M. (2002). "Integrating Toxicology and Ecology: Putting the 'Eco' into Ecotoxicology." *Marine Pollution Bulletin* 44,1: 7-15.

Chen, D.S. and K.M. Chan. (2009). "Changes in the Protein Expression Profiles of the Hepa-T1 Cell Line when Exposed to CU Super(2) Super (+)." *Aquatic Toxicology* 94,3: 163-76.

Chen, H-H., T. Ma, and I.K. Ho. (2001). "Effects of Developmental Lead Exposure on Inhibitory Avoidance Learning and Glutamate Receptors in Rats." *Environmental Toxicology and Pharmacology* 9,4: 185-91.

Chen, T-P. (2012). "Hong Kong's Killer Pollution." *The Wall Street Journal*. February 23, 2012. Available at: http://blogs.wsj.com/chinarealtime/2012/02/23/hong-kong's-killer-pollution (accessed March 18, 2012).

Cloquet, C., J. Carignan, G. Libourel, T. Sterckeman, and E. Perdrix. (2006). "Tracing Source Pollution in Soils using Cadmium and Lead Isotopes." *Environmental Science Technology* 40,8: 2525-30.

Cohen, A., H.R. Anderson, B. Ostro, K.D. Pandey, M. Krzyzanowski, N. Künzli, K. Gutschmidt, A. Pope, I. Romieu, J.M. Samet, and K. Smith. (2006). "The Global Burden of Disease Due to Outdoor Air Pollution." *Journal of Toxicology and Environmental Health, Part A: Current Issues* 68,13-14: 1301-7.

Cohn, J. and D.A. Cory-Slechta. (1993). "Subsensitivity of Lead-exposed Rats to the Accuracy-impairing and Rate-altering Effects of MK-801 on a Multiple Schedule of Repeated Learning and Performance." *Brain Research* 600,2: 208-18.

Cohn J., C. Cox, and D.A. Cory-Slechta. (1993). "The Effects of Lead Exposure on Learning in a Multiple Repeated Acquisition and Performance Schedule." *Nerotoxicology* 14,2-3: 329-46.

Colborn, T. (2004). "Neurodevelopment and Endocrine Disruption." *Environmental Health Perspectives* 112,9: 944-9.

Colborn, T., D. Dumanoski, and J.P. Meyers. (1997). *Our Stolen Future*. New York, NY: Plume.

Colborn, T., F.S. vom Saal, and A.M. Soto. (1993). "Developmental Effects of Endocrine-disrupting Chemicals in Wildlife and Humans." *Environmental Health Perspectives* 101,5: 378-84.

Constable, D.J.C., A.D. Curzons, and V.L. Cunningham. (2002). "Metrics to 'Green' Chemistry: Which are the Best?" *Green Chemistry* 4: 521-7.

Cordle, F., P. Corneliussen, C. Jelinek, B. Hackley, R. Lehman, J. McLaughlin, R. Rhoden, and R. Shapiro. (1978). "Final Report of the Subcommittee on Health Effects of PCBs and PBBs: Human Exposure to Polychlorinated Biphenyls and Polybrominated Biphenyls." *Environmental Health Perspectives* 24: 157-72.

Cory-Slechta, D.A., M. Garcia-Osuna, and J.T. Greenamyre. (1997). "Lead-induced Changes in NMDA Receptor Complex Binding: Correlations with Learning Accuracy and with Sensitivity to Learning Impairments Caused by MK-801 and NMDA Administration." *Behavioral Brain Research* 85,2: 161-74.

Croall, H. (2007a). "Victims of White Collar and Corporate Crime." In P. Davies, P. Francis, and C. Greer (eds), *Victims, Crime and Society*. London: Sage, 78-108.

——. (2007b). "Food Crime." In P. Beirne and N. South (eds), *Issues in Green Criminology*. Cullompton: Willan, 206-29.

——. (2009). "White Collar Crime, Consumers and Victimization." *Crime, Law and Social Change* 51: 127-46.

Crouch, G.I. (2001). "The Market for Space Tourism: Early Indications." *Journal of Travel Research* 40,2: 213-19.

Daily, G.C. and P.R. Ehrlich. (1992). "Population, Sustainability, and Earth's Carrying Capacity." *BioScience* 42,10: 761-71.

Daling, P.S., L-G. Faksness, A.B. Hansen, and S.A. Stout. (2002). "Improved and Standardized Methodology for Oil Fingerprinting." *Environmental Forensics* 3,3-4: 263-78.

Daly, H.E. (1998). *Beyond Growth: The Economics of Sustainable Development*. Boston, MA: Beacon Press.

Davis, D. (2002). *When Smoke Ran Like Water: Tales of Environmental Deception and the Battle Against Pollution*. New York, NY: Basic Books.

Day, W. (1983). "On the Difference Between Radical and Methodological Behaviorism." *Behaviorism* 11,3: 89-102.

Debelius, B., J.M. Forja, T.A. Del Valls, and L.M. Lubian. (2009). "Toxicity of Copper in Natural Picoplankton Populations." *Ecotoxicology* 18,8: 1095-103.

Denno, D. (1990). *Biology and Violence*. New York, NY: Cambridge University Press.

Denton, G.R.W. and C. Burdon-Jones. (1981). "Influence of Temperature and Salinity on the Uptake, Distribution and Depuration of Mercury, Cadmium and Lead by the Black-lip Oyster Saccostrea Echinata." *Marine Biology* 64: 317-26.

Diamond, J. (2005). *Collapse: How Societies Choose to Fail or Succeed*. New York, NY: Penguin.

Dickinson, J. (2007). *Inventory of New York City's Greenhouse Gas Emissions*. Mayor's Office of Operations, Office of Long-Term Planning and Sustainability. Available at: http://www.nyc.gov/planyc2030 (accessed March 13, 2012).

Dietrich, K.N., J.H. Ware, M. Salganik, J. Radcliffe, W.J. Rogan, G.G. Rhoads, M.E. Fay, C.T. Davoli, M.B. Denckla, R.L. Bornschein, D. Schwarz, D.W. Dockery, S. Adubato, and R.L. Jones. (2004). "Effect of Chelation Therapy on the Neuropsychological and Behavioral Development of Lead-Exposed Children after School Entry." *Pediatrics* 114,1: 19-26.

Dietrich, K.N., R.M. Douglas, P.A. Succop, O.G. Berger, and R.L. Bornschein. (2001). "Early Exposure to Lead and Juvenile Delinquency." *Neurotoxicology and Teratology* 23,6: 511-18.

Dietrich, K.N., K.M. Krafft, R.L. Bornschein, P.B. Hammond, O. Berger, P.A. Succop, and M. Bier. (1987). "Low-Level Fetal Lead Exposure Effect on Neurobehavioral Development in Early Infancy." *Pediatrics* 80,5: 721-30.

Difiglio, C. and L. Fulton. (2000). "How to Reduce US Automobile Greenhouse Gas Emissions." *Energy* 25: 657-73.

Doty, D.H. and W.H. Glick. (1994). "Typologies as a Unique Form of Theory Building: Toward Improved Understanding and Modeling." *Academy of Management Review* 18,2: 230-51.

Drinker, C.K., M.F. Warren, and G.A. Bennett. (1937). "The Problem of Possible Systemic Effects from Certain Chlorinated Hydrocarbons." *Journal of Industrial Hygiene and Toxicology* 19,7: 283-311.

Duffy, D.C. and A. Meier. (2003). "Do Appalachian Herbaceous Understories Ever Recover from Clearcutting?" *Conservation Biology* 6,2: 196-201.

Durkheim, E. (1951 [1897]). *Suicide: A Study in Sociology*, trans. J.A. Spaulding and G. Simpson. Glencoe, IL: Free Press.

Ehrlich, P. (1970). *The Population Bomb*. New York, NY: Ballantine.

Eiguren-Fernandez, A., A.H. Miguel, J.R. Fronies, S. Thurairatnam, and E.L. Avol. (2004). "Season and Spatial Variation of Polycyclic Aromatic Hydrocarbons in Vapor Phase and PM 2.5 in Southern California Urban and Rural Communities." *Aerosol Science and Technology* 38,5: 447-55.

El-Gendy, K.S., M.A. Radwan, and A.F. Gad. (2009). "In Vivo Evaluation of Oxidative Stress Biomarkers in the Land Snail, *Theba Pisana*, Exposed to Copper Based Pesticides." *Chemosphere* 77,3: 339-44.

Ellis, J.B. (2006). "Pharmaceutical and Personal Care Products (PPCPs) in Urban Receiving Waters." *Soil and Sediment Remediation* 144,1: 184-9.

Eman, K., G. Meško, and C.B. Fields. (2009). "Crimes Against the Environment: Green Criminology and Research Challenges in Slovenia." *Journal of Criminal Justice and Security* 11,4: 574-92.

Energy Information Administration. (2006). *Coal Production in the United States*. Available at: http://www.eia.doe.gov/cneaf/coal/page/coal_production_review.pdf (accessed April 2013).

Evans, G.W. and S.V. Jacobs. (1981). "Air Pollution and Human Behavior." *Journal of Social Issues* 37,1: 95-125.

Eyrikh, S., M. Schwikowski, and T. Papina. (2004). "Reconstruction of Mercury Air Contamination by Analysis of an Ice Core from Belukha Glacier, Siberian Altai." *Annual Report, 2004*. Paul Scherrer Institut, Switzerland. Available at: lch.web.psi.ch/pdf/anrep04/23.pdf (accessed April 2013).

Fatta, D., A. Nikolaou, and S. Meric. (2007). "Analytic Methods for Tracing Pharmaceutical Residues in Water and Wastewater." *TrAC Trends in Analytic Chemistry* 26,6: 515-33.

Field, B. (1997). *Environmental Economics*. Boston, MA: McGraw-Hill.

Fleming, J.R. (2005). *Historical Perspectives on Climate Change*. New York, NY: Oxford University Press.

Flynn, L. (2005). Poor Nations are Littered with Old PC's, Report Says." *New York Times*. October 24. Available at: http://www.nytimes.com/2005/10/24/technology/24junk.html (accessed April 2013).

Forastiere, F., M. Staoggia, C. Tasco, S. Picciotto, N. Agabiti, G. Cesaroni, and C.A. Percucci. (2006). "Socioeconomic Status, Particle Air Pollution and Daily Mortality: Differential Exposure or Differential Susceptibility?" *American Journal of Industrial Medicine* 50,3: 208-16.

Forbes, V.E. and T.L. Forbes. (1994). *Ecotoxicology in Theory and Practice*. New York, NY: Chapman and Hall.

Foster, J.B. (2000). *Marx's Ecology: Materialism and Nature*. New York, NY: Monthly Review Press.

———. (2002). *Ecology Against Capitalism*. New York, NY. Monthly Review Press.

Foster, J.B., B. Clark, and R. York. (2011). *The Ecological Rift: Capitalism's War on Earth*. New York, NY: Monthly Review Press.

Frank, N. and M.J. Lynch. (1992). *Corporate Crime, Corporate Violence*. Albany, NY: Harrow & Heston.

Fuller, S. (2006). *The New Sociological Imagination*. Beverly Hills, CA: Sage.

Gallagher, L.G., T.F. Webster, A. Aschengrau, and V.M. Vieira. (2010). "Using Residential History and Groundwater Modeling to Examine Drinking Water Exposure and Breast Cancer." *Environmental Health Perspectives* 118,6: 749-55.

Gallo, M.A. and J. Doull. (1991). "History and Scope of Toxicology." In M.O. Amdur, J. Doull, and C.D. Klaassen (eds), *Casarett and Doull's Toxicology: The Basic Science of Poisons*. New York, NY: Pergamon Press, 3-11.

Gamper-Rabindran, S. and C. Timmins. (2011). "Hazardous Waste Cleanup, Neighborhood Gentrification, and Environmental Justice: Evidence from Restricted Access Census Block Data." *The American Economic Review* 101,3: 620-24.

Gauderman, W.J., G.F. Gilliland, H. Vora, E. Avol, D. Stram, R. McConnell, D. Thomas, F. Lurmann, H.G. Margolis, E.B. Rappaport, K. Berhane, and J.M. Peters. (2002). "Association between Air Pollution and Lung Function Growth in Southern California Children: Results from a Second Cohort." *American Journal of Respiratory and Critical Care Management* 166: 76-84.

Gibbs, C., M. Gore, E. McGarrell, and L. Rivers III. (2010). "Introducing Conservation Criminology: Toward Interdisciplinary Scholarship on Environmental Crimes and Risks." *The British Journal of Criminology* 50,1: 124-44.

Gilbert, M.E. and S.M. Lasley. (2007). "Developmental Lead (Pb) Exposure Reduces the Ability of the NMDA Antagonist MK-801 to Suppress Long-term Potentiation (LTP) in the Rat Dentate Gyrus, in Vivo." *Neurotoxicology and Teratology* 29,3: 385-93.

Global Footprint Network. (2013). "World Footprint: Do We Fit on the Planet?" Global Footprint Network. Available at: http://www.footprintnetwork.org/en/index.php/GFN/page/world_footprint/ (accessed April 2013).

Global Witness. (2002). *The Logs of War: The Timber Trade and Armed Conflict. Economies of Conflict: Private Sector Activity in Armed Conflict*. Fafo Institute for Applied Social Science. Available at: http://www.unglobalcompact.org/

docs/issues_doc/Peace_and_Business/Logs_of_War.pdf (accessed April 2013).

Goodell, J. (2006). *Big Coal: The Dirty Secret behind America's Energy Future.* Boston, MA: Houghton Mifflin.

Goodstein, D. (2004). *Out of Gas: The End of the Age of Oil.* New York, NY: W.W. Norton.

Gottfredson, M.R. and T. Hirschi. (1990). *A General Theory of Crime.* Stanford, CA: Stanford University Press.

Gould, K.A. (1997). "Pollution and Perception: Social Visibility and Local Environmental Mobilization." *Qualitative Sociology* 16,2: 157-78.

Gould, K.A., D.N. Pellow, and A. Schnaiberg. (2008). *The Treadmill of Production: Injustice and Unsustainability in the Global Economy.* Herndon, VA: Paradigm Publishers.

Gould, K., A. Schnaiberg, and A.S. Weinberg. (1996). *Local Environmental Struggles: Citizen Activism in the Treadmill of Production.* Cambridge: Cambridge University Press.

Gouveia, N. and T. Fletcher. (2000). "Time Series Analysis of Air Pollution Mortality: Effects by Cause, Age and Socioeconomic Status." *Journal of Epidemiology and Community Health* 54: 750-55.

Grandjean, P., D. Bellinger, Å. Bergman, S. Cordier, G. Davey-Smith, B. Eskenazi, D. Gee, K. Gray, M. Hanson, P. Van Den Hazel, J.J. Heindel, B. Heinzow, I. Hertz-Picciotto, H. Hu, T.T-K. Huang, T.K. Jensen, P.J. Landrigan, I.C. McMillen, K. Murata, B. Ritz, G. Schoeters, N.E. Skakkebæk, S. Skerfving, and P. Weihe. (2008). "The Faroes Statement: Human Health Effects of Developmental Exposure to Chemicals in Our Environment." *Basic and Clinical Pharmacology and Toxicology* 102,2: 73-5.

Green, P., T. Ward, and K. McConnachie. (2007). "Logging and Legality: Environmental Crime, Civil Society and the State." *Social Justice* 34,2: 94-108.

Greer, J. and K. Bruno. (1996). *Greenwash: The Reality Behind Corporate Environmentalism.* Penang: Third World Network.

Griffin, J., R.C. Duncan, W.B. Riggan, and A.C. Pellom. (1989). "Cancer Mortality in U.S. Counties with Hazardous Waste Sites and Ground Water Pollution." *Archives of Environmental Health* 44,2: 69-74.

Grindon, C., R. Combes, M.T. Cronin, D.W. Roberts, and J. Garrod. (2006). "A Review of the Status of Alternative Approaches to Animal Testing and the Development of Integrated Testing Strategies for Assessing the Toxicity of Chemicals under REACH: A Summary of a DEFRA-funded Project Conducted by Liverpool John Moores University and FRAME." *Alternatives to Laboratory Animals* 34,1: 149-58.

Groombridge, N. (1998). "Masculinities and Crimes Against the Environment." *Theoretical Criminology* 2: 249-67.

Grove, R.H. (1997). *Ecology, Climate and Empire: Colonialism and Global Environmental History, 1400-1940.* Cambridge: The White Horse Press.

Guo, Y.L., G.H. Lambert, C-C. Hsu, and M.M.L. Hsu. (2004). "Yucheng: Health Effects of Prenatal Exposure to Polychlorinated Biphenyls and Dibenzofurans." *International Archives of Occupational and Environmental Health* 77,3: 153-8.

Hagan, F. (2011). *Introduction to Criminology*. Thousand Oaks, CA: Sage.

Hakkinen, P.J. and D.K. Green. (2002). "Alternatives to Animal Testing: Information Resources Via the Internet and World Wide Web." *Toxicology* 173,1-2: 3-11.

Hall, M. (2011). Environmental Victims: Challenges for Criminology and Victimology in the 21st Century. *Journal of Criminal Justice and Security* 4: 371-91.

——. (2013). *Victims of Environmental Harm: Rights, Recognition and Redress Under National and International Law*. Abingdon: Routledge.

Hallsworth, S. (2011). "Then They Came for the Dogs!" *Crime, Law and Social Change* 55,5: 391-403.

Halsey, M. (2004). "Against Green Criminology." *The British Journal of Criminology* 44,6: 833-53.

Hamilton, E.I. (2000). "Environmental Variables in a Holistic Evaluation of Land Contaminated by Historic Mine Wastes: A Study of Multi-element Mine Wastes in West Devon, England Using Arsenic as an Element of Potential Concern to Human Health." *Science of the Total Environment* 249,1-3: 171-221.

Harrison, B. and B. Bluestone. (1988). *The Great U-Turn*. New York, NY: Basic Books.

Harvey, A. and B. Salter. (2012). "Governing the Moral Economy: Animal Engineering, Ethics and the Liberal Government of Science." *Social Science and Medicine* 75,1: 193-9.

Hauck, M. (2008). Rethinking Small-scale Fisheries Compliance. *Marine Policy* 32,4: 635-42.

Hawken, P., A. Lovins, and L.H. Lovins. (2008). *Natural Capitalism: Creating the Next Industrial Revolution*. New York, NY: Back Bay Books.

Haynes, E.N., A. Chen, P. Ryan, P. Succop, J.P. Wright, and K.N. Dietrich. (2011). "Exposure to Airborne Metals and Particulate Matter and Risk for Youth Adjudicated for Criminal Activity." *Environmental Research* 111,8: 1243-8.

Henderson, R.K., D.J.C. Constable, and C. Jimenez-Gonzalez. (2010). "Green Chemistry Metrics." In P.J. Dunn, A.S. Wells, and M.T. Williams (eds), *Green Chemistry in the Pharmaceutical Industry*. Weinheim: Wiley-VCH, 21-48.

Hendriksen, C.F. (2002). "Refinement, Reduction, and Replacement of Animal Use for Regulatory Testing: Current Best Scientific Practices for the Evaluation of Safety and Potency of Biologicals." *ILAR Journal* 43,1: S43-S48.

Hendryx, M., E. Fedorko, and J. Halverson. (2010). "Pollution Sources and Mortality Rates Across Rural-Urban Areas in the United States." *The Journal of Rural Health* 26,4: 383-91.

Hillyard, P. and S. Tombs. (2007) "From 'Crime' to Social Harm?" *Crime, Law and Social Change* 48,1-2: 9-25.

Hirsch, H.V., D. Possidente, and B. Possidente. (2009). "Pb2+: An Endocrine Disruptor in Drosophila?" *Physiology and Behavior* 99,2: 254-9.

Hogan, M.J., M.A. Long, P.B. Stretesky, and M.J. Lynch. (2006). "Campaign Contributions, Postwar Reconstruction Contracts and State Crime." *Deviant Behavior* 27,3: 269-97.

Homyack, J.A. and C.A. Haas. (2009). "Long-term Effects of Experimental Forest Harvesting on Abundance and Reproductive Demography of Terrestrial Salamanders." *Biological Conservation* 142,1: 110-21.

Hough, M. (1995). *Cities and Natural Process: A Basis for Sustainability*. London: Routledge.

Houghton, R.A. (1991). "Tropical Deforestation and Atmospheric Carbon Dioxide." *Earth and Environmental Science* 19,1-2: 99-118.

Huanga, X., L. Lessner, and D.O. Carpenter. (2006). "Exposure to Persistent Organic Pollutants and Hypertensive Disease." *Environmental Research* 102,1: 101-6.

Hudson-Edwards, K.A. (2003). "Sources, Mineralogy, Chemistry and Fate of Heavy Metal-bearing Particles in Mining-affected River Systems." *Mineralogy Magazine* 67,2: 205-17.

Intergovernmental Panel on Climate Change (IPCC). (2001). *Climate Change 2001: Synthesis Report, Summary for Policy Makers*. Geneva: IPCC. Available at: http://www.ipcc.ch/pdf/climate-changes-2001/synthesis-spm/synthesis-spm-en.pdf (accessed October 2013).

Jacobson, J.L. and S.W. Jacobson. (1996). "Intellectual Impairment in Children Exposed to Polychlorinated Biphenyls in Utero." *The New England Journal of Medicine* 335: 783-9.

Jaffe, E.K., M. Volin, C.R. Bronson-Mullins, R.L. Dunbrack, Jr., J. Kervinen, J. Martins, J.F. Quinlan, Jr., M.H. Sazinsky, E.M. Steinhouse, and A.T. Yeung. (2000). "An Artificial Gene for Human Porphobilinogen Synthase Allows Comparison of an Allelic Variation Implicated in Susceptibility to Lead Poisoning." *Journal of Biological Chemistry* 275: 2619-26.

Jansson, B., L. Asplund, and M. Olsson. (1987). "Brominated Flame Retardants: Ubiquitous Environmental Pollutants?" *Chemosphere* 16,10-12: 2343-9.

Jarrell, M. and J. Ozymy. (2010). "Excessive Air Pollution and the Oil Industry: Fighting for Our Right to Breathe Clean Air." *Environmental Justice* 3,3: 111-15.

——. (2012). "Real Crime, Real Victims: Environmental Crime Victims and the Crime Victims' Rights Act (CVRA)." *Crime, Law and Social Change* 58,4: 373-89.

Jeffery, C.R. (1978). "Criminology as an Interdisciplinary Behavioral Science." *Criminology* 16,2: 149-69.

Jennings, W.G. (2010). "Sex Disaggregated Trajectories of Status Offenders: Does CINS/FINS Status Prevent Male and Female Youth from Becoming Labeled Delinquent?" *American Journal of Criminal Justice* 36: 177-87.

Jennings, W.G., M. Maldonado-Molina, and K.A. Komro. (2010). "Sex Similarities/Differences in Trajectories of Delinquency among Urban Chicago Youth: The Role of Delinquent Peers." *American Journal of Criminal Justice* 35: 56-75.

Jennsen, B. (2006). "Endocrine-disrupting Chemical and Climate Change: A Worst Case Combination for Arctic Marine Mammals and Seabirds?" *Environmental Health Perspectives* 114: 76-80.

Johnson, D.B., D.L. Eaton, P.W. Wahl, and C. Gleason. (2001). "Public Health Nutrition Practice in the United States." *Journal of the American Dietetic Association* 101,5: 529-34.

Jorgenson, A.K. and T.J. Burns. (2007). "The Political-Economic Causes of Change in the Ecological Footprints of Nations, 1991-2001: A Quantitative Investigation." *Social Science Research* 36,2: 834-53.

Jorgenson, J.L. (2001). "Aldrin and Dieldrin: A Review of Research on Their Production, Environmental Deposition and Fate, Bioaccumulation, Toxicity and Epidemiology in the United States." *Environmental Health Perspectives* 109,1: 113-39.

Kan, M. (2011). "IPhone Workers Still Sick after Chemical Poisoning." *PC World.* February 21. Available at: http://www.pcworld.com/article/220257/iphone_workers_still_sick_after_chemical_poisoning.html (accessed April 2013).

Karmen, A. (2010). *Crime Victims: An Introduction*. Belmont, CA: Wadsworth.

Katz, R.S. (2010). "The Corporate Crimes of Dow Chemical and the Failure to Regulate Environmental Pollution." *Critical Criminology* 18,4: 295-306.

Kauzlarich, D., R.A. Matthews, and W.J. Miller. (2002). "Toward a Victimology of State Crime." *Critical Criminology* 10,3: 173-94.

Kavlock, R.J., G. Ankley, J. Blancato, M. Breen, R. Conolly, D. Dix, K. Houck, R. Judson, J. Rabinowitz, A. Richard, R.W. Setzer, I. Shah, D. Villeneuve, and E. Weber. (2008). "Computational Toxicology: A State of the Science Mini Review." *Toxicological Science* 103,1: 14-27.

Kearney, M., R. Shine, and W.P. Porter. (2009). "The Potential for Behavioral Thermoregulation to Buffer 'Cold-blooded' Animals Against Climate Warming." *Proceedings of the National Academy of Sciences of the United States of America* 106,10: 3835-40.

Kennedy, R.F. Jr. (2005). *Crimes Against Nature: How George W. Bush and His Corporate Pals are Plundering the Country and Hijacking Democracy*. New York, NY: Harper Perennial.

Keys, T. (2008). "Green Chemistry: A Philosophy and a Business Model." *Society of Chemical Industry*. Available at: http://www.soci.org/News/Yorks-green-chem (accessed April 2013).

Kimbrough, R.D. (1987). "Human Health Effects of Polychlorinated Biphenyls (PCBs) and Polybrominated Biphenyls (PBBs)." *Annual Review of Pharmacology and Toxicology* 27: 87-111.

Kimbrough, R.D., J. Buckley, L. Fishbein, G. Flamm, L. Kasza, W. Marcus, S. Shibko, and R. Teske. (1978). "Final Report of the Subcommittee on Health

Effects of PCBs and PBBs: Animal Toxicology." *Environmental Health Perspectives* 24: 173-85.

Klaassen, C.D. and D.L. Eaton. (1991). "Principles of Toxicology." In M.O. Amdur, J. Doull, and C.D. Klaassen (eds), *Casarett and Doull's Toxicology: The Basic Science of Poisons*. New York, NY: Pergamon Press, 12-49.

Koren, H. and M. Bisesi. (2003). *Handbook of Environmental Health: Biological, Chemical and Physical Agents of Environmentally Related Diseases*. Boca Raton, FL: Lewis Publishers.

Kouznetsova, M., X. Huang, J. Ma, L. Lessner, and D.O. Carpenter. (2007). "Increased Rate of Hospitalization for Diabetes and Residential Proximity of Hazardous Waste Sites." *Environmental Health Perspectives* 115,1: 75-79.

Kramer, R. (2012). "Public Criminology and the Responsibility to Speak in the Prophetic Voice Concerning Global Warming." In E. Stanley and J. McCulloch (eds), *State Crime and Resistance*. London: Routledge, 41-53.

Kramer, R. and R. Michalowski. (2012). "Is Global Warming a State-Corporate Crime?" In R. White (ed.), *Climate Change from a Criminological Perspective*. New York, NY: Springer, 71-88.

Kramer, U., T. Koch, U. Ranft, J. Ring, and H. Benrendt. (2000). "Traffic Related Air Pollution is Associated with Atopy in Children Living in Urban Areas." *Epidemiology* 11,1: 64-70.

Krivo, L.J. and R.D. Peterson. (1996). "Extremely Disadvantaged Neighborhoods and Urban Crime." *Social Forces* 75,2: 619-48.

Lancaster, M. (2002). *Green Chemistry: An Introduction*. Cambridge: The Royal Society of Chemistry.

Lane, P. (1998). "Ecofeminism Meets Criminology." *Theoretical Criminology* 2: 235-48.

Lannig, G., J.F. Flores and I.M. Sokolova. (2006). "Temperature-Dependent Stress Response in Oysters, *Crassostrea Virginica*: Pollution Reduces Temperature Tolerance in Oysters." *Aquatic Toxicology* 79: 278-87.

Lapens, D.R., E. Topp, C.D. Metcalfe, H. Li, M. Edwards, N. Gottschall, P. Bollen, W. Cirnoe, M. Payne, and A. Beck. (2008). "Pharmaceutical and Personal Care Products in Tile Drainage Following Land Application of Municipal Biosolids." *Science of the Total Environment* 399,1-3: 50-65.

Laskar, J. (1995). "The Chaotic Motion of the Solar System." In J. Trân Thanh Vân, P. Bergé, R. Conte, and M. Dubois (eds), *Chaos and Complexity*. Gif-sur-Yvette Cedex: Editions Frontières, 53-62.

Laurance, W.F. and G.B. Williamson. (2001). "Positive Feedbacks among Forest Fragmentation, Drought, and Climate Change in the Amazon." *Conservation Biology* 15,6: 1529-35.

Lavelle, M. and M. Coyle. (1992). "Unequal Protection: The Racial Divide in Environmental Law." *National Law Journal* 21: S1-S11.

Lemieux, A.M. and R.V. Clarke. (2009). "The International Ban on Ivory Sales and Its Effect on Elephant Poaching in Africa." *British Journal of Criminology* 49,4: 451-71.

Lenton, T.M. (2011). "Early Warning of Climate Tipping Points." *Nature Climate Change* 1: 201-9.

Levin, E.D., M.L. Schneider, S.A. Ferguson, S.L. Schantz, and R.E. Bowman. (1988). "Behavioral Effects of Developmental Lead Exposure in Rhesus Monkeys." *Developmental Psychobiology* 21,4: 271-82.

Li, X.Y., P.S. Gilmour, K. Donaldson, and W. MacNee. (1996). "Free Radical Activity and Pro-Inflammatory Effects of Particle Air Pollution (PM10) in Vivo and in Vitro." *Thorax* 51,12: 12-16.

Liebsch, D., M.C.M. Marques, and R. Goldenberg. (2008). "How Long Does the Atlantic Rain Forest Take to Recover after a Disturbance? Changes in Species Composition and Ecological Features during Secondary Succession." *Biological Conservation* 141,6: 1717-25.

Liu, F. (2001). *Environmental Justice Analysis: Theories, Methods and Practice.* Boca Raton, FL: Lewis Publishers.

Long, M.A., M.J. Hogan, P.B. Stretesky, and M.J. Lynch. (2007). "The Relationship Between Post-War Reconstruction Contracts and Political Donations: The Case in Afghanistan and Iraq." *Sociological Spectrum* 27: 453-72.

Long, M., P. Stretesky, M.J. Lynch, and E. Fenwick. (2011). "Crime in the Coal Industry: Implications for Green Criminology and Treadmill of Production." Paper presented at the American Society of Criminology, Washington D.C.

——. (2012). "Crime in the Coal Industry: Implications for Green Criminology and Treadmill of Production." *Organization and Environment* 25,3: 328-46.

Lovelock, J. (1979). *Gaia: A New Look at Life on Earth.* Oxford: Oxford University Press.

——. (1991). *Scientists on Gaia.* Cambridge, MA: MIT Press.

——. (2007). *The Revenge of Gaia: Earth's Climate Crisis and the Fate of Humanity.* New York, NY: Basic Books.

——. (2009). *The Vanishing Face of Gaia: A Final Warning.* London: Allen Lane.

Lynch, J. and G. Davey Smith. (2005). "A Life Course Approach to Chronic Disease." *Annual Review of Public Health* 26: 1-35.

Lynch, M.J. (1990). "The Greening of Criminology: A Perspective for the 1990s." *The Critical Criminologist* 2,3: 3-4, 11-12 (reprinted in P. Beirne and N. South (eds). (2007). *Green Criminology.* Aldershot: Ashgate, 165-70).

——. (2000). "The Power of Oppression: Toward Understanding the History of Criminology as a Science of Oppression." *Critical Criminology* 9,1-2: 144-52.

——. (2004). "Toward a Radical Ecology of Urban Violence: Integrating Medical, Epidemiological, Environmental and Criminological Research on Class, Race, Lead (Pb) and Crime." In M. Zahn, H. Brownstein, and S. Jackson (eds), *Violence: From Theory to Research.* Cincinnati, OH: Anderson, 103-20.

——. (2007). *Big Prisons, Big Dreams: Crime and the Failure of the U.S. Prison System.* New Brunswick, NJ: Rutgers University Press.

——. (2013). "Reexamining Political Economy and Crime: Exploring the Crime Expansion and Drop." *Journal of Crime and Justice* 36,2: 250-64.

Lynch, M.J., R.G. Burns, and P.B. Stretesky. (2010). "Global Warming as a State-Corporate Crime: The Politicalization of Global Warming during the Bush Administration." *Crime, Law and Social Change* 54,3: 213-39.

Lynch, M.J. and W.B. Groves. (1995). "In Defense of Comparative Criminology: A Critique of General Theory and the Rational Man." *Advances in Criminological Theory. Volume 6*. New Brunswick, NJ: Transaction.

Lynch, M.J. and R.J. Michalowski. (2006). *Primer in Radical Criminology.* Boulder, CO: Lynne Rienner.

Lynch, M.J., M.K. Nalla, and K.W. Miller. (1989). "Cross Cultural Perceptions of Deviance: The Case of Bhopal." *Journal of Research in Crime and Delinquency* 26,1: 7-35.

Lynch, M.J., E.B. Patterson and K.K. Childs. (2008). *Racial Divide: Racial and Ethnic Bias in the Criminal Justice System*. Monsey, NY. Criminal Justice Press.

Lynch, M.J., H. Schwendinger, and J. Schwendinger. (2006). "The Status of Empirical Research in Radical Criminology." In F.T. Cullen, J.P. Wright, and K.R. Blevins (eds), *Taking Stock: The Status of Criminological Theory. Advances in Criminological Theory, Volume 15*. New Brunswick, NJ: Transaction, 191-215.

Lynch, M.J. and P.B. Stretesky. (2001). "Toxic Crimes: Examining Corporate Victimization of the General Public Employing Medical and Epidemiological Evidence." *Critical Criminology* 10,3 153-72.

———. (2003). "The Meaning of Green: Contrasting Criminological Perspectives." *Theoretical Criminology* 7,2: 217-38.

Lynch, M.J., P.B. Stretesky, and R.G. Burns. (2004a). "Determinants of Environmental Law Violation Fines Against Oil Refineries: Race, Ethnicity, Income and Aggregation Effects." *Society and Natural Resources* 17,4: 333-47.

———. (2004b). "Slippery Business: Race, Class and Legal Determinants of Penalties Against Petroleum Refineries." *Journal of Black Studies* 34,3: 421-40.

Lynch, V.D. (1966). "The Pharmacology of Addicting Drugs." *The Catholic Lawyer* 12: 121-30.

Lyndsay, R.W. and J. Zhang. (2005). "The Thinning of Arctic Sea Ice: Have We Passed a Tipping Point?" *Journal of Climate* 18: 4879-94.

Ma, J., M. Kouznetsova, L. Lessner, and D.O. Carpenter. (2007). "Asthma and Infectious Respiratory Disease in Children: Correlation to Residence Near Hazardous Waste Sites." *Pediatric Respiratory Review* 8,4: 292-8.

Mabey, N. and R. McNally. (1999). *Foreign Direct Investment and the Environment: From Pollution Havens to Sustainable Development*. World Wildlife Fund. Available at: http://www.oecd.org/dataoecd/9/48/2089912.pdf (accessed April 2013).

Maltby L. and C. Naylor. (1990). "Preliminary Observations on the Ecological Relevance of the Gammarus 'Scope for Growth' Assay: Effect of Zinc on Reproduction" *Functional Ecology* 4,3: 393-7.

Malvezzi C.K., E.G. Moreira, I. Vassilieff, V.S. Vassilieff, and S. Cordellini. (2001). "Effect of L-arginine, DMSA and the Association of L-arginine and DMSA on Tissue Lead Mobilization and Blood Pressure Level in Plumbism." *Brazilian Journal of Medical and Biological Research* 34: 1341-6.

Margai, F. and N. Henry. (2003). "A Community-Based Assessment of Learning Disabilities Using Environmental and Contextual Risk Factors." *Social Science and Medicine* 56,5: 1073-85.

Markowitz, G. and D. Rosner. (2002). *Deceit and Denial: The Deadly Politics of Industrial Pollution*. Berkeley, CA: University of California Press.

Marshall, J.D., T.E. McKone, E. Deakin, and W.W. Nazaroff. (2005). "Inhalation of Motor Vehicle Emissions: Effects of Urban Population and Land Area." *Atmospheric Environment* 39,2: 283-95.

Marshall, J.D., E. Nethery, and M. Brauer. (2008). "Within-Urban Variability in Ambient Air Pollution: Comparison of Estimation Methods." *Atmospheric Environment* 42,6: 1359-69.

Massey, D. and N. Denton. (1993). *American Apartheid: Segregation and the Making of the American Underclass*. Cambridge, MA: Harvard University Press.

Mayer, F.L., G.E. Marking, J.A. Brecken, T.K. Linton, T.D. Bills. (1991). *Physicochemical Factors Affecting Toxicity: pH, Salinity, and Temperature. Part 1 Literature Review*. EPA 600/X-89/033. Gulf Breeze, FL: U.S. Environmental Protection Agency.

McChesney, R.W. and D. Schillar. (2003). *The Political Economy of International Communications: Foundations for the Emerging Global Debate about Media Ownership and Regulations*. Technology, Business and Society, Programme Paper no. 11. Geneva: United Nations Research Institute for Social Development.

McDonnell, M.J., S.P.A. Pickett, P. Groffman, P. Bohlen, R.V. Pouyat, W.C. Zipperer, R.W. Parmelee, M.M. Carreiro, and K. Medley. (1997). "Ecosystem Processes along an Urban-Rural Gradient." *Urban Ecosystems* 1,1: 21-36.

McDonough, W. and M. Braungart. (2002a). *Cradle to Cradle: Remaking the Way We Make Things*. New York, NY: North Point Press.

——. (2002b). "Design for Triple Top Line: New Tools for Sustainable Commerce." *Corporate Environmental Strategy* 9,2: 251-8.

McGinnity, P., E. Jennings, E. de Eyto, N. Allott, P. Samuelsson, G. Rogan, K. Whelan, and T. Cross. (2009). "Impact of Naturally Spawning Captive-bred Atlantic Salmon on Wild Populations: Depressed Recruitment and Increased Risk of Climate-mediated Extinction." *Proceeding of the Royal Society, Biological Sciences* 276,1673: 3601-10.

McKenzie, L.M., R. Witter, L. Newman, and J. Adgate. (2012). "Human Health Risk Assessment of Air Emissions from Development of Unconventional Natural Gas Resources." *Science of the Total Environment* 1,424: 79-87.

McKibben, B. (2007 [1997]). *The End of Nature*. New York, NY: Anchor Books.

——. (2010). *Eaarth: Making a Life on a Tough New Planet*. New York, NY: Times Books.

McKinney, J.C. (1950). "The Role of Constructive Typology in Scientific Sociological Analysis." *Social Forces* 28,3: 235-40.

—— (1969). "Typification, Typologies, and Social Theory." *Social Forces* 48,1: 1-12.

Merchant, C. (2005). *Radical Ecology: The Search for a Livable World*. London: Routledge.

Meyer, C.B. (1988). "The Environmental Fate of Toxic Waste, the Certainty of Harm, Toxic Torts and Toxic Regulation." *Environmental Law* 19: 321-56.

Meyer J. and R. DiGiulio. (2002). "Patterns of Heritability of Decreased EROD Activity and Resistance to PCB 126-induced Teratogenesis in Laboratory-reared Offspring of Killifish (Fundulus heteroclitus) from a Creosote-contaminated Site in the Elizabeth River, VA, USA." *Marine Environment Research* 54: 621-6.

Mieczkowski, T. (ed.). (1999). *Drug Testing Technologies: Field Applications and Assessments*. Boca Raton, FL: CRC Press.

——. (2004). "Assessing the Potential of a 'Color Effect' for Hair Analysis of 11-nor-9-carboxy-Δ9-Tetrahydrocannibinol: Analysis of a Large Sample of Hair Specimens." *Life Sciences* 74: 463-9.

Mieczkowski, T. and C. Sullivan. (2007). "The Use of Bayes Coefficients to Assess the Racial Bias-Hair Analysis Conjecture for Detection of Cocaine and Cocaine Metabolites in Hair Samples." *Forensic Science Communications* 9,12: 1-16.

Mill, J. and A. Petronas. (2008). "Pre-and Peri-natal Environmental Risks for Attention-Deficit Hyperactivity Disorder (ADHD): The Potential Role of Epigenetic Processes in Mediating Susceptibility." *Journal of Child Psychology and Psychiatry* 49,10: 1020-30.

Mills, C.W. (1959). *The Sociological Imagination*. New York, NY: Oxford University Press.

Mitchell, M.S., M.J. Reynolds-Hogland, M.L. Smith, P. Bohall Wood, J.A. Beebe, P.D. Keyser, C Loehle, C.J. Reynolds, P. Van Deusen, and D. White Jr. (2008). "Projected Long-term Response of Southeastern Birds to Forest Management." *Forest Ecology and Management* 256,11: 1884-96.

Molina, P. (2003). *Endocrine Physiology*. New York, NY: McGraw-Hill Medical.

Moreira, E. G., Vassilieff, I., & Vassilieff, V. S. (2001). "Developmental lead exposure: behavioral alterations in the short and long term." *Neurotoxicology and teratology*, *23*, 5: 489-95.

Morello-Frosch, R. and B.M. Jesdale. (2005). "Separate and Unequal: Residential Segregation and Estimated Cancer Risks Associated with Ambient Air Toxins in US Metropolitan Areas." *Environmental Health Perspectives* 114,3: 386-93.

Moriarty, F. (1983). *Ecotoxicology: The Study of Pollutants in Ecosystems*. London: Academic Press.

Motavalli, J. (2011). "A History of Greenwashing: How Dirty Towels Impacted the Green Movement." *Daily Finance*. February 12. Available at: http://www. dailyfinance.com/2011/02/12/the-history-of-greenwashing-how-dirty-towels-impacted-the-green/ (accessed April 2013).

Nakajima, S., Y. Saijo, S. Kato, S. Sasaki, A. Uno, N. Kanagami, H. Hirakawa, T. Hori, K. Tobiishi, T. Todaka, Y. Nakamura, S. Yanagiya, Y. Sengoku, T. Iida, F. Sata, and R. Kishi. (2006). "Effects of Prenatal Exposure to Polychlorinated Biphenyls and Dioxins on Mental and Motor Development in Japanese Children at 6 Months of Age." *Environmental Health Perspective* 114,5: 773-8.

Narag, R.E., J. Pizarro, and C. Gibbs. (2009). "Lead Exposure and Its Implications for Criminological Theory." *Criminal Justice and Behavior* 36,9: 954-73.

National Academy of Science. (1993). *Population Summit of the World's Scientific Academies*. Washington, DC: National Academies Press. Available at: http://www.nap.edu/openbook.php?record_id=9148 (accessed April 2013).

Navas-Acien, A., E.K. Silbergeld, R. Pastor-Barriuso, and E. Guallar. (2008). "Arsenic Exposure and Prevalence of Type 2 Diabetes in US Adults." *Journal of the American Medical Association* 300,7: 814-22.

Neal, A.P. and T.R. Guilarte. (2009). "Molecular Neurobiology of Lead ($Pb^{2}+$): Effects on Synaptic Function." *Molecular Neurobiology* 42,3: 151-60.

Needleman, H.L., C. Gunnoe, A. Leviton, R. Reed, H. Peresie, C. Maher, and P. Barrett. (1979). "Deficits in Psychologic and Classroom Performance of Children with Elevated Dentine Lead Levels." *New England Journal of Medicine* 300,13: 689-95.

Needleman, H.L., C. McFarland, R.B. Ness, S.E. Fienberg, and M.J. Tobin. (2002). "Bone Lead Levels in Adjudicated Delinquents: A Case Control Study." *Neurotoxicology and Teratology* 24,6: 711-17.

Needleman, H.L., J.A. Riess, M.J. Tobin, G.E. Biesecker, and J.B. Greenhouse. (1996). "Bone Lead Levels and Delinquent Behavior." *Journal of the American Medical Association* 275,5: 363-9.

Nemerow, N.L. (1963). *Theories and Practices of Industrial Waste Treatment*. Reading, MA: Addison-Wesley.

Nemerow, N.L. and F.J. Agardy. (1998). *Strategies of Industrial and Hazardous Waste Management*. New York, NY: Van Nostrand Reinhold.

Nevin, R. (2000). "How Lead Exposure is Related to Temporal Changes in IQ, Violent Crime and Unwed Pregnancies." *Environmental Research* 83,1: 1-22.

———. (2007). "Understanding International Crime Trends: The Legacy of Preschool Lead Exposure." *Environmental Research* 104,3: 315-36.

———. (2009). "Trends in Preschool Lead Exposure, Metal Retardation and Scholastic Achievement: Association or Causation?" *Environmental Research* 109,3: 301-10.

Nielsen, A.L., M.T. Lee, and R. Martinez. (2005). "Integrating Race, Place and Motive in Social Disorganization Theory: Lessons for the Comparison of

Black and Latino Homicide Types in Two Immigrant Destination Cities." *Criminology* 43,3: 837-72.

Nobre, C.A. and L.D.S. Borma. (2009). "Tipping Points for the Amazon Forest." *Current Opinion in Environmental Sustainability* 1,1: 28-36.

Noyes, P.D., M.K. McElwee, H.D. Miller, B.W. Clark, L.A. Van Tiem, K.C. Walcott, K.N. Erwin, and E.D. Levin. (2009). "The Toxicology of Climate Change: Environmental Contaminants in a Warming World." *Environment International* (Pre-publication draft release).

Nriagu, J.O. (1990). "Global Metal Pollution, Poisoning the Biosphere?" *Environment* 32,7: 7-33.

Nurse, A. (2013). "Privatising the Green Police: The Role of NGOs in Wildlife Law Enforcement." *Crime, Law and Social Change* 59,3: 305-18.

O'Connor, J. (1973). *The Fiscal Crisis of the State*. New York, NY: Macmillan.

O'Donnell, J. (1985). *The Origins of Behaviorism: American Psychology, 1870-1920*. New York, NY: New York University Press.

Obach, B. (2007). "Theoretical Interpretations of the Growth in Organic Agriculture: Agricultural Modernization or Organic Treadmill?" *Society and Natural Resources* 20,3: 229-44.

Olympio, K.P.K., P.V. Oliveira, J. Naozuka, M.R.A. Cardoso, A.F. Marques, W.M.R. Günther, and E.J.H. Bechara. (2010). "Surface Dental Enamel Lead Levels and Antisocial Behavior in Brazilian Adolescents." *Neurotoxicology and Teratology* 32,2: 273-9.

Osborne, S.J., C.M. Shy, and B.M. Kaplan. (1990). "Epidemiologic Analysis of a Reported Cancer Cluster in a Small Rural Population." *American Journal of Epidemiology* 132,1: S87-S95.

Ozawa, H., A. Ohmura, R.D. Lorenz, and T. Pujol. (2003). "The Second Law of Thermodynamics and the Global Climate System: A Review of the Maximum Entropy Production Principle." *Reviews of Geophysics* 41: 1018-33.

Ozymy, J. and M.L. Jarrell. (2011). "Upset over Air Pollution: Analyzing Upset Event Emissions at Petroleum Refineries." *Review of Policy Research* 28,4: 365-82.

———. (2012). "Upset Events, Regulatory Drift, and the Regulation of Air Emissions at Industrial Facilities in the United States." *Environmental Politics* 21,3: 451-66.

Pacyna, E.G., J.M. Pacyna, F. Steenhuisen, and S. Wilson. (2006). "Global Anthropogenic Mercury Emission Inventory for 2000." *Atmospheric Environment* 40,22: 4048-63.

Palanza, P., F. Morellinia, S. Parmigiania, and F.S. vom Saal. (1999). "Prenatal Exposure to Endocrine Disrupting Chemicals: Effects on Behavioral Development." *Neuroscience and Biobehavioral Reviews* 23,7: 1011-27.

Park, R.E., E.W. Burgess, and R.D. McKenzie. (1925). *The City: Suggestions for Investigation of Human Behavior in the Urban Environment*. Chicago, IL: University of Chicago Press.

Parker, L. (2007). "Mining Battle Marked by Peaks and Valleys." *USA Today*. April 18. Available at: http://www.usatoday.com/news/nation/2007-04-18-mines_N.htm (accessed October 13, 2008).

Parmesan, C. (2006). "Ecological and Evolutionary Responses to Recent Climate Change." *Annual Review of Ecological Systems* 37: 637-69.

Patra, R.W., J.C. Chapman, R.P. Lim, and P.C. Gehrke. (2007). "The Effects of Three Organic Chemicals on the Upper Thermal Tolerances of Four Freshwater Fishes." *Environmental Toxicology and Chemistry* 26,7: 1454-9.

Pavlov, I. (1927). *Conditioned Reflexes*. London: Routledge and Kegan Paul.

——. (1929). *Lectures on Conditioned Reflexes: Twenty Five Years of Objective Study of the Higher Nervous Activity Behavior of Animals*. Moscow: International Publishers.

Pearce, F. (2008). *With Speed and Violence: Why Scientists Fear Tipping Points in Climate Change*. Boston, MA: Beacon Press.

Pearce, F. and S. Tombs. (1993). "US Capital versus the Third World: Union Carbide and Bhopal." In F. Pearce and M. Woodiwiss (eds), *Global Crime Connections*. Toronto: University of Toronto Press, 187-211.

Pelletier, M. (2002). *Monitoring the State of the St. Lawrence River*. Quebec: Minister of the Environment. Available at: http://www.planstlaurent.qc.ca/sl_obs/sesl/publications/fiches_indicateurs/sediments_lsf_2002_e.pdf (accessed April 2013).

Pellow, D.N. (2000). "Environmental Inequality Formation." *American Behavioral Scientist* 43: 581-601.

——. (2004). *Garbage Wars: The Struggle for Environmental Justice in Chicago*. Cambridge, MA: MIT Press.

Peters, A., D.W. Dockery, J.E. Muller, and M.A. Mittleman. (2001). "Increased Particulate Air Pollution and the Triggering of Myocardial Infarction." *Circulation* 103: 2810-15.

Peters, J.M., E. Avol, W. Navida, S.J. London, W.J. Gauderman, F. Lurmann, W.S. Linn, H. Margolis, E. Rappaport, H. Gong, and D.C. Thomas. (1999). "A Study of Twelve Southern California Communities with Differing Levels and Types of Air Pollution. II. Effects on Pulmonary Function." *American Journal of Respiratory and Critical Care Management* 159: 760-67.

Petit, T.L. and D.P. Alfano. (1979). "Differential Experience Following Developmental Lead Exposure: Effects on Brain and Behavior." *Pharmacology, Biochemistry and Behavior* 11,2: 165-71.

Phillips, B. (2001). *Beyond Sociology's Tower of Babble: Reconstructing the Scientific Method*. Piscataway, NJ: Adline Press.

Phillips, B., H. Kincaid, and T. Scheff (eds). (2002). *Toward a Sociological Imagination: Bridging Specialized Fields*. Lanham, MD: University Press of America.

Pires, S. and R.V. Clarke. (2011). "Are Parrots CRAVED? An Analysis of Parrot Poaching in Mexico." *Journal of Research in Crime and Delinquency* 49,1: 122-46.

Pond, G., M. Passmore, F. Borsuk, L. Reynolds, and C. Rose. (2008). "Downstream Effects of Mountaintop Coal Mining: Comparing Biological Conditions Using Family and Genus Level Macroinvertebrate Bioassessment Tools," *Journal of the North American Benthological Society* 27: 717-37.

Pope, C.A., R.T. Burnett, M.J. Thun, E.E. Callie, D. Krewski, K. Ito, and G.C. Thurston. (2002). "Lung Cancer, Cardiopulmonary Mortality, and Long-Term Exposure to Fine Particulate Air Pollution." *Journal of the American Medical Association* 287: 1123-41.

Popkin, R. (1986). "Two 'Killer Smogs' The Headlines Missed." *The EPA Journal* 12: 27-9.

Porter, W.P., S. Budaraju, W.E. Stewart, and N. Ramankutty. (2000). "Calculating Climate Effects on Birds and Mammals: Impacts on Biodiversity, Conservation, Population Parameters, and Global Community Structure." *American Zoology* 40: 597-630.

Portner, H.O. (2002). "Climate Variations and the Physiological Basis of Temperature Dependent Biogeography: Systemic to Molecular Hierarchy of Thermal Tolerance in Animals." *Comparative Biochemistry and Physiology: Part A, Molecular and Integrative Physiology* 132, 4: 739-61.

Powell, D.L. and V. Stewart. (2001). "Children: The Unwitting Targets of Environmental Injustice." *Pediatric Clinics of North America* 48,5: 1291-305.

Preston, B.L., R.C. Warren, S.M. Wooten, R.D. Gragg, and B. Walker. (2001). "Environmental Health and Antisocial Behavior: Implications for Public Policy." *Journal of Environmental Health* 63,9: 9-19.

Putnam, H. (1965). "Brains and Behavior." In R.J. Butler (ed.), *Analytical Philosophy*. Oxford: Blackwell, 1-19.

Quentin-Baxter, M. and D. Dewhurst. (1992). "An Interactive Computer Based Alternative to Performing a Rat Dissection in the Classroom." *Journal of Biological Education* 26,1: 27-33.

Raaschou-Nielson, O., O. Hertle, B.L. Thomsen, and J.H. Olsen. (2001). "Air Pollution from Traffic at the Residence of Children with Cancer." *American Journal of Epidemiology* 153,5: 433-43.

Raine, A. (1993). *The Psychopathology of Crime: Criminal Behavior as a Clinical Disorder*. San Diego, CA: Academic Press.

Rand, G.M. and S.R. Petrocelli. (1985). *Fundamentals of Aquatic Toxicology: Methods and Applications*. Princeton, NJ: FMC Corp.

Rand, M. (2008). *Criminal Victimization, 2007* (NCJRS 224390, December, 2008). Washington, DC: US Department of Justice. Available at: http://www.ojp.usdoj.gov/bjs/pub/pdf/cv07.pdf (accessed April 2013).

Reece, E. (2006). *Lost Mountain: A Year in the Vanishing Wilderness*. New York, NY: Riverhead Books.

Rees, W.E. (1997). "Urban Ecosystems: The Human Dimension." *Urban Ecosystems* 1,1: 63-75.

Regan, T. (2004). *The Case for Animal Rights*. Berkeley, CA: University of California Press.

Reiman, C. and P. de Cariatt. (2005). "Distinguishing between Natural and Anthropogenic Sources for Elements in the Environment: Regional Geochemical Surveys Versus Enrichment Factors." *Science of the Total Environment* 337,1-3: 91-107.

Reiman, J. (2006). *The Rich Get Richer and the Poor Get Prison.* Boston, MA: Allyn & Bacon.

Ren, C., P.S. Vokonas, H. Suh, S. Fang, D.C. Christiani, and J. Schwartz. (2010). "Effect Modification of Air Pollution on Urinary 8-Hydroxy-2'-Deoxyguanosine by Genotypes: An Application of the Multiple Testing Procedure to Identify Significant SNP Interactions." *Environmental Health* 9: 78-97.

Reuters. (2012). "Geithner Says U.S. Economy Showing Signs of Expansion." *New York Times Online.* March 15. Available at: http://www.nytimes.com/2012/03/16/business/geithner-says-us-economy-showing-signs-of-growth.html (accessed April 2013).

Reyes, J.W. (2007). "Environmental Policy as Social Policy? The Impact of Childhood Lead Exposure on Crime." *The B.E. Journal of Economic Analysis and Policy* 7,1. Available at: http://www.nber.org/papers/w13097 (accessed April 2013).

Reynolds, P., J. van Behren, R. Gunier, D.E. Goldberg, and A. Hertz. (2004). "Residential Exposure to Traffic and Childhood Cancer." *Epidemology* 15,1: 6-12.

Reynolds, P., J. van Behren, R. Gunier, D.E. Goldberg, A. Hertz, and D.F. Smith. (2003). "Childhood Cancer Incident Rates and Hazardous Air Pollutants in California: An Exploratory Study." *Environmental Health Perspectives* 111,4: 663-8.

Rice, D.C. (1996). "Behavioral Effects of Lead: Commonalities between Experimental and Epidemiologic Data." *Environmental Health Perspectives* 104,2: 337-351.

Richards, V.L. and T.L. Beitinger. (1995). "Reciprocal Influences of Temperature and Copper on Survival of Fathead Minnows, Pimephales Promelas." *Bulletin of Environmental Contamination and Toxicology* 55: 230-36.

Ridker, R.G. and J.A. Henning. (1967). "The Determinants of Residential Property Values with Special Reference to Air Pollution." *The Review of Economics and Statistics* 49,2: 246-57.

Rifkin, J. (1995). *The End of Work: The Decline of the Global Labor Force and the Dawn of the Post-Market Era.* New York, NY: Putnam.

Rijnsdorp, A.D., M.A. Peck, G.H. Engelhard, C. Möllmann, and J.K. Pinnegar. (2009). "Resolving the Effect of Climate Change on Fish Populations." *ICES Journal of Marine Science* 66,7: 1570-83.

Rodricks, J. (2007). *Calculated Risks: The Toxicity and Human Health Risks of Chemicals in Our Environment.* Cambridge: Cambridge University Press.

Rogan, W.J. and N.B. Ragan. (2003). "Evidence of the Effect of Environmental Chemicals on the Endocrine System in Children." *Pediatrics* 112,1: 247-52.

Rogers, H. (2010). *Green Gone Wrong: How Our Economy is Undermining the Green Revolution.* New York, NY: Scribner.

Roos-Barraclough, F., A. Martinez-Cortizas, E. Garcia-Rodeja, and W. Shotyk. (2002). "A 14,500 Year Record of the Accumulation of Atmospheric Mercury in Peat: Volcanic Signals, Anthropogenic Influences and a Correlation to Bromine Accumulation." *Earth Planet Science Letter* 202,2: 435-51.

Rosen, C.M. (1995). "Businessmen Against Pollution in Late Nineteenth Century Chicago." *Business History Review* 69: 351-97.

Rosner, D. and G. Markowitz. (1989). *Dying for Work: Workers' Safety and Health in Twentieth-Century America.* Bloomington, IN: Indiana University Press.

——. (1994). *Deadly Dust: Silicosis and the Politics of Occupational Disease in Twentieth-Century America.* Princeton, NJ: Princeton University Press.

Roth, R. (2011). "Biology and the Deep History of Homicide." *British Journal of Criminology* 51,3: 535-55.

Ruggiero, V. and N. South. (2010). Green Criminology and Dirty Collar Crime. *Critical Criminology* 18,4: 251-62.

——. (2013). "Green Criminology and Crimes of the Economy: Theory, Research and Praxis." *Critical Criminology* 21,3: 359-73.

Ruhl, L., A. Vengosh, G.S. Dwyer, H. Hsu-Kim, A. Deonarine, M. Bergin, and J. Kravchenko. (2009). "Survey of the Potential Environmental and Health Impacts in the Immediate Aftermath of the Coal Ash Spill in Kingston, Tennessee." *Environmental Science and Technology* 43,16: 6326-33.

Sampson, R.J. and W.B. Groves. (1989). "Community Structure and Crime: Testing Social-Disorganization Theory." *American Journal of Sociology* 94: 774-802.

Schantz, S.L. and J.J. Widholm. (2001). "Cognitive Effects of Endocrine-disrupting Chemicals in Animals." *Environmental Health Perspectives* 109,12: 1197-206.

Schaper, M. and J. Jofre. (2000). "Comparison of Methods for Detecting Genotypes of F-Specific RNA Bacteriophages and Fingerprinting the Origins of Faecal Pollution in Water Samples." *Journal of Virological Methods* 89,1-2: 1-10.

Schnaiberg, A. (1980). *The Environment: From Surplus to Scarcity*, New York, NY: Oxford University Press.

Schwetz, B.A., J.M. Norris, G.L. Sparschu, U.K. Rowe, P.J. Gehring, J.L. Emerson, and C.G. Gerbig. (1973). "Toxicology of Chlorinated Dibenzo-p-dioxins." *Environmental Health Perspective* 5: 87-99.

Selin, N.E., D.J. Jacob, R.M. Yantosca, S. Strode, L. Jaegle, and E.M. Sunderland. (2008). "Global 3-D Land-Ocean-Atmosphere Model for Mercury: Present-day Versus Preindustrial Cycles and Anthropogenic Enrichment Factors for Deposition." *Global Biochemical Cycles* 22: 1-13. Available at: http://dash. harvard.edu/bitstream/handle/1/3554408/Jacob_LandOceanAtmosphere. pdf?sequence=1 (accessed April 2013).

Selvia, M. and A. Perosa. (2008). "Green Chemistry Metrics: A Comparative Evaluation of Dimethyl Carbonate, Methyl Iodide, Dimethyl Sulfate and Methanol as Methylating Agents." *Green Chemistry* 10: 457-64.

Semlitsch, R.D., C.A. Conner, D.J. Hocking, T.A.G. Rittenhouse, and E.B. Harper. (2008). "Effects of Timber Harvesting on Pond-Breeding Amphibian Persistence: Testing the Evacuation Hypothesis." *Ecological Applications* 18: 283-9.

Semlitsch, R.D., B.D. Todd, S.M. Blomquist, A.J.K. Calhoun, J.W. Gibbons, J.P. Gibbs, G.J. Graeter, E.B. Harper, D.J. Hocking, M.L. Hunter Jr., D.A. Patrick, T.A.G. Rittenhouse, and B.B. Rothermel. (2009). "Effects of Timber Harvest on Amphibian Populations: Understanding Mechanisms from Forest Experiments." *BioScience* 59: 853-62.

Sergeev, A.V. and D.O. Carpenter. (2005). "Residential Proximity to Environmental Sources of Persistent Organic Pollutants and First-time Hospitalizations for Myocardial Infarction with Comorbid Diabetes Mellitus: A 12-year Population-based Study." *International Journal of Occupational Medicine and Environmental Health* 113,6: 756-61.

——. (2010). "Increased Hospitalizations for Ischemic Stroke with Comorbid Diabetes and Residential Proximity to Sources of Organic Pollutants: A 12-Year Population-Based Study." *Neuro-epidemiology* 35,3: 196-201.

——. (2011). "Increase in Metabolic Syndrome-Related Hospitalizations in Relation to Environmental Sources of Persistent Organic Pollutants." *International Journal for Research on Environmental Health* 8,3: 762-76.

Serra, A. and H. Guasch. (2009). "Effects of Chronic Copper Exposure on Fluvial Systems: Linking Structural and Physiological Changes of Fluvial Biofilms with the In-stream Copper Retention." *Science of the Total Environment* 407,19: 5274-82.

Sherman, L. (2005). "The Use and Usefulness of Criminology, 1751-2005: Enlightened Justice and Its Failures." *The Annals of the American Academy of Political and Social Science* 600,1: 115-35.

Shoulars, K., M.A. Rodriguez, T. Thompson, J. Turk, J. Crowley, and B.M. Markaverich. (2008). "Regulation of the Nitric Oxide Pathway Genes by Tetrahydrofurandiols: Microarray Analysis of MCF-7 Human Breast Cancer Cells." *Cancer Letter* 264,2: 265-73.

Silver, P.G. and M.D. Behn. (2008). "Intermittent Plate Tectonics?" *Science* 319,5859: 85-8.

Singer, P. (1990). *Animal Liberation*. New York, NY: New York Review of Books.

Sipes, I.G. (2002). *Comprehensive Toxicology, Volume 14*. Waltham, MD: Elsevier.

Sipes, I.G. and A.J. Gandolfi. (1991). "Biotransformation of Toxicants." In M.O. Amdur, J. Doull, and C.D. Klaassen (eds), *Casarett and Doull's Toxicology: The Basic Science of Poisons*. New York, NY: Pergamon Press, 88-126.

Situ, Y. (1997). "A Pathway to the Knowledge of Environmental Crime: Learning Through Service." *Journal of Criminal Justice Education* 8,2: 243-351.

Skinner, B.F. (1965 [1953]). *Science and Human Behavior*. New York, NY: The Free Press.

——. (1974). *About Behaviorism*. New York, NY: Knopf.

Smith, V.K. and J.C. Huang. (1993). "Hedonic Models and Air Pollution: Twenty-Five Years and Counting." *Environmental and Resource Economics* 3: 381-94.

Snyder, S.A., P. Westerhoff, Y. Yoon, and D.L. Sedlak. (2004). "Pharmaceuticals, Personal Care Products, and Endocrine Disruptors in Water: Implications for the Water Industry." *Environmental Engineering Science* 20,5: 446-69.

Sokolova, I.M. (2004). "Cadmium Effects on Mitochondrial Function are Enhanced by Elevated Temperatures in a Marine Poikilotherm, Crassostrea Virginica Gmelin (Bivalvia: Ostreidae)." *Journal of Experimental Biology* 207: 2639-48.

Sollund, R. (2008). *Global Harms: Ecological Crime and Speciesism*. Portland, OR: Book News.

South, N. (1998). "A Green Field for Criminology? A Proposal for a Perspective." *Theoretical Criminology* 2: 211-33.

———. (2007). "The 'Corporate Colonisation of Nature:' Bio-Prospecting and Bio-Piracy and the Development of Green Criminology." In P. Beirne and N. South (eds), *Issues in Green Criminology*. Cullompton: Willan, 230-47.

South, N. and A. Brisman. (2013). *Routledge International Handbook of Green Criminology*. New York, NY: Routledge.

Staats, A.W. (1994). "Psychological Behaviorism and Behaviorizing Psychology." *Behavioral Analysis* 17,1: 93-114.

Stitt, B.G. and D. Giacopassi. (1995). "Assessing Victimization from Corporate Harms." In M. Blankenship (ed.), *Understanding Corporate Criminality*. New York, NY: Garland, 57-84.

Stretesky, P.B. (2006). "Corporate Self-policing and the Environment." *Criminology* 44: 671-708.

Stretesky, P.B. and M.J. Hogan. (1998). "Environmental Justice: An Analysis of Superfund Sites in Florida." *Social Problems* 45: 268-87.

Stretesky, P.B., J.E. Johnston, and J. Arney. (2003). "Environmental Inequality: An Analysis of Large-Scale Hog Operations in 17 States, 1982-1997." *Rural Sociology* 68,2: 231-52.

Stretesky, P.B., M.A. Long, and M.J. Lynch. (2013). *The Treadmill of Crime: Political Economy and Green Criminology*. Abingdon: Routledge.

Stretesky, P.B. and M.J. Lynch. (1999). "Environmental Justice and the Prediction of Distance to Accidental Chemical Releases in Hillsborough County, Florida." *Social Science Quarterly* 80,4: 830-46.

———. (2001). "The Relationship Between Lead and Homicide." *Archives of Pediatric and Adolescent Medicine* 155,5: 579-82.

———. (2003). "Environmental Hazards and School Segregation in Hillsborough, 1987-1999." *The Sociological Quarterly* 43,4: 553-73.

———. (2004). "The Relationship Between Lead and Crime." *Journal of Health and Social Behavior* 45,2: 214-29.

———. (2009a). "A Cross-National Study of the Association Between Per Capita Carbon Dioxide Emissions and Exports to the United States." *Social Science Research* 38: 239-50.

——. (2009b). "Does Self-policing Reduce Chemical Emissions?" *The Social Science Journal* 46,3: 459-73.

——. (2011a). "Does Self-Policing Improve Environmental Compliance?" In L. Paddock, D. Qun, L. Kotze, D.L. Markell, J. Markowitz, and D. Zaelke (eds), *Compliance and Enforcement in Environmental Law: Toward More Effective Implementation* (Select Proceeding of the 4th International Union for Conservation Academy, Environmental Law Colloquium). Northampton, MA: Edward Elgar, 223-44.

——. (2011b). "Coal Strip Mining, Mountaintop Removal, and the Distribution of Environmental Violations across the United States, 2002-2008." *Landscape Research* 36,2: 209-30.

Sykes, G. and D. Matza. (1957). "Techniques of Neutralization: A Theory of Delinquency." *American Sociological Review* 22,6: 664-70.

Szasz, A. (1986). "Corporations, Organized Crime, and the Disposal of Hazardous Waste: An Examination of the Making of a Criminogenic Regulatory Structure." *Criminology* 24: 1-27.

Szockyj, E. and J.G. Fox (eds). (1996). *Corporate Victimization of Women*. Boston, MA: Northeastern University Press.

Takemura, N. (2007). "'Criticality of Environmental Crises' and Prospect of 'Complexity Green Criminology.'" *Toxin University of Yokohama Research Bulletin* 17: 5-11.

Tansley, A.G. (1935). "The Use and Abuse of Vegetational Concepts and Terms." *Ecology* 16: 284-307.

Tchounwou, P.B., A.K. Patlolla, and J.A. Centeno. (2003). "Invited Review: Carcinogenic Health Effects Associated with Arsenic Exposure—A Critical Review." *Toxicological Pathology* 31,6: 575-88.

Thorndike, E. (1898). *Animal Intelligence: An Experimental Study of the Associative Process in Animals*. New York, NY: Macmillan.

Truhaut, R. (1977). "Ecotoxicology: Objectives, Principles and Perspectives." *Ecotoxicology and Environmental Safety* 1,2: 151-73.

Tsapakis, M. and E.G. Stephanou. (2005). "Occurrence of Gaseious and Particulate Arocromatic Hydrocarbons in the Urban Atmosphere: Study Sources and Ambient Temperature Effect on the Gas/Particle Concentration Distribution." *Environmental Pollution* 133,1: 147-56.

Umemura, T., S. Kai, R. Hasegawa, K. Kanki, Y. Kitamura, A. Nishikawa, and M. Hirose. (2003). "Prevention of Dual Promoting Effects of Pentachlorophenol, an Environmental Pollutant, on Diethylnitrosamine-induced Hepato- and Cholangiocarcinogenesis in Mice by Green Tea Infusion." *Carcinogenesis* 24,6: 1105-9.

United Nations. (2009). "WHO Warns of Growing Chemical Risks to Developing World." United Nations Environment Programme. Available at: http://www.unep.org/Documents.Multilingual/Default.asp?DocumentID=585&ArticleID=6169&l=en (accessed April 2013).

United Nations Department of Economic and Social Affairs, Population Division. (2009). "World Population Prospects: The 2008 Revision." *Population Newsletter* 87. Available at: http://www.un.org/esa/population/publications/popnews/Newsltr_87.pdf (accessed April 2013).

US EPA. (2004). *Cleaning Up the Nation's Waste Sites: Markets and Technological Trends*. US EPA Technological Innovation and Field Services Division. Washington, DC: US EPA.

USGS. (2004). "Magnitude 9.1: Off the West Coast of Northern Sumatra." Available at: http://earthquake.usgs.gov/earthquakes/eqinthenews/2004/us2004slav/#summary (accessed July 10, 2010).

van der Zee, S., G. Hoek, H.M. Boezen, J.P. Schouten, J.H. van Wijnen, and B. Brunekreef. (1999). "Acute Effects of Urban Air Pollution on Respiratory Health of Children with and without Chronic Respiratory Symptoms." *Occupational Environmental Medicine* 56: 802-12.

van Solinge, T.B. (2008). "Eco-Crimes: The Tropical Timber Trade." *Studies of Organized Crime* 7,1: 97-111.

——. (2010). "Deforestation Crimes and Conflicts in the Amazon." *Critical Criminology* 18,4: 263-77.

Vázquez, A. and S. Peña de Ortiz. (2004). "Lead (Pb+2) Impairs Long-term Memory and Blocks Learning-induced Increases in Hippocampal Protein Kinase C Activity." *Toxicology and Applied Pharmacology* 200,1: 27-39.

Veblen, T. (1899 [1994]). *The Theory of the Leisure Class*. New York, NY: Penguin Books.

Wade, T.J., R. Calderon, K.P. Brenner, E. Sams, M. Beach, R. Haugland, L. Wymer, and A.P. Dufour. (2008). "High Sensitivity of Children to Swimming-Associated Gastrointestinal Illness: Results Using a Rapid Assay of Recreational Water Quality." *Epidemiology* 19,3: 375-83.

Wadsworth, M.E.J. (1997). "Health Inequalities in the Life Course Perspective." *Social Science and Medicine* 44,6: 858-69.

Walker, C.H., S.P. Hopkins, R.M. Sibley, and D.B. Peakall. (2006). *Principles of Ecotoxicology*. Boca Raton, FL: Taylor & Francis.

Wallace, H. and C. Roberson. (2011). *Victimology: Legal, Psychological and Social Perspectives*. Englewood Cliffs, NJ: Prentice-Hall.

Wallis, V. (2010). "Beyond 'Green Capitalism.'" *Monthly Review* 61,9: 32-48.

Walsh, A. and L. Ellis. (2006). *Criminology: An Interdisciplinary Approach*. Thousand Oaks, CA: Sage.

Walters, R. (2006). "Crime, Bio-Agriculture and the Exploitation of Hunger." *The British Journal of Criminology* 46,1: 26-45.

——. (2007). "Food Crime, Regulation and the Biotech Harvest." *European Journal of Criminology* 4,2: 217-35.

——. (2010). "Toxic Atmospheres: Air Pollution, Trade and the Politics of Regulation." *Critical Criminology* 18,4: 307-23.

——. (2011). *Eco Crime and Genetically Modified Food*. Abingdon: Routledge.

Walther, G., E. Post, P. Convey, A. Menzel, C. Parmesan, T.J.C. Beebee, J-M. Fromentin, O. Hoegh-Guldberg, and F. Bairlein. (2002). "Ecological Responses to Recent Climate Change." *Nature* 416: 389-95.

Wang, Z. and M.F. Fingas. (2003). "Development of Oil Hydrocarbon Fingerprinting and Identification Techniques." *Marine Pollution Bulletin* 47,9-12: 423-52.

Wang, Z., S. Stout, and M.F. Fingas. (2006). "Forensic Fingerprinting of Biomarkers for Oil Spill Characterization and Source Identification." *Environmental Forensics* 7,2: 105-46.

Wargo, J. (1996). *Our Children's Toxic Legacy: How Science and the Law Fail to Protect Us from Pesticides*. New Haven, CT: Yale University Press.

Watson, J. and R. Rayner. (1920). "Conditioned Emotional Reaction." *Journal of Experimental Psychology* 3,1: 1-14.

White, R. (2002). "Environmental Harm and the Political Economy of Consumption." *Social Justice* 29,1/2: 82-102.

———. (2007). "Green Criminology and the Pursuit of Social and Economic Justice." In P. Beirne and N. South (eds), *Issues in Green Criminology*. Cullompton: Willan, 32-54.

———. (2008a). *Crimes Against Nature: Environmental Criminology and Ecological Justice*. Cullompton: Willan.

———. (2008b). "Depleted Uranium, State Crime and the Politics of Knowing." *Theoretical Criminology* 12,1: 31-54.

———. (ed.). (2010). *Global Environmental Harm: Criminological Perspectives*. Cullompton: Willan.

———. (2011). *Transnational Environmental Crime: Toward an Eco-Global Criminology*. Abingdon: Routledge.

———. (2012). "Green Criminology." In J. Muncie and E. McLaughlin (eds), *The Sage Dictionary of Criminology*. London: Sage, 208-10.

Wilkins, E.T. (1954). "Air Pollution Aspect of the London Fog of December 1952." *Quarterly Journal of the Royal Meteorological Society* 80,344: 267-71.

Winneke, G., A. Brockhaus, and R. Baltissen. (1977). "Neurobehavioral and Systemic Effects of Longterm Blood Lead-elevation in Rats." *Archives of Toxicology* 37,4: 247-63.

Wittmer, H., B.N. McLellan, R. Serrouya, and C.D. Apps. (2007). "Changes in Landscape Composition Influence the Decline of a Threatened Woodland Caribou Population." *Journal of Animal Ecology* 76,3: 568-79.

Wohlersa, J., A. Engel, E. Zöllnera, P. Breithauptc, K. Jürgensd, H-G. Hoppec, U. Sommere, and U. Riebesell. (2009). "Changes in Biogenic Carbon Flow in Response to Sea Surface Warming." *Proceedings of the National Academy of Sciences of the United States of America* 106,17: 7067-72.

World Health Organization. (2002). *World Health Report*. Geneva: WHO. Available at: http:www.who.int/whr/2002/en (accessed April 2013).

Wright, J.P., D. Boisvert, and J. Vaske. (2009). "Blood Lead Levels in Early Childhood Predict Adulthood Psychopathy." *Youth Violence and Juvenile Justice* 7: 208-22.

Wright, J.P., K.N. Dietrich, M. Douglas Ris, R.W. Hornung, S.D. Wessel, B.P. Lanphear, M. Ho, and M.N. Rae. (2008). "Association of Prenatal and Childhood Blood Lead Concentrations with Criminal Arrests in Early Adulthood." *PLoS Medicine* 5,5: 732-40.

Wyatt, T. (2011). "The Illegal Trade of Raptors in the Russian Federation." *Contemporary Justice Review* 14,2: 103-23.

——. (2012). *Green Criminology and Wildlife Trafficking: The Illegal Fur and Falcon Trades in Russia Far East.* Saarbrücken: LAP Lambert Academic Publishing.

Yong, E. (2012). "Replication Studies: Bad Copy." *Nature* 485,7398: 298-300.

Zakrzewski, S.F. (2002). *Environmental Toxicology.* New York, NY: Oxford University Press.

Zilney, L.A., D. McGurrin, and S. Zahran. (2006). "Environmental Justice and the Role of Criminology: An Analytic Review of 33 Years of Environmental Justice Research." *Criminal Justice Review* 31,1: 47-62.

Zimmer, C., E. Labruyere, V. Meas-Yedid, N. Guillen, and J.C. Olivo-Martin. (2002). "Segmentation and Tracking of Migrating Cells in Videomicroscopy with Parametric Active Contours: A Tool for Cell-based Drug Testing." *IEEE Transactions on Medical Imaging* 21,10: 1212-21.

Ziska, L.H., P.R. Epstein, and W.H. Schlesinger. (2009). "Rising CO_2, Climate Change, and Public Health: Exploring the Links to Plant Biology." *Environmental Health Perspectives* 117,2: 155-8.

Index